up before daylight:

Life Histories from the Alabama Writers' Project, 1938–1939

Farm family waiting to go home. Enterprise, 1939. Wolcott, FSA.

up before daylight:

Life Histories from the Alabama Writers' Project, 1938–1939

Edited by James Seay Brown, Jr.

The University of Alabama Press

Publication of this book was made possible, in part, by financial assistance from the Andrew W. Mellon Foundation.

Library of Congress Cataloging in Publication Data
Main entry under title:
Up before daylight.

  Bibliography: p.
  Includes index.
  1. Alabama—Social life and customs—Addresses, essays, lectures. 2. Alabama—Social conditions—Addresses, essays, lectures. 3. Alabama—Biography —Addresses, essays, lectures. 4. Oral history. I. Brown, James Seay, 1944–   . II. Alabama Writers' Project. F326.U65   976.1:062   81–21988
ISBN 0-8173-0092-9   AACR2
ISBN 0-8173-0099-6 (pbk.)

Contents

Dedicated to Claude Hayes,
Ellin Kelly, and Harold Daffron,
who taught me about the thirties in Alabama

Preface

Walking up a trail in a little-used part of Oak Mountain State Park, just south of Birmingham, a hiker can see a series of frame buildings with handsome stone chimneys. A few are burned out and most are in disrepair, relics of a Civilian Conservation Corps camp from the Depression. It makes an attractive and sad puzzle, all this organization and idealism forgotten and gone to ruin up on a brushy hill.

Like the CCC, the Federal Writers' Project was a Depression relief effort. As one of its minor undertakings, the Alabama branch of the Writers' Project turned out, in just over a year's time in 1938 and 1939, a hundred or so "life histories" of everyday Alabamians. Three of these were published in 1978 in Tom Terrill's and Jerrold Hirsch's edition of life histories, *Such As Us: Southern Voices of the Thirties.* Twenty-eight more of these Alabama life histories make up the heart of the book in hand. Seeded and cultivated in the hothouse of a government relief project, they were "laid by" these forty years. Harvest has been the easiest part of all.

The editor appreciatively acknowledges support from a Samford University Research Fund grant that made possible a research trip to Chapel Hill in August 1979 and a subsequent SURF grant to help with manuscript production. Similar support from the Department of History and Political Science at Samford, chaired by David M. Vess, facilitated a subsequent trip to the Library of Congress and the National Archives. The University of North Carolina at Chapel Hill permitted me to reproduce twenty-five accounts from the manuscripts room of the Southern Historical Collection, and the Alabama State Department of Archives and History granted permission to publish three more. Miss Sarah Ann Warren of the manuscripts division of the state archives in Montgomery and Steve Hensen of the Harwell G. Davis Library at Samford were especially helpful. I owe particular thanks to Wayne Flynt, former colleague and now head of the Department of History at Auburn University, who suggested the topic and provided help and encouragement. Jerrold Hirsch was kind enough to share time and insights with me. And finally, W. T. Couch, the grand old man who started all this, warmly welcomed me in his home for an evening of questions and conversation. The book itself and any mistakes or shortcomings in it are my own responsibility.

J. BROWN

up before daylight:

Life Histories from the
Alabama Writers' Project, 1938–1939

Introduction

The Origin of the Federal Writers' Project

When Wall Street crashed in 1929 and the Great Depression spread worldwide in 1930, conventional economic wisdom said to cut government expenditures and balance national budgets. That policy was tried in most industrial countries and its failure was spectacular. In fact, those countries emerged quickest from the Depression whose governments found ways to get money into circulation and people into some kind of work. The clearest example may have been Germany with its superhighway construction.

By the summer of 1932 the Hoover administration in the United States was moving in this direction. An emergency act sent $300 million in loans to the states for direct relief and work relief.[1] In September presidential candidate Franklin Roosevelt gave a remarkable campaign speech in which he said the frontier was gone and "equality of opportunity as we have known it no longer exists." Among American traditions he listed was the right to make a living.[2] The idea and the man captured a considerable popular mandate later that fall in the first presidential election of the Depression.

Within two months after Roosevelt took office, the Federal Emergency Relief Administration was created, with more money for relief and a permanent administration headed by veteran social worker Harry Hopkins.[3] In the winter of 1933–34 the new Civil Works Administration experimented briefly with a work relief program run along the lines of a traditional public works program. Successor to all these was the Works Progress Administration—the famous WPA—set up in May 1935 to "coordinate" the work relief effort. Coordination in this case included increasing control from Washington; every WPA worker was on the payroll of the federal government, as was the head of the WPA in each state.[4]

One of the touchiest areas of relief was in fact handled directly from Washington, bypassing even the state WPA heads. This was Federal Project Number One, which provided relief in the areas of art, music, theater, and writing. Thad Holt, first Alabama director of the WPA, remarked that most state WPA heads simply were not interested in arts relief, and if they had not been administered directly from Washington these projects would have died from neglect in most states. "Federal One," as it was known, was approved by the president in September 1935 and lasted four years until its demise in 1939. It was the first federal subsidy of the arts and a most visible and controversial part of the entire WPA.[5]

Included in Federal One was the Federal Writers' Project, hereafter usually labeled FWP. Henry Alsberg from the old Federal Emergency Relief Administration was its director. He had degrees from Columbia University in arts and in law, and he had been a journalist of some distinction and an even more successful creative writer. From the beginning his main concern—indeed, the activity that justified the FWP—was the production of an American Guide Series about the states and cities. The Guide Series was to be a revealing yet sympathetic picture of an area's geography, history, and culture, organized around the theme of highway tours and written by local writers. A staunch New Dealer, Alsberg saw the guides emphasizing the common people and the potential of the democratic tradition of the United States.[6]

From this ongoing major project peripheral projects sprouted like buds. Folklore studies began as an integral part of guide writing and research, especially in 1936–37 when John Lomax was adviser on folklore and folkways. Under his tutelage, the ex-slave narrative project begun in Florida took shape as a powerful individual study, beyond the scope of the guide proper. Something of the same thing happened in Negro studies under the influence of Sterling Brown, who was made editor for this subject in early 1936. In 1938 a nationwide project called "social-ethnic studies" similarly was promoted by Morton W. Royse. The "life histories" project in the southern states also was born in 1938, brainchild of FWP Regional Director W. T. Couch.[7] It was as part of this southern life histories project that the Alabama life stories were written.

W. T. Couch and the Life History Idea

William T. Couch was born in 1901 and spent a good deal of his life in and around universities. Even before his graduation from The University of North Carolina in 1925 he became assistant director of the University Press there, and from 1932 to 1945 he served as its director.

Couch recounts a story that reveals him as an impatient supporter of academia even in his early years with the University Press. When he started with the UNC Press in 1925, he recalls, his employer told him, albeit with regret, that he could not deal seriously with matters of race, religion, or economics. "What then could you do?" was a question Couch remembers asking himself. In 1927 the Board of Governors of the Press approved for publication a manuscript of plantation stories from around Columbia, South Carolina, called *Congaree Sketches*. After approval of the manuscript, the author told Couch that he would like to have an introduction in the book by Paul Green, recent winner of the Pulitzer Prize in drama and known for his outspoken views on racial injustice. Couch duly got the introduction, which included the analogy that, by keeping the Negro in the ditch, the white man in the South had to stay there too.[8] Couch remembers thinking, "Oh my God," and figuring the Press's Board of Governors would never pass it. So, he sent it on to the printer and shipped out approximately five hundred advance copies and perhaps two hundred more to reviewers. Custom required also that he send a copy to the university president's office and to each member of the Board of Governors. Shortly thereafter he was summoned to the president's office and there found assembled the entire Board. In Couch's account every Board member agreed with a letter of condemnation from the dean of the graduate school. Couch told the president that withdrawal of the offending book would be difficult, with seven hundred copies already in circulation. That won his case, but more interesting is what he left unsaid.

I didn't say, "What is the university anyway?" I knew that that would not be appropriate for me to sit there and tell leading members of the faculty—we had the top members of the faculty [on the Press Board]—and tell them that if the university couldn't discuss the basic problems of the community in which it existed, and couldn't carry on a dialogue with its public on this subject, it wasn't doing its job.[9]

The life histories project W. T. Couch sponsored later in the Federal Writers' Project seems to have been an attempt to use nonscholars to open new areas to rigid university scholars as well as to the general public.

At about this same time Couch was in contact with a powerful new regional school of social science associated with Howard Odum, Guy Johnson, Rupert Vance, and other North Carolinians. This group blended geography, economics, sociology, and folklore studies to investigate the ways in which the region had evolved. Their goal was not mere armchair reflection, but rather to use this intelligence to regenerate the economy and society of the American South. The South had been hit particularly hard by the Depression, rivaled only, perhaps, by the Dust Bowl states and the northern ghettoes. Unemployment and malnutrition were not new in the South, but conditions in the early 1930s were serious enough to give an air of desperation to the work of these serious social scientists. The last few pages of Rupert Vance's 1932 masterwork *Human Geography of the South* are an impassioned cry for a folk renaissance on the model of Ireland, where consciousness of folk culture lay behind all the political moves that brought autonomy by 1921, or Denmark, where the same theme working through the "folk high schools" brought economic and political revival by 1900.[10]

Couch, a close personal friend of Vance, was thinking along these same lines at least by the time he organized and edited his *Culture in the South* anthology in 1934. As UNC Press director his formulation of the basic problem was perhaps less scholarly but just as direct: he began wondering why folks no longer could make a living on a fifty-acre farm.[11]

Early in June 1938, Couch got word that he soon would be appointed director of the seven southeastern states' region of the Writers' Project.[12] He immediately began to use this organization as a test vehicle for his new ideas. On July 11, 1938, a six-page memorandum concerning proposed FWP work was circulated from the regional office to all states listed as "southern" in the census. Unsigned because Couch was not officially appointed until August, it is manifestly his work. Here the Alabama Writers' Project got its first statement on Couch's idea of writing biographies of the common people, along with a list of occupations, topics, and cultural groups that had been neglected by the academic world and that might profitably be studied. His opening suggestion that tenant farmers be interviewed includes perhaps the best short description of his life history idea to be found in his papers.

Very little trustworthy material on this subject is available. The kind of story that can be collected is best illustrated by the case history on page 260ff. of *Human Factors in Cotton Culture* by Rupert B. Vance. This case history was written by Ben Dixon McNeill and first published in the *News and Observer,* daily newspaper of Raleigh, from which it was taken by Mr. Vance. Mr. McNeill has had no technical sociological training and had no sociological supervision when he wrote his case history. It was written purely as a newspaper job, but its value has been recognized for sociological as well as newspaper purposes.

This case is cited because of the possible objection that only sociologists can get case histories that are worth getting. The fact is that when sociologists get such material they generally treat their subjects as abstractions, and while an enormous amount of statistical material is available on tenants, there are not available at the present time in print anywhere as many as one-half dozen accurate case histories of actual tenant farmers.

This kind of material needs only to be mentioned in order for its importance to be realized. The fact that it has not been collected means that the existing scholarly discipline which might engage in the collection of such materials have had their attention directed elsewhere; and, in fact, their present attitude toward their subject matter and their techniques are such as to preclude their conceiving of such work as is described here or their doing the work satisfactorily after it has been described.

The approach to this subject by the workers on the Federal Writers' Project will be from a human point of view corresponding closely with the point of view of the journalists except that certain simple techniques will be established and followed in order to assure the greatest possible accuracy in the histories that are collected.

Couch also suggested as subjects farm owners and their families; cotton mill workers and their villages; such service workers as waitresses, grocery clerks, and elevator boys in the towns and cities; steel mill and coal mine workers; lumber workers; and fishermen. The rest of the list was a miscellany of locations, groups, and topics, such as slums, legal cases on landlord-tenant relations, eating habits, southern health and disease, poor whites, "Negroes who have achieved distinction," and finally folklore, songs, and legends. Couch wanted to get enough material to publish four or five volumes under the general title "Life in the South."[13]

Some of the life histories for which he called were generated by the North Carolina project even before Couch officially was named director. He sent them to Henry Alsberg in early August, and Alsberg used them in the final push to get Couch appointed. Alsberg was excited about the initial results but thought them "a little sentimental" and "slightly patronizing." He wanted "a harder, more clearly drawn picture of the people and more facts about their lives."[14]

On August 25, 1938, W. T. Couch received official notification of his new job; that same day he wrote letters to all the southeastern state directors, outlining a personal trip to visit each.[15] Shortly thereafter, a small, typescript "Manual for the Collection of Life Histories" was sent to each southern state headquarters. An extended outline of questions to be asked by the interviewers, originally compiled by Ida Moore of the North Carolina staff, was appended. Couch expressed his desire for "an accurate, honest, interesting and fairly comprehensive view of the kind of life that is lived by the majority of people in the south." Perhaps the most important part of the manual was the paragraph dealing with writing techniques and the interviewers' attitude toward their subject.

> Insofar as possible, the stories should be told in the words of the persons who are consulted. The effort should be made to get definite information. Avoid generalities such as "those who are industrious and ambitious can do well," "had not made good use of opportunities"—wherever possible expand such wording to give detail, that is, exactly what industry and ambition might have done or what the opportunities were that could have been used. In general avoid the expression of judgment. The writer will, of course, have to exercise judgment in determining the course of a conversation through which he gains information, but aside from this, he should keep his own opinions and feelings in the background as much as possible. For instance, if he sees

people living under conditions which he thinks are terrible, he should be most careful not to express his opinion in any way and thus possibly affect the opinion of the person to whom he is talking. He must try to discover the real feeling of the person consulted and must record this feeling regardless of his own attitude toward it. Any story in which this principle is violated will be worthless.[16]

Couch would come back to this avoidance of "the expression of judgment" many times in the following year in his dealings with the Alabama Writers' Project, both in the preparation of the long-delayed state guide and in the life stories project. In a way, however, as part of the movement of the 1920s and 1930s that labeled itself variously "liberal" or "progressive," Couch seemed to be calling for a new kind of judgment. In the main, he himself had found dignity and resilience in the common folks of whatever economic level or cultural group, and he was suspicious of the mindset of those who did not find it. Stereotypes of blacks and poor whites concerned him particularly. For example, Erskine Caldwell's 1932 *Tobacco Road,* a best seller and then a highly successful play, galled Couch because this sort of portrayal of people beyond help worked against reform. When in 1937 Caldwell (with Margaret Bourke-White) published *You Have Seen Their Faces,* Couch concluded a blistering critique with this sentence: "If we ever pass out of the present era of sentimental slush, of undiscriminating sympathy on the one hand and of merriment over psychopaths on the other, Mr. Caldwell's works will be forgotten."[17] This was part of the background and emotional wellspring of the life history idea in 1938.

The Alabama Writers' Project

Meanwhile, in Alabama the Writers' Project had been three years taking shape. In early October 1935, Federal One officials in Washington named Myrtle Miles of Columbiana, Alabama, head of the Alabama Writers' Project. Her career had been in journalism and public relations, including managing the New York Central Women's Bureau of Public Relations.[18] As former editor of the society page for the *Birmingham News* she had some reputation in social as well as professional circles, at least in central Alabama.[19]

Miles immediately faced the task of assembling some 100 writers to produce the Alabama state guide. There were two huge obstacles: first, 90 percent of the writers had to be on the relief rolls and listed there by profession as writers, and second, the 250,000-word book needed to be done in the six months initially allotted to the Federal One projects.[20] For four years Miles struggled to find qualified writers on relief or to get exemptions for nonrelief writers. By her own estimate at one point in 1938, she had 3 qualified writers on her staff.[21] Numbers of writers allowed her on the project fluctuated erratically from as high as 110 in March 1936 to as low as 30 in June 1937.[22] The average monthly wage was less than seventy dollars.[23] Birmingham did become a working editorial center, staffed largely with out-of-work journalists, but Miles's planned division of the state under district supervisors never materialized.[24]

One of Miles's recruiting ventures bears quoting in her words, both for its insights into the times and her own attitudes. Alsberg had written that she ought to look up the writer Covington Hall, who was living around Mentone, and this was her reply:

> I drove my car out of Mentone through a mountain jungle as thick as may be found in Alabama, taking a native with me to guide the way through cornfields and winding paths that led through brooks and brush that left one wondering at times whether I would ever get back. In a cabin put together of boards and metal sheets and logs I found Mr. Hall. He was preparing at the moment to walk the several miles required to get him out to the big road and the home of a friend who had agreed to give him a lift to Fort Payne where I had indicated I would be the day following. We talked as long as I felt safe in staying, in view of the uncertainties of my return to Mentone. I found him a thoroughly interesting person, a personality as individual as any I have encountered in a long time.[25]

Like other state directors, Myrtle Miles faced the psychological pressures of management in the Depression, when a pink slip might threaten family survival. Less than two years into the project, Miles wrote Alsberg that work had "been complicated by almost unbelievable oddities in disposition and character."[26] One writer lifted project work and sold it free-lance under his own name to a newspaper.[27] Another wrecked the only government car to which they had access.[28] And all through this period Miles's mother, in her nineties, was very ill and required considerable attention.[29]

Possibly the single most disheartening series of events was the refusal of the state government to consider publishing the guide. Without even looking at the manuscript, Governor Bibb Graves refused to sponsor it. The Alabama State Department of Archives and History under Marie Bankhead Owen seemed hostile to the Writers' Project and especially the proposed guide, possibly because Owens considered the guide a threat to her own history of Alabama as an adoption choice by the public schools.[30]

When Couch took over as regional director, he too despaired of the Alabama guide, but for reasons of quality.[31] After seven months of close administrative contact with Miles, some of which will be described below, Couch felt he understood what was wrong. "The present editor," he wrote Alsberg, "is a charming person, has good managerial ability, is careful, conscientious and intelligent, but knows nothing about writing or editing."[32] By this time Couch had revitalized the Tennessee staff, which had been in even worse condition, and had two of its editors working full-time on the Alabama guide. He manipulated assistant directors, desperately asked for exemptions for nonrelief people, and kept a running correspondence of advice and suggestions, but the guide was not to be published until two years after his tenure as regional director.[33]

As peripheral projects grew, they partly complemented but also partly competed with work on the guide. Alabama writers produced 117 ex-slave narratives in more than four hundred pages of typescript, for example.[34] The Alabama writers even got nonwriting assignments. In March 1939, Ben Botkin sent down his itinerary for a three-month recording expedition of the Joint Committee on Folk Arts for Federal One. They had heavy recording equipment loaded in a Ford station wagon and requested that Ruby Pickens Tartt get ready to introduce them to

singers at Livingston, Rhussus Perry to singers around Tuskegee, Lawrence Evans to singers in the Swedish colony of Silver
Hill, and so on.[35] At the same time that work on the life histories
was getting underway in the fall of 1938, Myrtle Miles wrote
Couch that the Alabama Writers' Project was about to begin
work on a state encyclopedia and was working already on an
almanac and a book on the origin of place names.[36] Many of
these projects were stillborn, but in 1938 and 1939, along with
the guide, they were competitors for Couch's pet project, the life
histories.[37] Given these pressures, it is remarkable that anything
at all was produced.

The Alabama Life Histories

Couch first visited the Alabama project in September 1938.
He apparently spent most of his time with Miles and her
Birmingham-based staff discussing the life histories project.[38]
Within two months of that visit, Miles mailed the first Alabama
life history drafts to the regional office and asked Couch for a
critique.[39] In reply, Couch commented extensively on fifteen of
the stories. His major criticism was of preconceived value judg-
ments and of high-flown literary style as opposed to simple
descriptive writing. One of the stories to receive this sort of
detailed criticism was "Sam, the Turpentine Chopper" by
Lawrence Evans of Fairhope. The life history originally opened
with this paragraph:

> The sand-trail stopped abruptly. On one side an old cemetery,
> gone to ruin after the Civil War, reared huge monuments as high
> as cedars over gaping holes, where lizards and toads lived among
> the bones of those who had dwelt in peace and plenty in this
> land. On the other side, a squat turpentine camp, called the
> quarters, sprawled on the slope of a hill.[40]

Couch's criticism of that account ran like this:

> This story has some of the best and some of the worst qualities
> of any you have submitted. On page 1 the author is literary in a
> big way. If he were writing for some other purpose his style
> might be suitable, but atmosphere of a literary kind—that is, the

kind someone thinks up while sitting in his room chewing a pencil—is precisely what we do not want. The second sentence in the first paragraph illustrates exactly what is to be avoided. In the third sentence the author has a turpentine camp sprawling on the slope of a hill. It would be best merely to let the camp be on the hill. In the past too many camps have sprawled and readers are now tired of "sprawling" camps. In the second paragraph the second sentence reads, "Here 8 miles from a highway and 16 miles from a town was a country slum." This kind of statement should not be made. The author should give his description and let the reader draw his conclusions as to whether the place described is a slum or not. In the next sentence I have to object to the "rude" shack "crouched low." These terms are terribly hackneyed. The author will find that if he will talk to the people living in such a community they will give him out of their own mouths descriptions fresh, interesting, vivid, and far more to the point than anything he can get by "crouching" and "sprawling." From this sentence on the story is much better. Four lines below occur the words "disreputable," "forlorn," and "lopsided" referring to an iron bed. The term "lopsided" is a descriptive term and if the author has actually seen the bed and it is lopsided, then he is justified in using the term. The terms "disreputable" and "forlorn" are emotive terms expressing feeling, and as used in this sentence they express the feeling of the author. Now it happens that one of the first principles of this work is that the author is to keep his feeling out of the stories. His task is to try to get the people on paper as they see themselves; to get them to tell their own story in their own words as much as possible, and to suppress his own feelings and attitudes.

Couch pointed out technical writing problems in most of the fifteen accounts and expressed concern about the brevity of many; but in general he claimed to be "very pleased" with the work done.[41]

Couch was back in Birmingham November 20–23 as program chairman for the controversial Southern Conference for Human Welfare. He was among the one thousand southerners, black and white, who ignored Birmingham's Jim Crow law for two days, voted to have future meetings only in cities with no such laws, and heard Harry Hopkins's Deputy Administrator Aubrey Williams say, "I am not sure that class warfare is not all right"—all of which created a sensation in the national press. Couch earlier had planned to take time off to drive with Myrtle Miles to Cullman and Marshall counties to organize writers there. Appointed chair of the committee to permanently organize the conference, he probably had little time for the Writers' Project.[42]

In mid-December Miles sent in another sheaf of life histories and a week later got a brief but enthusiastic note from Couch that he was "very favorably impressed."[43] That same month the Alabama staff was allowed an increase from forty to fifty writers. Couch had made some very specific suggestions for additions, names apparently received from noted professional writers from Alabama such as James Saxon Childers.[44] Miles gamely fought through the mountain of paperwork required and continued sending in life histories.[45] All this effort was in addition to other project work, and first, last, and always was work on the guide.

By the end of January 1939 Couch had accumulated enough life histories from the region, possibly including some from Alabama, to give them to his friend Rupert Vance for a reading. Vance's reaction to the work was positive; he thought they might be integrated into a volume without further editing and "give us something of a real biography of the common man of the South."[46] Couch immediately began publication plans; the tentative title "These Are Our People" later gave way to *These Are Our Lives*.[47] By this time Couch had begun giving Alabama life histories to a writer on the Tennessee staff for final editing.[48] In mid-February the Tennessee editor wrote Couch asking to be notified if any Alabama life histories were to be edited for the first volume. The next day and presumably before he received this letter, Couch sent out an announcement that the first volume of life histories had been compiled and was on its way to the printer.[49]

By this narrow margin no Alabama life stories appeared in *These Are Our Lives,* but the project still continued to gain momentum in the state. Walter Cutter, assistant regional director, and James Aswell of the Tennessee project visited Alabama especially to help with the life histories. Aswell wrote that he and Cutter believed "the Alabama staff now knew precisely what to do with life histories."[50] The Alabama staff appreciated the help, judging by Lawrence Evans's response. He wrote

Miles an enthusiastic letter from his home in Fairhope, thanking her for the visit and the criticism of "an expert like Cutter." Evans thought Cutter's editing of the country doctor story "makes it look like a real live story and I have compared copies eagerly today. It's fine."[51] Miles continued to send life histories to Couch at regular intervals, and toward the end of March Couch wrote about his plans for the Alabama material.

> I am now working on plans for the second volume of life histories. This volume is to supplement the first one and in conjunction with it is going to give a fairly complete picture of types of life throughout the south.
>
> We do not have any good stories of both Negroes and whites working in coal and iron in the Birmingham area. I wish you would attempt to get us a few of these stories. I believe you can find some way to do this without interfering with work on the Guide Book.
>
> In the second volume we shall publish several Alabama stories that have already been submitted.[52]

In late April Couch sent Miles two copies of *These Are Our Lives,* just off the press, and asked her to gather the staff for a May 1–2 visit he planned to make to the state. The publication of *These Are Our Lives* to immediate acclaim from critics of the stature of Charles Beard must have made this a high point in Couch's regional directorship.[53]

Couch's plans, however, were quickly interrupted. A conservative backlash to the New Deal had been building all through the thirties. Roosevelt's attempt to pack the Supreme Court in the wake of his successes in the 1936 elections had caused enormous resentment in some quarters. A retrenchment in federal spending in 1937 brought an immediate recession that aided the anti–New Deal forces. In the spring and summer of 1938 Roosevelt personally had campaigned in the primaries against "unregenerate" southern senators and congressmen; the campaign was unsuccessful and won the label "purge," comparing it with events that same year in Stalinist Russia. In 1939 the reaction exploded in Congress in Representative Martin Dies's House Un-American Activities Committee and Representative Clifton Albert Woodrum's special subcommittee of the Appropriations Committee.

Federal One was a primary target of the anti–New Deal forces. It was effectively killed by the relief act passed in June by Congress that ruled against any project sponsored solely by the WPA. W. T. Couch desperately mobilized what support he could in defense of the FWP, his branch of Federal One, but it was too late. Ironically, amid a flood of congratulatory letters and telegrams on *These Are Our Lives,* he got word that as of September the FWP would be divided among the state WPA organizations and would do work on state-sponsored projects only.[54]

Alabama materials, including the Birmingham-area coal mining stories Couch had requested, continued to arrive at his office through August 1939. These eventually were left with Couch's other FWP material in the UNC library. Ninety Alabama life history manuscripts appear in those papers.[55] Perhaps ten others rest in the state archives in Montgomery, some caught by the project's closing, like the August 24, 1939, "Janey Gets Her Desires," and others perhaps simply lost in the files.[56] It is difficult to separate clearly categories of writing—life histories from ex-slave narratives, for example—and chances are that some projects written as fish wound up looking more like fowl. The life history of a Washington County Cajan turpentiner, to name one, began as a response to the folklore manual.[57] So, in all, there are perhaps one hundred life histories from Alabama, written in less than a year's time from September 1938 through August 1939. They are nearly invisible next to the popular and published ex-slave narratives, although in most cases they are longer and more detailed.

Evaluating the Life Histories

By today's categories, the life histories are an interesting cross between oral history and creative writing. The interviewers had no tape recorders and most probably were ignorant of shorthand. The lengthy quotations, many times in dialect, must be less than verbatim. Despite Couch's warnings, some writers obviously strained to reach creative heights, especially in setting the initial and final scenes. Forced metaphors abound, such as a bayou "resting complacently on her sandy, dredged bottom."

Yet among the Alabama writers were a few good nonfiction writers. Covington Hall, socialist activist and a leading radical

writer in the South for twenty-five years before his brief employment on the Alabama project, was possibly the most sophisti-
cated of these; he was concerned with economic and social
patterns as well as personalities. Lawrence Evans, a younger
writer, had a degree in herpetology and a minor in journalism
from the University of Southern California, and he already had
written for National Geographic Society and Smithsonian expeditions. François Ludgere Diard of Mobile, local historian as
well as newspaperman, had established a regional reputation as
a writer. Veteran newspaper writers were well represented,
especially in the Birmingham editorial offices of the project.

Only one of the Alabama life history authors, Ruby Pickens
Tartt, was a talented and perhaps aspiring creative writer.
Otherwise the accounts tend to be pedestrian in prose but
correspondingly simple and straightforward in description, right
down to the point of enumeration—a list of farm tools, a list of
pantry supplies. Lack of literary sophistication in this case
seems to lead more to factual accuracy than to creative fiction.
And some of these (literarily) simple accounts are more interesting to this writer than James Agee's impassioned and introspec-
tive prose in *Let Us Now Praise Famous Men.*[58]

At the same time in these accounts paternalism and a conde-
scending humor toward black people is the rule rather than the
exception. In fact, the treatment of black subjects in all writers'
projects in the South was a concern of New Deal liberals from
the beginning of the FWP. In some cases there was clear
discrimination against black writers, but more commonly it
seems as if the idea of hiring black writers never came to mind.[59]
Writers tended to present "the attitude of the 'average' middle-
class southerner toward racial problems."[60] An acrimonious
correspondence was carried on between Myrtle Miles and Sterling Brown of the Office on Negro Affairs on this issue; the
Alabama Writers' Project eventually got three black writers,
although only one—Rhussus Perry—wrote life histories.[61]

A patronizing attitude toward the poor is not uncommon in
these pages. This attitude seems especially strange in light of
the fact that the writers were taken from the relief rolls. Many
apparently saw themselves as urban intelligentsia only temporarily jobless. Despite Couch's belief that a few simple rules
would keep a writer's personality in the background, personality

exercised a major influence in simple choice of subject. Jack
Kytle, writer and assistant director of the project, was fascinated
by the down and out, for example; most of his subjects are of
this type, and here his writing is enthusiastic but also openly
didactic.[62]

Perhaps what Couch was after was as simple as a sympathetic
hearing for the inarticulate. Although these Alabama accounts
were never selectively chosen by Couch's office for publication,
it seems to this editor that the most valuable ones are indeed the
most sympathetic ones. Usually the interviewer was of the same
race, sex, and even political persuasion as the interviewed; good
examples are Covington Hall's portrait of his old friend, "The
Andrew Jackson of Southern Labor," Nettie S. McDonald's
sensitive picture of a long-naturalized immigrant, "Mary
Worked in the Mines in Belgium," Woodrow Hand's grudgingly
respectful "Johnnie Fence, Truck Miner," and forty-three-year-
old Rhussus L. Perry's admiring study of an older black woman,
"Janey Gets Her Desires."

Although these Alabama life histories are uneven in quality
and length, all but the worst have an attractive immediacy about
them. Often flawed by the intrusion of writers' personalities and
values into the narrative, they are at the same time free from the
attitudes of the past forty years of reflection on the Depression.[63]
They were never meant to be a statistically accurate sample of
the population, and pressures of time and money made them
even less representative than W. T. Couch had hoped. At the
same time, a great value of these accounts is the sheer variety of
people and occupations described. Here are the expected tenant
farmers and miners and cotton mill workers, but also river
fishermen, teachers, weatherstrippers, nurserymen, day care
workers, country doctors, cooks, sculptors, and hotel hostesses.
Southern loyalty to place is a truism and a point of regional
pride, but these pages are just as full of the footloose—hoboes,
immigrants, migrants, and those who frequently moved to and
from neighboring states. The dignity and resilience of even the
rural poor emerge as clearly as Couch believed they would,
though here too is an occasional *Tobacco Road* type. At the same
time, most of the accounts show the enormous shaping force
the past had on each individual, making Couch's own vision of
reform seem idealistic.

Part of Couch's vision, though, survives. In his first statement of the life history idea to the writers' projects of the southern states, he spoke of an attempt "to collect such material purely for its human interest." In that sense at least, perhaps a reader will agree, the Alabama Writers' Project series of life histories remains a real success.[64]

Notes to the Introduction

1. William F. McDonald, *Federal Relief Administration and the Arts: The Origins and Administrative History of the Arts Projects of the WPA* (Columbus: Ohio State University Press, 1969), p. 15. This was the July 21, 1932, Emergency Relief and Construction Act.

2. Howard Zinn, ed., *New Deal Thought* (Indianapolis: Bobbs-Merrill Co., 1966), pp. 45, 50.

3. Monty Penkower, *The Federal Writers' Project: A Study in Government Patronage of the Arts* (Urbana: University of Illinois Press, 1977), p. 9.

4. McDonald, *Federal Relief Administration and the Arts,* pp. 60, 65, 104.

5. Interview with editor, Birmingham, June 9, 1980. See also McDonald, *Federal Relief Administration and the Arts,* pp. 14, 129–31, and Penkower, *Federal Writers' Project,* p. 10.

6. McDonald, *Federal Relief Administration and the Arts,* pp. 663–65.

7. See McDonald, "The Programs of the FWP," in *Federal Relief Administration and the Arts,* pp. 693–750, for a succinct account; see also Penkower, *Federal Writers' Project,* pp. 144–50, and Susan Dwyer-Shick, "The Development of Folklore and Folklife Research in the Federal Writers' Project, 1935–1943," *Keystone Folklore Quarterly* 20 (Fall, 1965): 11–17.

8. The book was Edward C. L. Adams's *Congaree Sketches; scenes from Negro life in the swamps of the Congaree and tales by Tad and Scip of heaven and hell with other miscellany* (Chapel Hill: University of North Carolina Press, 1927). Paul Green had won the Pulitzer Prize for "In Abraham's Bosom" that same year.

9. Interview with W. T. Couch, Chapel Hill, August 9, 1979, quoted by permission. Tape in possession of editor.

10. Rupert B. Vance, *Human Geography of the South: A Study in Regional Resources and Human Adequacy* (Chapel Hill: University of North Carolina Press, 1932). Couch still discusses this book as one of the most important the UNC Press published in his fifteen years there (telephone conversation with editor, June 22, 1980).

11. W. T. Couch, ed., *Culture in the South* (Chapel Hill: University of North Carolina Press, 1934). Couch remembers the origins of the life history idea not as something he got from Rupert Vance or any other single source. If one had certain questions, this approach was simply a logical way to answer them. "Nobody could write about the South, the real South, without seeing the individual poor," he said, especially the poor whites and blacks (quoted from notes taken in telephone conversation, June 22, 1980). William Stott, in his

provocative *Documentary Expression and Thirties America* (New York: Oxford University Press, 1973), p. 119, argues that the shock of the Depression created an urgency about social problems; the attempt to treat them directly and on a human level was the genesis of the "documentary" approach, in which he includes Couch's life history series. Theodore Dreiser, for example, wrote no fiction from the onset of the Depression until Pearl Harbor; he turned instead to economics.

12. Alsberg to Couch, June 6, 1936, in Federal Writers' Project, Papers of the Regional Director William Terry Couch, Southern Historical Collection, University of North Carolina (hereafter cited as FWP—Couch Papers). See also in these papers George W. Coan, Jr., to Couch, August 24, 1938. The states were North and South Carolina, Georgia, Florida, Alabama, Tennessee, and Virginia.

13. [Couch] to Directors of State Writers' Projects, "Memorandum Concerning Proposed Plans for Work of the Federal Writers' Project in the South," in Life Histories/Stories, General Information, Procedure folder, WPA Alabama Writers' Project, Manuscripts Division, Alabama State Department of Archives and History (hereafter cited as AWP). Here, too, Couch stated his intention to get material for four or five volumes to be published under the series name "Life in the South."

14. Couch to Alsberg, August 5, 1938; and Alsberg to Couch, September 8, 1938, FWP—Couch Papers.

15. Couch to Directors of Writers' Projects in the southeastern states, August 25, 1938.

16. See the four-page "Manual for the Collection of Life Histories" and the accompanying three-page outline for life histories, n.d., in Life Histories/Stories, General Information, Procedure folder, WPA, AWP. The manual and instructions are published as an appendix in FWP's *These Are Our Lives*, pp. 417–21, and in Tom E. Terrill and Jerrold Hirsch, eds., *Such As Us: Southern Voices of the Thirties* (Chapel Hill: University of North Carolina Press, 1978), pp. 283–87.

17. See Erksine Caldwell, *Tobacco Road* (New York: Charles Scribner's Sons, 1932); Caldwell and Margaret Bourke-White, *You Have Seen Their Faces* (New York: Viking Press, 1937); and W. T. Couch's review article, "Landlord and Tenant," in the *Virginia Quarterly Review* 14 (Spring, 1938): 309–12.

18. Jakob Baker to Thad Holt, October 8, 1935, in "Alabama–Arizona 1935–39" in Administrative Correspondence, Records of the Central Office, Records of the FWP, Records Group 69, National Archives (hereafter cited as FWP—Central Office).

19. Interview with Thad Holt, Birmingham, June 9, 1980.

20. See Mabel S. Ulrich, "Salvaging Culture for the WPA," *Harper's Monthly Magazine* 178 (May, 1939): 655, for a sketch of the initial guide plans sent to each state.

21. Couch to Alsberg, September 26, 1938, FWP—Couch Papers, reporting Miles's comments. This apparently was not unusual. In the same letter Couch

described the Tennessee project as in worse shape, having had only two quality writers, both of whom had since resigned. Another neighboring project, in Georgia, pleaded with Washington for a lenient interpretation of professional listing on the relief rolls for the same reason; see Penkower, *Federal Writers' Project,* p. 59.

22. Alsberg to Miles, February 26, 1936, "Alabama–Arizona 1935–39," and Miles to Alsberg, June 26, 1937, "Alabama 1935–39," Administrative Correspondence, FWP—Central Office.

23. Miles to Alsberg, October 8, 1938, FWP—Couch Papers.

24. The only district that functioned as intended was Mobile, under François Ludgere Diard. He was made supervisor December 14, 1935; see Miles to Alsberg of that date, FWP—Couch Papers. For a brief description of how the position of district supervisor failed in Montgomery and north Alabama see Miles to Alsberg, October 8, 1938, FWP—Couch Papers.

25. Miles to Alsberg, August 12, 1938, in "Alabama 1935–39," Administrative Correspondence, FWP—Central Office.

26. Miles to Alsberg, August 28, 1937, in "Alabama–Arizona 1935–39," Administrative Correspondence, FWP—Central Office.

27. Miles to Duke Merritt, June 8, 1936, in "Alabama–Arizona 1935–39," Administrative Correspondence, FWP—Central Office, an angry letter in regard to the use of Dr. Roland Harper's botanical material in the June 7 issue of the *Birmingham News.*

28. Miles to Couch, May 19, 1939, FWP—Couch Papers.

29. Lyle Saxon to Alsberg, August 24, 1937, in "Alabama–Arizona 1935–39," Administrative Correspondence, FWP—Central Office.

30. Penkower, in *Federal Writers' Project,* p. 156, says: "Alabama's governor delayed sponsorship of the state guide because of the efforts of the state archives department to get a different volume approved as the state textbook." See also Saxon to Alsberg, August 24, 1937, cited in note 29 above.

31. Couch to Alsberg, September 26, 1938, FWP—Couch Papers. His comment on guide copy was: "In poor shape as far as I read it."

32. Couch to Alsberg, March 3, 1939, FWP—Couch Papers.

33. On March 2, 1939, Couch wrote James Aswell of the Tennessee staff (see FWP—Couch Papers): "The situation in Alabama is serious. For any staff to work for three years and not have anything ready for publication is sufficient to warrant severe measures." Later that month Aswell, who had complained earlier about the "flossy" and "lavender and old lace" writing for the proposed guide, wrote Couch (FWP—Couch Papers, March 23, 1939) this facetious complaint: "P.S. Sir! Alabama is driving me nuts! I cannot sleep at night for Alabama! I cannot eat for the bad taste of Alabama in my mouth! My walk is palsied from Alabama! My speech is halt and hoarse with Alabama! If you hear of wells and reservoirs poisoned and mass murder in Alabama, you may know that the worm has turned. . . ."

Interestingly, Aswell's attitude toward the life histories being generated in Alabama at this same time was considerably more positive, and he was "greatly impressed" by the abilities of some of the writers he came to know in

Birmingham (see Aswell to William R. McDaniel, February 23, 1939, FWP—Couch Papers). The guide itself was finally sponsored by the State Planning Commission under a later governor, Frank Dixon; see Alabama Writers' Project, *Alabama: A Guide to the Deep South* (New York: Hastings House, 1941).

34. Federal Writers' Project, *Slave Narratives: A Folk History of Slavery in the United States from Interviews with Former Slaves,* vol. 5, *Alabama and Indiana Narratives,* ed. George P. Rawick (Westport, Conn.: Greenwood Publishing Co., 1973; reprinted from 1941). Gertha Couric of Eufaula, Ila B. Prine of Mobile, and Ruby Pickens Tartt of Livingston were as prolific writers here as they were in the subsequent life histories project, between them accounting for 46 of the 117 ex-slave narratives from Alabama. A good deal of Tartt's material in particular appeared in the famous national edition of FWP's *Lay My Burden Down: A Folk History of Slavery,* ed. Ben Botkin (Chicago: University of Chicago Press, 1945); see list of informants including those from Alabama, pp. 271–84.

35. Botkin to Miles, March 18, 1939, FWP—Couch Papers. The month before Miles wrote that she had "never heard from Dr. B. A. Botkin since the day I took him to see Mrs. Tartt in Livingston, at which time she had four Negro singers to present a program of songs" (Miles to Alsberg, February 6, 1939, "Alabama 1935–39," Administrative Correspondence, FWP—Central Office).

36. Miles to Couch, October 4, 1938, FWP—Couch Papers. At least one writer was interested in creative writing, judging by the fact that Luther Clark's piece "Lookin' for Three Fools" was published in *American Stuff* (New York: Viking Press, 1937), the FWP anthology produced from the Washington office; see Miles to Alsberg, October 13, 1938, FWP—Couch Papers.

37. Other than the state guide, the only Alabama Writers' Project publications were four pamphlets on recreation, hunting, fishing, and health (see Evanell K. Powell, *WPA Writers' Publications: A Complete Bibliographic Checklist and Price Guide of Items, Major and Minor, of the Federal Writers' Project and Program* [Palm Beach: n.d.], p. 1), and these most likely were written after September 1939 when Federal One was shut down and the projects given over to state WPA administrators.

The life histories program was conducted only in the southern states under Couch. The closest parallel in the rest of the nation was the social-ethnic survey under Dr. Morton W. Royse, who in 1935 became national editor of the FWP for this project. An expert on European minorities, Royse saw America as a mosaic of cultures, and in collaboration with folklorist Ben Botkin he proposed a series of group studies. The social-ethnic survey was firmly shelved by Couch's office in favor of the life histories that Couch considered better fitted for understanding the problems facing the South. In May 1939 a harried Myrtle Miles replied to an inquiry from Royse on the state of the social-ethnic survey in Alabama. She noted that the staff had mailed a few in the previous fall but had understood from Couch's office that this project was to be discontinued. In a plaintive conclusion she said, "I am sorry about this as we make an effort to understand and remember every instruction given us by field supervisors, regional directors, and all other visitors who have come to help us." She promised to try to finish work on a German colony, and thought something might be done with Cajans; "but we were in a better position to do this a few months ago when one of our more capable workers was living near Cajan country" (Miles to Royse, May, 29, 1939, FWP—Couch Papers). Obviously, even projects *not* involving Alabama writers consumed time and energy, at least on the part of the director.

38. Couch to State Directors, August 25, 1938, FWP—Couch Papers.

39. Miles to Couch, November 5, 1938, FWP—Couch Papers.

40. The life histories begin in Box 9 of Couch's FWP papers, alphabetically arranged by state.

41. Couch to Miles, November 12, 1938, FWP—Couch Papers. Four days later Couch sent a memo to all state directors saying some ninety life histories had been generated in North Carolina, twenty-eight in Alabama, and none elsewhere. The Alabama project had reacted more quickly to the life histories proposal than any other state except Couch's home base of North Carolina. His evaluation of the Alabama material was: "Several of these are excellent and publishable practically as they are. About half need some revision to cut out generalizations and terms expressing the feelings of writers; most of them need to be increased to a length of at least 10 to 15 pages. . . ." (See November 16, 1938, memo in Life Histories/Stories, General Information, Procedure folder, WPA, AWP.)

42. See Mary Weber to Couch, November 9, 1938, in response to his plans for that month; Couch to Alsberg, November 10, 1938, and Miles to Couch, November 14, 1938, FWP—Couch Papers.

43. Miles to Couch, December 15, 1938, FWP—Couch Papers.

44. See James Saxon Childers to Couch, November 18, 1938; Miles to Couch, January 19, 1939; and Couch to Miles, November 4, 1938, FWP—Couch Papers. In this last letter Couch mentions his contacts with Gould Beech of the *Birmingham News* and Hudson Strode of the University of Alabama and suggests that Miles contact them for recommendations of qualified writers.

45. Miles to Couch, letters of January 11, 18, and 23, 1939, FWP—Couch Papers. The project was upgraded to some extent—two university graduates were added and given life history assignments—but by and large the specific writers Couch recommended either were not on the relief rolls, found other jobs, or were reluctant to take a short-term job that might require moving to Birmingham or other expensive travel. Myrtle Miles pursued these leads with a visible determination but little success; perhaps here more than any other place Couch's plans went awry.

46. Vance to Couch, January 28, 1939, FWP—Couch Papers.

47. Federal Writers' Project, *These Are Our Lives, as told by the people and written by members of the Federal Writers' Project of the Works Progress Administration in North Carolina, Tennessee, and Georgia* (Chapel Hill: University of North Carolina Press, 1939). The preface was by W. T. Couch.

48. Couch to Aswell, January 23, 1939, FWP—Couch Papers. Here Couch wrote: "At present time there is no one on the Alabama staff who is able to get material into good final form. A large portion of the copy is fairly good but very little if any, in my opinion, is good enough to be published in its final form."

49. McDaniel to Couch, February 17, 1939, and undated Couch memo to State Directors from approximately the same date, FWP—Couch Papers. Myrtle Miles and participating Alabama writers must have been disappointed. The previous November Couch had spoken of having every southeastern state represented in the book (see November 18, 1939, memo, Couch to State Directors, in Life Histories/Stories, General Information, Procedure folder, WPA, AWP).

50. With Myrtle Miles they drove as far as Mobile, visiting staff writers; see Miles to Couch, February 18, 1939, and Aswell to McDaniel, February 23, 1939, FWP—Couch Papers.

51. Evans to Miles, February 23, 1939, FWP—Couch Papers. This life history is the final account in the present volume.

52. Couch to Miles, March 24, 1939, FWP—Couch Papers.

53. Couch to Miles, April 26, 1939, FWP—Couch Papers. See also "Book Review," *Time* 33 (May 1, 1939): 88.

54. Jerry Mangione, *The Dream and the Deal* (Boston: Little, Brown & Co., 1972), pp. 289–330. Couch wrote letters (FWP—Couch Papers) on May 4, 1939, to state directors and University of North Carolina President Frank Graham asking them to use their influence with their congressmen. Couch in his letter to Miles seemed especially stung by the FWP's being labeled a Communist agency, and he quoted the following editorial from the *Memphis Commercial Appeal*: "The Writers' Project, as everyone knows, is a Communist organization operating under the guise of overthrowing the American system and establishing Communism."

55. See Appendix.

56. In the Autauga County file is a seven-page typed manuscript that is almost certainly a life history; it is by Gertrude Brooks Milford on the daughter of a coal miner, and its December 11, 1939, date explains why it does not appear in the papers of the regional director. In the Conecuh County file is a three-page unsigned story of William George Riley, ninety-four-year-old Confederate veteran, possibly a life history. In the Escambia County file in folder one, Annie Lee Bowman has an account of Mr. and Mrs. W. D. Owens of Atmore, five pages typed on legal paper, dated December 14, 1939. In folder two is a shorter story of T. A. Graham, also of Atmore, dealing with the concerns of turkey hunting and the liquor business.

In the Jefferson County files, which also include editorial department work, is a story signed simply S. J., dated September 14, 1938, about an old couple who play dominoes while their son, thirty-nine, runs the farm. There are two stories by Nettie S. McDonald, one of Bill and Louise Borderland, a Birmingham baker and his wife, half the seven pages describing the baby they just had, and a fifteen-page manuscript on Miss Bessie Longshore. Wilson Heflin of the editorial department has a thirteen-page typed manuscript on Walter B.

Murray, printer from Leighton; the setting is a funeral, and the reminiscences make good reading except that it is a fifth carbon and hard to decipher.

In the Lee County files are several one- and two-page biographies by Preston Klein, some of ex-slaves and some of noted people, possibly for the tour guide. Others, though brief, more nearly fit the life history category. In the Mobile County files, François Ludgere Diard has a fourteen-page typed manuscript on Edden Bodden, veteran sailor. Most of the action takes place out of state, although it includes a great sailor yarn of a brawl. Diard also has a ten-page sketch of Tainer Lee; although the main subject is folklore and hoodoo, overall it resembles a life history. In the miscellaneous manuscripts folder from Mobile County, Benjamin Baker has a story on ninety-year-old Captain John Durgan in four typed pages, possibly a life history attempt.

In the Perry County file Susie R. O'Brien has an account of Mrs. Ira Reynolds. In the Sumter County file Ruby Pickens Tartt has an interesting account of L. B. Runkle of Livingston, who gave up the janitor business to become a fisherman. The last two accounts are almost certainly life histories. Finally, one of the accounts that never reached the regional office is published in this volume, Rhussus Perry's "Janey Gets Her Desires," from Macon County. All of these accounts are from the appropriate county files in the Alabama Writers' Project—WPA material in the manuscripts division of the Alabama State Department of Archives and History in Montgomery.

57. Miles to Alsberg, October 13, 1938, FWP—Couch Papers. In an undated two-page memo that followed the "Manual for the Collection of Life Histories" to each southern state (see Life Histories/Stories, General Information, Procedure folder, WPA, AWP), Couch says of an interview with an ex-slave that it is an ex-slave narrative if its focus is on slavery, but if the focus is on the present, it is a life history: "In the life histories the emphasis is on the present and the past is treated only to throw light on the present."

In the Elmore County file of AWP materials is a five-page typed article on a family of wealthy recluses. At first glance it seems to be a life history, but penciled across the top is the note, "place in Elmore Co. file—*not* in Life Stories." Perhaps this means it was slated for the tour guide; in any case, it is clear that even project workers had trouble differentiating projects. That may have reflected a certain confusion even on the national level. Botkin, for example, saw the life histories as a folklore project; see his "WPA and Folklore Research: 'Bread and Song,' " *Southern Folklore Quarterly* 3 (March, 1939): 10.

58. James Agee and Walker Evans, *Let Us Now Praise Famous Men* (Boston: Houghton Mifflin, 1960; originally published in 1941). In most research there is the discovery of interesting material not quite on the subject at hand. In an interview with Thad Holt, Birmingham, June 9, 1980, the editor was given an account of the genesis of *Let Us Now Praise Famous Men.* Holt, in 1935 head of the Alabama WPA, had had some contact with *Fortune* writer Florence Horn, who was reporting on Harry Hopkins. Holt suggested to her a story on sharecroppers, a social and economic class he had come to see as the heart of rural poverty in the Deep South. He himself had become interested in

sharecroppers through CCC work, and he thought their story had never been told. Holt forgot that suggestion until he got a telegram from *Fortune* editor Eric Hodgins asking for help on the project. Holt wired back, "sure," and the next telegram said James Agee was assigned to the story, and would Holt please start him off. Holt set up a luncheon in Montgomery with four of the largest landowners in the state, two of them his wife's kinsfolk; these four included the two single largest cotton farmers in Alabama, according to Holt: Will Howard Smith of Prattville and Jack McLemore of Mt. Meigs. Of course, Holt recalls, this was just the opposite social stratum for which Agee was looking. Holt remembers "Jimmy" as quiet and a little too polite to ask tough questions of the landlords. Agee went on to Selma, the heart of the black belt, and disappeared from view. A month later, Holt got a telegram from *Fortune* asking where in the world Agee was. Holt still has his correspondence and the telegrams relating to these incidents. He does not remember meeting Walker Evans.

59. Daniel M. Fox, "The Achievement of the Federal Writers' Project," *American Quarterly* 13 (Spring, 1961): 11.

60. The Georgia director said in 1969, "I wonder why we did not have Negro representation on our State staff, but in the 1930's it didn't seem so urgent, if indeed we ever thought of it" (see Penkower, *Federal Writers' Project*, p. 67). Of all the southeastern states, only Virginia had an active black component.

61. Sterling Brown wrote the following to Couch, October 19, 1939 (FWP—Couch Papers): "According to the State Director of Alabama, there has been great difficulty in finding Negroes in Alabama eligible for positions on the Federal Writers' Project. She states ' . . .members of the race who are fortunate enough to have Institute training are not on relief,' and 'it would be unwise to give a Negro this job . . . there is considerable racial sensitiveness in Tuskegee and vicinity.' "

Earlier (according to Penkower, *Federal Writers' Project*, p. 142) Miles had complained: "Dr. Brown has a chip on his shoulder"; and "Alabamans understand the general Negro situation here better than a critic whose life has been spent in another section of the country, however studious he may be." The Alabama Writers' Project's three black writers were Louise Porter of Mobile, Levi Shelby of Tuscumbia, and Rhussus Perry of Macon County (see Miles to Couch, January 4, 1939, FWP—Couch Papers). Perry was hired October 4, 1938, after several pointed suggestions from the regional and national FWP offices to get a certified black writer from the Tuskegee area. Mrs. Perry (now Mrs. Saunders) was the only black writer of Alabama life histories; she says she never met Miles personally (telephone conversaton with editor, February 4, 1980).

62. See Kytle's "A Dead Convict Don't Cost Nothin' " and "I'm Allus Hongry" in this volume, typical of his work on the life histories project.

63. Even Studs Terkel's popular history, *Hard Times: An Oral History of the Great Depression* (New York: Pantheon Books, 1970), is a reflective work.

64. The names of all primary characters in the following life histories have

been changed (even though many of them were already altered in the original manuscripts), as well as specific addresses. The only exception to this is Arthur Lee Emerson, the subject of "The Andrew Jackson of Southern Labor." Because of his labor activity, he was already something of a public figure, and since the life history deals in part with this public activity, his true name has been kept. All of these accounts are presented entire, again with the single exception of one paragraph in "The Andrew Jackson of Southern Labor," which deals with recognizable individuals probably still living.

Part One

Small Town and Farm Folk
of North Alabama

Covington Hall was at one time "the leading radical writer and journalist in the South." He was a friend of Big Bill Haywood of the International Workers of the World and a central figure in the 1912 struggles of the Brotherhood of Timber Workers in Louisiana.[1] When Myrtle Miles interviewed Hall a quarter of a century later in 1938 in the "mountain jungle" around Mentone, he was in a Thoreau-style retreat and eminently certifiable for the relief rolls. He probably picked the Mentone area for his retreat because it was the home of Arthur Lee Emerson, the principal organizer of the 1912 timber workers and by this time an old friend. By the time Hall left the Alabama Writers' Project in early December 1938, he had written four life histories.[2] The two longest are printed here. The first is perhaps most interesting for Hall's sketch of the mountain economy of northeastern Alabama and of Bill Dollar's attitudes toward religion. The second is a sympathetic study of Arthur Lee Emerson in decline and obscurity.

Bill Dollar, Farmer-Miner

by Covington Hall

"No, Arthur, hit haint so. That haint true. He does some moonshinin' an' bootleggin' an' gets drunk now an' then, but he's a fine man. He works hard and takes care of his family," said Bill Dollar, answering a query as to a neighbor whose conduct was under fire in the community. In making these statements, Bill spoke earnestly, judging his friend, not by his personal prejudices, but by the ethical standards generally accepted by the mountain people.

Bill is one of them. He was "bawn an' raised" near where he now lives. He left home only once, when he worked for a year or so in the coal mines of Harlan County, Kentucky, and West

---

[1]See Grady McWhiney, "Louisiana Socialists in the Early Twentieth Century: A Study of Rustic Radicalism," *Journal of Southern History* 20 (August, 1954): 320, n. 26; see also F. Ray Marshall, *Labor in the South* (Cambridge: Harvard University Press, 1967), pp. 97–98, and Joseph R. Conlin, *Big Bill Haywood and the Radical Union Movement* (Syracuse: Syracuse University Press, 1969), p. 116.

[2]Miles to Weber, December 6, 1938, FWP—Couch Papers.

Virginia. Almost from the hour in which he crawled out of the cradle he has toiled in the fields and mines, being at present employed in a small coal mine about four miles to the east of Mentone when not tilling his land. "I have been farmin' an' minin' ever sence I can remember," he says, "an' I still don't know which one is the worse to make a livin' at." He is still doing so, though today he is nearing the three score and ten limit.

When times are hard, as they often are, he may do some moonshining and bootlegging as a side line, excusing himself, if he ever bothers to, by quoting the biblical admonition to the effect that "a man who does not care for his family is worse than an infidel." And Bill is "a good family man," a kind and indulgent husband and father. He is also very religious, being a member of the Church of God, or "Holy Roller," persuasion. In union territory, he is a staunch union man, holding firmly to the belief that John L. Lewis[3] is, or will be, the saviour of the coal diggers, "who," he avers, "have as tough a time diggin' and livin' out of the ground as do the farmers. Everybody else," he swears, "lives offen us farmers an' miners an' all we gits for our labor is a grubstake, an' a po' one." But he keeps to his diggin's, trusting to God and President Lewis to remedy conditions; how, he doesn't know. Only of this he said he is certain: that "things can't go on much longer like they is goin', 'cause they is too onjust in the sight of God."

Bill Dollar is typical of those who have been trapped in the southern mountains, where, when their forebears came, getting a living was comparatively easy, the abundance of game in the forests and fish in the streams, plus the "gyardin', 'tater an' co'n patches," assuring a plentiful supply. Their log or weatherboard cabins never lacked warmth, for all one had to do "in the good old days" to keep the fire glowing was step into the woods with his axe. His fuel supply was free, costing only what labor he and his sons chose to devote to the task.

---

[3]John L. Lewis was president of the United Mine Workers beginning in 1920, but his most dramatic activity was from 1933 to 1937, when he organized southern miners, formed the Congress of Industrial Organizations, and won landmark agreements from companies the size of U.S. Steel. More than a year before this life history was written, however, a recession broke the CIO's momentum and Lewis's power began to wane; see Irving Bernstein, *The Turbulent Years: A History of the American Worker 1933–1941* (Boston: Houghton Mifflin, 1970), pp. 397–98, 784–85.

Baptist church. Gadsden, 1940. Vachon, FSA.

Gradually, however, the old life changed. The game disappeared from the forests and an important source of cash income vanished, that derived from the sale of furs. The streams were fished out. The fields widened. The summer people came, bought homes and became residents and, with them, the stock laws preventing the use of the woods as common pasture. The large herds of sheep and goats were lost, still further limiting the free meat supply and cutting off another cash crop, wool. The trees were hewn into crossties for the railroads, or logged off to sawmills in the valley or turned into rough lumber by portable mills on the spot. The game, the fish, the goats and sheep and timber being "et up," the people lost their economic independence.[4] So Bill and his neighbors turned to farming for a living.

[4]Shortage of game seems to have been the prime reason that camp hunting, presumably for commercial purposes, was prohibited in DeKalb County in 1876. Closed seasons

Having no agricultural experience beyond scratching a corn-field and "plantin' by the moon," unused to planning far ahead, unable to secure financing except at interest rates ranging from ten to fifteen percent per annum, they found farming, as Bill insists, "mainly a heap o' work for nothin'." All the majority have been able to eke out of it is a bare subsistence. Even when they can add to their meager cash income by working in small nearby mines or mills, or on WPA, or on whatever temporary jobs they find, their standard of living is unbelievably low. Few of Bill's kind, though they have now begun to raise cotton, possess decent bedding or comfortable clothing. All this deprivation, however, they look upon as "the will of God."

This, "Hit's God's work and will," is the attitude of Bill and his generation toward the big families with which they are "blest." Bill's opinion of birth control is that "hit's ag'inst the law set down in The Book. God sont 'em," he says, "an' hit ain't for man to meddle with God's doin's." And that settles it as far as he is concerned. If he and his ever heard of Margaret Sanger,[5] and quite a few have, they speak of her ideas with horror, since the ministers of all their sects denounce her in unmeasured terms as a modern "Jezebel come to corrupt our women folks to disobey our Lord's commandment to 'go forth, multiply and replenish the earth.' " Bill and his generation heed this warning, but many of the young people, they regretfully admit, "is strayin' away from the strict an' narrow path."

This "fallin' away" by the young men and women worries their elders considerably; but "believin'," as their forefathers and mothers did, that babies "is sont of God," and that "God he'ps them as what he'ps themselves an' others," Bill and his frail little wife have stuck to it, "raisin' somehow, we don't know

---

were initiated for deer, turkey, dove, and quail in 1895; see *Acts of the General Assembly of Alabama, session of 1876–7* (Montgomery: Barrett & Brown, State Printers, 1877), p. 181, and *Acts . . . session of 1894–5* (Montgomery: Roemer Printing Co., 1895), p. 5. Open range law for the state of Alabama was done away with in 1941, though almost all counties abolished it before then. The developments summarized here by Covington Hall are otherwise difficult to document for a single county, although this overall pattern was perhaps typical for much of the nation.

[5]Margaret Sanger (1883–1966) had become a household name to millions of Americans for her dramatic activities of 1914 to 1921 and later on behalf of birth conrol as part of the path to women's liberation; see David M. Kennedy, *Birth Control in America: The Career of Margaret Sanger* (New Haven: Yale University Press, 1970), pp. 82, 106.

how," five sons and a daughter. Two sons and the girl have married, settled down in the community and are giving Bill and his wife many grandchildren of whom they are proud.

Most of the old folks on "The Mountain," as its inhabitants affectionately call Lookout, have little book knowledge. The education of few of them went beyond simple "readin', ritin' and 'rithmetic." Many are illiterate. But elders take great interest in the schools. The great majority say, "a boy or girl without eddication haint got no chance in the worl' today." The children emulate their parents in this. They will work and scrape and deny themselves to save a few pennies with which to purchase books and other necessaries and then trudge through sleet and snow six or seven miles rather than miss a day in classes. But when they receive their high school diplomas, as many do, and though they love their mountain home, they are unlike their parents in that the majority are not satisfied to "settle down" there. They hear the call of the mills and factories in the restless world below and, the blood of the pioneers being in their veins, more and more of them answer it every year. When the Textile Code was promulgated with its promise of steady jobs and good wages,[6] they poured into the mill town, returning bitterly disappointed when they found they were not wanted.

When Bill was asked what he thought of so many young folks leaving the mountain, "I don't like hit," he said. "Of course, the youngsters haint to be blamed. There haint nothin' much for them to do here no more. So most of them is onsatisfied, 'specially them as has some eddication. Course most of the cabins we folks hereabouts lives in haint much as a home, as fur as homes go, but they is *ourn,* which is more'n most town an' city people can say. But the younguns don't see that. They hears all about the high wages, short hours an' good times in town, an' so heads for hit. Most of them will be disapp'inted. Most of us is wherever we be. We all got to take our chance. I don't blame them an' nobody else can. Farmin' an' minin' is both hard lives, an' hit's gittin' harder every year for a man to dig a livin' out of

---

[6]President Roosevelt signed the National Industrial Recovery Act on June 16, 1933, an act enabling codes to be established by management *and* organized labor in the various industries through the mediation of the federal government. The Textile Code was one of the immediate responses, adopted the following month; see Bernstein, *Turbulent Years,* pp. 34–35, and Marshall, *Labor in the South,* p. 166.

either for hisself an' family. No, I don' like hit an' I don' blame the young folks; but I wush we could keep 'em all here at home," he ended wistfully.

The last time I saw him he was looking peaky. I asked him if he was ill. "No," he said, "I'm all right, only I nearly got kilt last week." "How? What happened?" I asked. "A fall of rock in the mine hit me an' busted my collarbone an' bruised me up. But I'm all right now. Goin' back to the mine Monday." "Better lay off and take it easy a few days more," I suggested. "Kain't afford to," he said, a smile wrinkling his strong, gaunt face. "Me an' the old woman an' what kids is lef' at home has got to eat. An' eatin' costs money. You know that. Kain't 'ford to lose the wages I've already missed, collarbone or no collarbone. So long. Hope I'll be seein' you ag'in soon."

Bill, contrary to general belief, is not shiftless. Neither is his wife. Both are up before the sun, Bill on his way to the field or mine and Mrs. Dollar busy about her endless housework, which includes watching over and taking care of the chickens, cows, babies and dogs, not to mention washing, scrubbing and, now and then, helping out with a hoe.

Their cabin home sits on the edge of their field, close to the woods. It is made of plain plank, roofed with shingles. It has no front porch or gallery. It is entered from two rickety steps. It is only partly ceiled. The flooring is fairly good, but the sun shines through the roof and cracks in the walls let in more than sufficiency of fresh air. There are no partitions between the rooms, no pictures on the walls. A stone chimney rises in the center of the house. Its wide, deep fireplace, filled with ash, oak or hickory logs, gives them all the heat they seem to need and lends a cheerful aspect to the almost furnitureless interior. The kitchen is a long, narrow room built on the rear of the cabin. Nearby is a rickety barn, sheltering one cow, one mule and a few chickens. The hog pen is close by—the Dollars, like all their neighbors, being fond of and heavy consumers of pork. The dwelling has a few oaks in front of it and is bordered by an orchard containing a few peach and apple trees. Few townfolk would envy them their home, but they were heartbroken when the mortgage was foreclosed, the place sold to another "hard-scrabbler" and they had to move into a rented house.

Losing their home was a tragedy to them, but it is not the only tragedy they have known. Their oldest son was shot and killed in the early 1930s by a neighbor who charged him with seducing and then refusing to marry (a "mortal crime" on the mountain) his fifteen-year-old daughter. The wronged girl committed suicide and this, with the fact that all said, "the boy was a bad 'un an' got what he deserved," hurt them greatly. Next, their daughter's first husband, a boy who was noted far and wide for his "glorious singing voice," got mixed up in the whiskey business and was killed in a fight with a revenue officer.

Yes, the Dollars have know tragedy, more than their fair share. But they rarely talk of it. They "bear the burdens the Lord has sent" with the stoicism of true Calvinists. Their hospitality is unfailing. If an invitation to come in and sit awhile is accepted, they will insist on the caller having "a bit to eat with us," bringing out cakes and honey, or other homemade luxury, to tempt the palate. They do not keep bees. The honey comes from bee trees Bill found and robbed, he being one of the famed "bee trailers" of DeKalb County.

Like all mountain people, once they learn to know a person, the Dollars are sociable and friendly. With a friend they will share their last peck of meal, or go even further and loan their prize coon dog or fox hound. They will minister to the sick and reverently bury the dead. But provoke their enmity and the feudist boils up. Then there is nothing they will not do to "git even." In this, as in nearly all other matters, they proceed according to their own law, judging right and wrong with primitive directness. Beyond this code and the Ten Commandments, the only other laws they respect are those of the Federal Government, and then only the statutes relating to the illicit distilling of whiskey. These laws they fear but, at the same time, resent as an infringement of their individual liberty. They "kain't see where hit is any of the Gov'ment's business what I do with my c'on, whether I make hit into cowfeed or likker. Hit's mine, hain't hit?" they growl. The argument is convincing to all save the internal revenue officers who have all but destroyed the once flourishing "white mule" traffic, thus cutting off an important source of cash income.

Whether it is due to this and all the other woes that have harried him and his throughout their lives, I do not know; but Bill has got religion. He has "j'ined the Holy Rollers," and, as the making, selling and using of whiskey, tobacco and like "vile stuff" is anathema to the Church of God, Bill has repented and reformed. The church has done for him through love and sympathy what the state could not do through force and fear of prison. And so Bill "keeps the faith," courageously striving, he says, to "make the sperrit triumphant over the flesh."

The Andrew Jackson of Southern Labor

by Covington Hall

Arthur Lee Emerson is five feet eleven inches tall. He is rawboned in build. He has keen, clear blue-gray eyes. He has probably had more babies named after him than all other Southern labor and farmer leaders combined. He was born in Tennessee. He never knew his father and his mother died when he was a child. He was placed in an orphan asylum in Chattanooga, the matron of which called him "my boy" to her dying day. He was taken to Lookout Mountain when he was fourteen years old by Dr. Parker, who reared him. Dr. Parker, who was always proud of his foster son, was a well-educated man of decided character. Tiring of cities and hospitals, he had settled near Mentone and married (twice) before he took Arthur out of the asylum. He had one daughter, but she married when young and left the mountain. Both his wives died, leaving the doctor and Arthur alone in the woods. The social instincts of both, however, being strong, they did not lead lonely lives, and they educated each other. The doctor died in his eighty-seventh year, interested to the last in all that was happening in the world. Arthur—that is what everyone calls him—cared for him to the end as best he could.

Emerson is now in his fifty-eighth year and, from the day when a boy of eighteen, he organized and led a strike of Georgia strawberry pickers, he has been active and deeply interested in farmer and labor movements. He won the berry pickers' strike, securing better wages and treatment for the workers, but was himself discharged and blacklisted. "That didn't bother me," he says. "I could always take care of myself."

For several years he worked at different jobs near home and then headed west, roaming the nation from Mentone, Alabama, to Portland, Oregon, and back again, making his way as a lumber worker. In time he became a skilled woodworker and building carpenter. He was working at this trade in West Louisiana when the panic of 1907 hit the country. Taking advantage of it, the lumber companies drastically cut the wages and lengthened the hours of the employees. As a result of this, there was a spontaneous, south-wide walk-out. It was unorganized. The workers simply went home and stayed there until, on the promise that the old wages and hours would be reinstated as soon as business conditions justified it, they returned to work. The promise was not kept and ever-increasing discontent and restlessness resulted. Spontaneous and sporadic strikes broke out in Louisiana. Attempts were made to organize unions. All petered out; but the lumber companies, fearing the idea might take and hold, began to compel their employees and all applying for work to take the "yellowdog oath."[7] This oath, subscribed to before a notary or justice of the peace, pledged that under no circumstances would the worker "ever join a labor union of any kind." This merely increased the already smouldering discontent, for thousands of workers had begun to look to unionization as their "only salvation from starvation on the job," as they put it. They were soured and resentful.

Emerson had joined one of the sporadic unions, but had dropped out. Then one day a contractor friend he was working for, and who was building an addition to a mill, came to him with a slip of paper in his hand, and said, "Arthur, I don't want to ask you to sign this, but they say I and all my men have got to sign it."

"What is it?" Arthur asked.

"Here it is," his friend said, handing him the "yellowdog oath."

"No," Arthur exploded. "I won't degrade my manhood by signing any such pledge."

"I thought you wouldn't," said his friend.

Talking to me of it, Arthur said, "I was so mad and fed-up, so sick and tired of it all, I threw my tools in the box and left it with a friend. Then, determined to do something about it, I went out preaching organization. I started first with the woods crews. I found the big majority ready to move, but they kept saying, 'See Jay Smith and let us know what he says.' I hunted up Jay and finally met him. He agreed and we called a meeting of men we

---

[7]The "yellowdog contracts" were held valid in the federal courts, enforceable by injunction in perpetuity, as late as 1928; see Bernstein, *The Lean Years: A History of the American Worker 1920–1933* (Boston: Houghton Mifflin, 1960), p. 131.

thought we could trust. About twenty-five attended. It was decided to organize the Brotherhood of Timber Workers and issue a call to everybody working in, around, or for the mills, to join. They flocked in by the thousands, and that is how the Brotherhood got started."

So began the summer of 1910, the most spectacular period of Emerson's career, for he and Smith soon found themselves leading, not a labor union, but a revolt of the people of the Louisiana and Texas pine country against the "Lumber Barons," as the owners of the industry were dubbed. Not only lumberjacks but farmers, merchants, lawyers and doctors joined the Brotherhood. The struggle that ensued was an epic one. It lasted for more than three years. It was for his activity in this "timber war," as both sides styled it, that Emerson earned the title of "Andrew Jackson of the Southern Labor Movement."

Nervous, quick-tempered, often going into paroxysms of rage when balked, he was idolized by his followers and obeyed unquestioningly on every order he issued. When asked why they so blindly followed him, they would reply: "Ef Arthur tells you to do something, he'll do it himself. Ef he tells you, 'you be thar an' I'll be thar,' he'll be thar." And he always was. Whites, Negroes and Mexicans all looked upon him as a messiah come to deliver his people from bondage, for he was one of them.

Desperate, unable to stem the tide, the lumber companies early in 1911 declared a lockout, closing down for seven months fifty or more of the largest mills in West Louisiana and East Texas. "But," said Arthur, "the men were not whupped. Weak and hungry, they came back fighting, sticking to our demands for better conditions and wages paid in United States money."

The struggle continued, both sides becoming more and more bitter, until, on July 7, 1912, a riot occurred at the sawmill village of Grabo, Louisiana. The Brotherhood had called a strike here, but the mill was operating with strikebreakers furnished by a detective agency of national scope. The union had not planned a meeting at Grabo that day, but at Carson, a few miles away. The meeting at Carson was broken up by loyal workers of the company and its "Good Citizen League" allies from the surrounding territory. Emerson and all others attempting to speak had their voices drowned out by the opposing mob yelling and beating on small circular saws and tin shields made especially for such occasions. These tactics had been used by the lumber companies previously and were humorously referred to by the union workers and farmers as "tincannings."

Unable to speak, Emerson and the 800 men, women and children with him headed home for DeRidder, a sub-headquarters of the Brotherhood. Runners sent ahead of the march reported to Emerson that gunmen were lying in wait to shoot at his wagon as it passed through a strip of woods on the route, so he ordered the march changed to the Grabo road. About 400 of the 800 in the crowd followed him. When they reached Grabo they halted and ate lunch, after which it was decided to "hold a speaking." One or two spoke before Emerson without trouble, but when he rose and had been talking only a few minutes, shots were fired from one of the company's buildings at the wagon on which he stood. He said, "I threw up my hands and yelled, 'Don't shoot! Don't shoot! For God's sake stop! There are women and children in the crowd!' " The firing, however, soon became general on both sides, ending only when the unionmen charged the company's office and routed their opponents. Several men were killed on both sides and many wounded, how many was never exactly known. Three men were left dead on the field of battle, two unionmen and one strikebreaker. One unionman was mortally wounded and died shortly after the fight. Only ten or twelve of the Brotherhood men were armed, mostly with pistols, one or two with shotguns or rifles, "because," says Emerson, "we did not expect trouble that day."

As a result of this riot, Emerson and fifty-seven other lumber workers and farmers were immediately arrested, taken to Lake Charles, the parish seat, jailed, and later indicted for "conspiracy to murder." On this charge, Emerson and eight other "ringleaders" were brought to trial that autumn. The trial lasted about two months, with all labor and farmer organizations lining up behind the defense, and this was despite the fact that the 1912 convention of the Brotherhood affiliated it with the Forest & Lumberworkers Union of the Industrial Workers of the World. The case was bitterly contested by both prosecution and defense attorneys. It was finally given to the jury, composed of eight farmers from the rice district, two businessmen and two nonunion workingmen. The jury was out one hour, when it returned with a unanimous verdict of "not guilty." This verdict freed not only the nine "ringleaders," but all other indicted men. None of the companies' men who took part in the battle were ever indicted.

Worn down by the long, gruelling strife, Emerson suffered a nervous collapse, and shortly after his acquittal went home to Lookout Mountain to rest and recuperate. It took him several months to do so; but as soon as he felt better, he returned to Louisiana in 1913 and made one more trip through the lumber country in an endeavor to reorganize the Brotherhood. Failing, he resigned his office as General Organizer and went to Tennessee. There he studied law and on his graduation began to practice in Chattanooga.

He married, and rapidly forged to the front in the law profession, becoming in a short time a power in the labor movement and in the Democratic Party of the city and county. Success seemed to attend all his efforts, but at the moment he thought he had won out, he suffered a stroke of paralysis. This happened in 1921. He was training a basketball team in the YMCA gymnasium when the stroke came. He never lost consciousness, but his left side was crippled and his speech badly affected. This affliction made it impossible for him to function longer either as a lawyer or labor organizer.

Heartbroken at the sudden eclipse of his prospects and hopes, he spent some time in northern hospitals seeking to regain his health; but, getting little relief, went home to the mountain, hoping its invigorating climate and pure waters would restore his strength. He has been there ever since, his wife and a friend having bought the old home place.

There, though he has regained much of his strength, he has never been able to rest content. Always the urge is on him to return to the old exciting and successful life, only to come back, "because my speech wouldn't let me go on," he explains. During the winter months when there is little to do save feed the chickens, chop firewood and hang around the house, he is like a caged panther longing for the open.

It has been eighteen years now since his tragedy occurred, but he has never given up hope of coming back. Having no predelictions for farming, he has desperately striven to get a living for his family out of the soil and from eggs and chickens. I have seen him, when the pain in his left side was terrible, leave his plow and lie down in the row until it eased. Then he would go on, he and Old Sam, his mule, until sundown. Once he built up a flock of 500 leghorn hens. These he nursed from the time the chicks were delivered until they were grown. On sunny days when he went to feed them he would sit down and lean against the henhouse. The hens, when they had finished eating, would come around, hop up on his knees and shoulders and he would talk to them saying, "Never mind; my daughters will yet save us." But this, too, was not to be. The entire flock was lost when in the panic of 1929 eggs dropped to five and ten cents a dozen and broilers and fryers to ten and fifteen cents a pound, and were hard to sell out even at that.

In the tragic winters that followed 1929, the family depended mainly on cornbread, cowpeas, and sorghum molasses to hold body and soul together. Milk and butter from their two cows, which they managed somehow to hold on to, with what fruits and vegetables they had been able to can, were the only luxuries they knew. Biscuits were rarely seen on the table, for flour costs money and money was scarce with them. Their clothing and bedding became, as Mrs. Emerson put it, "mostly rags." But still they struggled on, making only one appeal for relief, which was denied. Many of their neighbors suffered like privations. The general cry was, "My God! what's a man who's willin' to work to support his family and kain't get no payin' job or must sell his crops for nothin going to do? What's the world comin' to, anyhow?" President Roosevelt's election with his plea for the "forgotten man" and his prompt relief measures cheered them, "for," they said, "he is the first high-up that has ever showed any sympathy for our lot."

Somehow or other, the Emersons with the help of friends managed to exist, and their prospects have improved somewhat lately. There are seven persons in the family, Emerson, his wife, her eighty-year-old mother, three boys and a girl, all grown. They managed to send the children through high school. To this end, no sacrifices have been too great for the parents to bear. Emerson's clothes in rags, he worries that he cannot send them to the university. The children, like their parents, are eager for education.[. . .]

The farm originally contained 160 acres, but a friend took over forty in 1936 to save them from the mortgage. Only four acres were cleared when the family moved on the place in 1921. Since then about 35 acres have been put under cultivation, all of it cleared by Emerson and the boys, who are strapping young men and have worked ever since they could handle a hoe. Emerson and the friend who bought the forty are now busy planning for next year, having in mind the sale of plant sets, broilers and eggs to begin with. They, too, "want no more cotton."

The family lives in an ancient log cabin having five rooms and a kitchen of sorts. It is meagerly furnished with only the household goods bought in prosperous days. On the walls hang a few pictures. Photographs of the family and friends adorn the mantelpiece of the big stone fireplace in the sitting room, in which there is a case filled with books. Dumas is there, a series of novels by noted foreign authors, the Harvard Library classics, Montesquieu's *Spirit of the Laws, Don Quixote,* Ridpath's *History of the World,* and other works of equal merit are on the shelves. All the children love to read, especially one son who has read every volume in the bookcase and is hungry for more. A daily paper and several weeklies and monthly magazines come to the house and are read by all the family. All listen in on a radio one of the boys recently purchased for his mother. Emerson has been planning a new house ever since he returned to the farm in 1921, but has never gotten around to building it, mainly because of lack of money.

The home is not on the public road. It faces a by-road that passes through the yard about fifty yards from the dwelling. On the front of the cabin there is a small, roofed porch, entered by steps made of two large unhewn stones. In front of this and on both sides is a flower garden filled with roses, lilies, honeysuckle, gladioli, jonquils, hollyhocks, and numerous other flowers and shrubs. From early spring to late fall the sight makes one forget the poverty which the beauty covers for a while. In the surrounding woods grow and blossom many kinds of wild flowers and flowering trees, dogwood, azaleas, mountain laurel, and others native to the section. In autumn all the colors of the rainbow blaze on the forest. There is some compensation then for the hard living. In the spring Mrs. Emerson, her mother and daughter busy themselves in the garden. They never tire of the task and are happy when their plants reward their labors with fine and abundant blooms. In the winter they always set out a supply of feed for the birds in boxes fixed in an old dead peachtree or on the porch.

When they first settled on the farm few birds were to be seen around the place, but now many come for breakfast and supper and if the boxes are empty, protest until their wants are satisfied. Last winter a partridge with a late brood discovered the barn. Peas were scattered on the snow for the brood, and every day the mother and her brood were there. The lands are not posted, but as everyone has been asked not to shoot the quail and squirrels these are rarely molested, for the mountain people still respect each other's wishes in such matters. If, however, some sportsman is heard banging away, one of the boys promptly heads for where the shooting is going on, and his protests are heeded. Seldom is an appeal to law needed.

The Emersons, though poor, are of good families. Christine, his wife, is the daughter of a Louisiana physician and the granddaughter of a Georgia planter, who was a slaveholder and a major in the Confederate army. Arthur has no fixed or strong religious beliefs, merely saying when one questions him thereon: "I believe there is some power over the universe, but I don't know what it is. I believe that if a man tries to do the right thing, it well help him." And he lets it go at that. Christine, however, is a convert to the Seventh Day Adventist creed and a devout member of that church. She will stand for Arthur and the boys working on Sunday, but not on her Sabbath, which is a Saturday. All work on the farm comes to a halt on that day, for "so it is commanded by the Scriptures." She is not, however, intolerant, and there being no Adventist congregation in the community, they usually attend the services of the nearby Wesleyan Methodist church to which most of their friends belong.

Beyond the part the children take in church affairs, they have few amusements other than radio plays and a motion picture show now and then. Their greatest excitement comes when a football, baseball, or basketball game occurs between Valley Head High and some other school. Then, as all the children have been on the teams, the discussion is endless as to which team will win and afterwards why it won or lost. All are ardent sportsmen. Preparing for a game, they and their friends practice in the yard until it is too dark to find the ball, when they reluctantly leave off. At such time Mrs. Emerson must use both threats and strategy to get them to stop long enough to bring in stove wood. None of them are musical, though they join in the singing at church and at the occasional 'sings' in the community. Their main complaint at present is inability to "get work at living wages." This is the general complaint of the young mountain men and women. They "see nothing in farming," they say, and so are restless to get out and try a better standard of living. The Emersons, like all the rest, would like to keep them at home, but bow to the inevitable.

Emerson frequently hears the bugles of battle calling and is wild to answer; but though the spirit is willing, the flesh is no longer strong enough to carry on as of old. And so the Andrew Jackson of Southern Labor goes back to the field instead of the forum and battle line.

Charles Donigan of Sheffield, described by Myrtle Miles as a "capable" writer, wrote only this one life history. The life history itself is stilted and pedestrian, the kind of oral history that results when the interviewer grimly pursues a fixed list of questions. At the same time it is detailed and is most interesting for its picture of 1938 farming methods in the Tennessee River Valley.

F. W. Kachelhofer, Farmer

by Charles Donigan

Frederick William Kachelhofer lives with his wife and two daughters on what is known as Leighton Road several miles north of Leighton, Alabama. His house is about sixty feet from the highway. This road is graveled from Leighton north to the Tennessee River. The rural route does not pass in front of his house so he has a box on the road going west to Sheffield, Alabama. All of these points are in Colbert County, Alabama.

Mr. Kachelhofer rents (money rent) eighty acres of fairly good land with house, barn, chicken house and other outhouses. The improvements are not in good condition. A good creek flows through the place and he uses a well for water. The house was dilapidated when he first rented it about three years ago, and he has repaired it as far as he was able, painting it inside and out and repapering the walls. The roof is old but does not leak. The old house has two rooms in front with two shed rooms to the rear and an attic room upstairs. A porch is across the front, and doors open from each of the front rooms on to it. One of the front rooms has a large wood-burning fireplace. A heater is installed in the other front room. One of the rear rooms is used as kitchen and the other as a bedroom. There is no heat in this room except through a door into the kitchen. One of the front rooms is used as a living room and is nicely furnished with piano, couch, table, chairs and bookcase. The other is the dining room. There is also a bed and wardrobe in this room. A TVA electric line passes along the road in front of Mr. Kachelhofer's house, but the house is not wired. He uses a mantle coal oil lamp and ordinary lamps.

F. W. Kachelhofer was born in Barton County, Kansas, in 1889 and moved with his parents to Colbert County, Alabama, within one-fourth mile of where he now lives, in 1898. His wife, May Smith Kachelhofer, was born in Lauderdale County, Alabama, in 1893.

The oldest daughter is Stacie Kachelhofer, whose birthday is in November. She would not allow her father to tell the date of her birth, but she was born in Colbert County, Alabama, about twenty-three years ago. She was graduated from Colbert County High School in 1936 and then completed a correspondence business course. The younger daughter is Andrea, whose birthday is in April. She also objected to giving year of birth but she is about twenty-one. Andrea completed the eleventh grade in Colbert County High School, but did not finish because she got a job and contributed a part of her earnings so Stacie could graduate. They are both pretty, industrious, refined and highly respected girls.

Mr. Kachelhofer's father, grandfather and great grandfather were natives of Baden, Germany. He said that his father was one of a family of five boys and girls, that he lived in Baden, Germany, in a house and barn built together and that he had heard his father say he worked an ox and a horse together. Mr. Kachelhofer said that a schoolmate of his father came over to this country and settled in Ohio and wrote his father who then came over himself. One other member of his father's family, a brother, also came over to this country. Mr. Kachelhofer's father's name was Frederick Joseph Kachelhofer, born in Baden, Germany, in 1853. He died in Colbert County about 1936 or 1937. Mrs. Mary Hassell Kachelhofer's father was a farmer in Baden, with a family of four girls and two boys. Mr. Hassell came to this country on account of the California gold discovery and crossed the country to California in 1849. He then went back to Germany and brought all his family over to settle in Kansas where he homesteaded, building at first a sod house. Frederick Joseph Kachelhofer, who moved to Kansas from Ohio, had known the Hassell family in Germany, and they were married after they reached Kansas.

Mr. Kachelhofer said, "My father took a German language newspaper and saw an advertisement about fine farming country in Alabama and warm climate, and since there had been several crop failures in Kansas, he decided to go to Alabama and look the country over. After he convinced himself that this was good country, he sold out and moved to Colbert County in 1898, and bought 310 acres of land east of Sheffield and south of the Tennessee River on the River Road."

Mrs. Kachelhofer's paternal grandfather brought his family of three boys and several girls from South Carolina, and homesteaded in Lauderdale County, near Waterloo, Alabama, in the 1820s. His own maternal grandfather, Josiah Cane, was a school teacher who came from North Carolina and settled in Lauderdale County, where he married the widow Gray in 1857.

Mr. Kachelhofer believes in large families. He said, "A family that includes seven or eight children is better off financially. I

Tenant farm. Walker County, 1937. Rothstein, FSA.

believe an extra large family is better than a small one. I think it is a sin to limit children." Both Mr. and Mrs. Kachelhofer are proud of their two fine girls and of each other. He showed a pride in his ancestry for he spoke of his mother's father being a "forty-niner" and of his father's grandfather fighting against Napoleon.

He attended school fourteen years which he said was pretty good in his day, but both he and his wife would like to have their daughters college educated if they could afford it. They say a college education would be an economic advantage. They say, however, that the public school system in Colbert is efficient.

He said that his chief ambition is to own a home. He does not now own a car. He used to own one but had to give it up during the depression. The present income of the family is greater in dollars but will not buy as much as his income would when he first started out in life for himself. He says their actual needs to be covered by income are "living expenses of myself and family," and he added that his income covers that. He is apparently a thrifty man who expends his income with judgment and apportions it wisely in his living. Mr. Kachelhofer said, "I think that in order to live adequately a family should have an income of $2,500 a year."

He expressed pride in the fact that he is a farmer. He is also a first-class mechanic, and was in the garage and automobile repair business for a while in Leighton, Alabama. He moved just before the depression with his family, to South Bend, Indiana, and held a factory job. His wife also worked while there, but after a year or two they decided to return to Alabama and begin farming again. In regard to land ownership, he said, "I don't believe land should be owned in too large tracts. I think ownership should be well distributed."

In speaking of different types of life and different environments he said, "I have tried both farm and city life and each has its advantages. In town I made good money and when the day's work was done, I had nothing to worry about. But when you get out of a job, I don't know what then. When you are sick you are up against it. Expenses still go on. In the country on the farm, if something happens to keep you from working for a day or two, everything goes on pretty much as usual; crops continue to grow. Besides in the country it is healthier; there is better air, water, fresher food. Education for children in the country, now that buses pass the door, about equals that of city children. If living in town my children might be able to get jobs, but I might not, because of age, while in the country on a farm I have a job as long as I can work regardless of age. Also children have jobs on a farm; all the work they can do."

Speaking of politics, Mr. Kachelhofer said, "I always vote in all primaries and all general elections. I cast my ballot for the man I think best for the office. I use my own judgment and am not influenced by others; but I always vote for the man I think is the best Democratic candidate and I always vote the Democratic ticket. I think the trend of political thought is from a conservative to a liberal policy."

About religion he said, "Considered as a whole, religion has a beneficial influence on morals. I approve of all clean forms of sports, such as football, baseball, tennis, golf, etc. I think dancing in the home is all right but do not approve of dancing in night clubs or public places. It is all right to go automobile riding, provided no expenses are indulged in. Playing cards and similar games are all right if no gambling is involved. Attending picture shows and the theater except on Sunday is all right and probably has some educational value. I contribute all I am able in money and farm produce to my church. I would feel very grateful if I was in need and worthy, for any aid extended to me by my church. Both my family and myself are regular members." Mr. Kachelhofer and his family attend a U.S.A. Presbyterian Church which is less than a half-mile from where they live. Some time ago I was talking with him about a government loan he is trying to obtain so that he may buy a farm; and he said he was afraid purchase of the farm he now rents and for which he has applied, would not be approved on account of the cost. I then suggested another farm several miles away. His answer was, "I wouldn't want to get that far away from my church."

Mr. Kachelhofer said that he had spent in all about two hundred dollars for doctors and medicines with no hospital expense. He said, "The health of myself and family has always been good, due partially to good medical care and to good home doctoring and nursing. Work has helped to keep us all healthy. I have never made a study of balanced diet but I believe in it. My wife, as far as possible, plans her meals with a balanced diet in view. Our income is sufficient, together with produce we raise and can, and with milk, butter, eggs, meat, etc., for a completely balanced diet."

The Kachelhofer home of four rooms is always kept clean and in first class order. All members of his family are very neat and clean of person. The home is orderly and is comfortably furnished and the kitchen has a good wood-burning range, safe, shelves, table and utensils. Beds are all comfortable and with good mattresses and covers and the dining room table always has perfectly clean linen or a cotton damask cloth spread. I did not see the attic room, but was told it is fully equipped. There is no bathroom in the house, the family using a tub for bathing. They take an interest in everything they have, buying new pieces of furniture as they can afford, and Mr. Kachelhofer keeps it all in good repair.

"In regard to my farming operations," he said, "I raise cotton, corn, hay, garden truck, hogs, calves, and chickens. I break all my tillable land in the late fall and winter, and break up my cotton land again about April first; then I double cut it with a disk harrow; then go over it with a section harrow; then between the middle of April and the first of June I plant my cotton, which in 1938 was eighteen acres, with a two-row planter, applying fertilizer with the same operation. I cultivate with a spring-tooth cultivator when cotton gets up about three or four inches, which is usually around the middle of May. I follow the first cultivation immediately with first chopping; then I wait about a week and cultivate again. Then I wait for about two weeks, usually until the tenth of June, and chop again. I follow this chopping immediately with a cultivation, then in about ten days I cultivate again and July first run over the middles. This lays the cotton by. Then about September first we start picking cotton. Two or three pickings are necessary to get all the cotton. My family do most of the chopping and picking. I have to hire some of it, but not much."

"In planting my corn, which in 1938 was twenty acres, I break up again about five acres around March twentieth, then section harrow it and plant it with a two-row planter. Between

May first and fifteenth I break up the other fifteen acres for
corn, section harrow it and plant with a two-row planter. I
cultivate my corn when it gets about four inches high, and in
about ten days or two weeks I cultivate again. When corn gets
from knee to waist high I thin out and hoe and follow with
another cultivation which lays it by. I side-dress it just before
the last cultivation with nitrate of soda, one hundred pounds to
the acre. In November I gather corn and put it in the crib."

"My hay is mostly meadow hay, about four acres, which I cut
when ready and as soon as cured I haul it to the barn. I get
usually two cuttings. I have one-half acre in garden and raise
cabbage, carrots, onions, tomatoes, beans, peas, turnips, spin-
ach, beets, cucumbers, mustard, lettuce, radishes, eggplants,
squash, okra, sweet pepper, and hot pepper. In addition to a
garden, I raise in separate patches sweet and Irish potatoes,
sorghum for syrup, watermelons, canteloupes, popcorn and
pumpkins."

"I use and own the following stock and tools:
3 mules
3 cows
1 calf
15 hogs and pigs
25 chickens
1 wagon
1 hay rake
1 lot misc. tools
1 mowing machine
1 cultivator
1 2-row planter
2 1-row planters
2 plows
1 tractor (out of commission)
1 feed mill
1 harrow
"After laying by, my wife and daughters do most of their
canning while I make my hay. As for amusements we don't have
so much time left. However, we go fishing, go to picnics, go
visiting, go to parties, and church entertainments. I usually
settle with my landlord in cash about November first. I rent in

all about eighty acres. As soon as I can get a government loan already applied for, I expect to buy my own place."

"We always rise in summertime about four a.m., eat breakfast, and get to the field about five o'clock. We knock off for lunch about 11:30 and return to the field about one o'clock, finish up about thirty minutes before sundown; then we do the evening chores, eat supper and retire as soon as possible unless something happens to prevent it. In the winter we don't get up so early."

"Among our amusements are hunting, picnicking, going to parties, picture shows and school entertainments, going to town, visiting neighbors and relatives in the next county. Of course my daughters do their share of courting. The courting couples use our living room for this purpose, then go to church together, go riding, go to town, to picture shows and visiting. I spend most of my spare time at home with my family, but go to town occasionally and also to the neighborhood stores."

R. V. Waldrep, a member of the editorial department in Birmingham, was the most prolific life history writer in Alabama. Nine of his eleven accounts came from Red Bay and surrounding parts of Franklin County in July and August of 1939. All the subjects were male but cover a variety of occupations and personalities: dry goods storekeeper, hermit, rural postman, doctor, farmers black and white, drugstore loafer, and others. In light of the criteria set up by W. T. Couch, these may be, unfortunately, the worst of the Alabama life histories. Waldrep had some of the literary pretensions bemoaned by Couch and was seemingly more interested in communicating his own personality to the reader than that of the person being interviewed. The following account is his best at letting the informant speak for himself.

I'll Be An Old Man Tomorrow

by R. V. Waldrep

"I believe in letting your boys do what they want to. If you put them in something they don't like they won't learn as fast and never will do any good. I let my boys do what they wanted to. I give them that Cook Correspondence Course in Chicago—I give it to Edwin and Carl, and B. H., he picked up what he knew from them." Mr. Shanks really believes what he is thinking and saying; but as a matter of fact, his boys just grew, as he didn't have a word or take a drop of authority. He might have done something for the boys if he had wanted to, but it never occurred to him to do anything.

Mr. Shanks is one of these scrawny, little, thin, leathery guys, looking as if he has been fried crisp and brittle like bacon—good bacon. He is a talker, quite intelligent and fluent, too. He was talking about himself, and the things he had done, and the boys he had trained. The correspondence course he was telling about was in electricity. The boys received little motors, diagrams of the ignition of cars, and diagrams of house wiring.

"The boys are all healthy. Jay eats the most; B. H. never did eat anything much. But Jay, he could eat more than anybody I ever saw. For breakfast, I never do want more'n two fried eggs, three biscuits, some bacon and some coffee. When supper comes I like nothing more than cornbread and milk. That's all I ever eat, and I reckon I'm healthy." He stood there small and scrawny, and tough as a string of rawhide. His hands, one horribly mutilated, were gnarled, bony, and stiff to the shake. His neck came out of his shirt as lean as his wrist, and as tough.

"Whiskey won't hurt a fellow, I reckon. I was raised in a house where we kept a jug under the head of the bed, and I have always kept one under my bed. It ain't done me no harm, and I'll be an old man tomorrow!" His shriveled face creased in a grin, and he said happily, "I'll be sixty-seven. You know, you're an old man when you git to be sixty-five. I'll be sixty-seven tomorrow. I come in at night from the sawmill so tired I can't hardly wiggle, and I take me a little drink, and then I eat me a hearty supper, and I go to bed. I sleep good. Then, when I get up, I take me another drink, eat me a good breakfast, and I feel good all day. I ain't no drunkard, and it's all right if I ain't a drunkard."

He laughed, "I said I went directly to bed, but I don't. I set up and read, sometimes to eleven o'clock, and I always git up at four. I reckon if a feller gits out of bed at four all his life, he just tumbles and tosses if he don't git up every time at four. I allus get up at four, no matter when I go to bed." He reads western magazines, and has been doing it all his life. His wife reads to him, when he is too tired.

He was happy as he began to remember his early days. He would talk all day about that, anybody could see, for his voice took on strength and vitality like that of a young man. "About that whiskey," he went on, "I had it on and off with that preacher down in Jacksonville, in Calhoun County!" He paused to rock his memory with glee, as he was asked whether he had ever made any speeches about prohibition.

"No, I didn't make no speeches; I was working in those days, contracting and sawmilling. But we won that time; we beat in the election. I'd come in from work and write articles in the paper to the preachers." The memory made the old man happy, and his fried-bacon body seemed to sing like taut rawhide twitted by a breeze. "They preached me to hell, and I'd answer

'em every time, and get the best of it, too. We won that time." He
stopped for a question, and said no, it wasn't when they voted *in*
prohibition: "It was around 1905 or somewhere and we won it."

He drifted about in his memories without prodding. He
skipped the years, bounced along happily, glad to be heard, for
he is usually a solitary figure on the streets there in Red Bay.
Rarely do people talk to him and take interest in his affairs. Now
he talked.

"I didn't marry until I was up in the thirties. I never did settle
down to then, and I didn't drink as much after I got married; but
when I was sawmilling all over Mississippi and Alabama, I was
something! I spent money! I spent every dollar I made, and I
made $150 a day sometimes. We'd go to Birmingham every
Saturday. We'd go out to Red Light. That town! Was there
women? The damndest town ever I was in! It was tough! It was
over there past that old L&N Depot that we was. No, there
wasn't no 26th Street then. The tough place was Red Light, we
called it."

He took off his hat, and the hair was thin and gray, but the
scalp was tough and tanned. He pulled his cheap, boy-like,
straw hat down on his head again. "I was up from South
Mississippi—I was working down there in a mill that had six
hundred men, nearly all niggers, counting the ones in the
woods. We was cutting pines. I was up in Birmingham, and I
got to talking to a man from Vina. He's the Goddamdest liar that
ever lived! There never was a liar like him. He got to telling me
about the timber up here; he told me how many thousand and
thousand of feet of timber there was here. I listened, since I was
nearly through in South Mississippi; timber was pretty near all
cut down there."

"Well, he told me so much about that timber, and I was
looking for a good timber country to settle down in, that I
brought my family and hauled everything to Vina. There was
Edwin, Carl, and Jay in the family then. B. H. was born there in
Vina. That man is the damndest liar ever I saw." He growled in
his throat like a little pup, his old eyes looked from the glasses,
the black, celluloid-rimmed glasses. "I moved. That man didn't
own a foot of the timber! Yeah, there was a good deal of timber,
but he didn't own a foot, and I had my whole family up here. So I

had to get out and buy up a section of timber and go to work. I couldn't do anything else." He paused. "Later on I worked for another man in Vina there."

Now, he launched back to earlier days with the ease that years give; things seemed to be scrambled in his mind—sensations, experiences, hates scattered through many years were all one connected memory—but they all made sense to him. He untied the bundle of experiences without a fumble. "My father was a sawmill man. I was born in Texas, and raised in Calhoun County. All my people are in Calhoun County. I go back there some. And I'm going back again pretty soon. They're buried out there—my people." His voice was the same in discussing his old home county, but a close attention to the tone brought out the softness of a sentiment. Attention to his eyes showed there was a film come over them, and the creases down the lean scrawny jaw moved ever so little. Perhaps his voice was lower, too. "I married my wife when I was in my thirties. She's a Davidson, from Burleson."

He went back to earlier days, and he was in Texas. "I helped to run telephone lines in Texas, and when we got that finished, I went back over the same lines and put up the poles and wire for a postal telegraph line. Boy, I was free and easy them days. I had money, but I could take seven hundred dollars to town and to the saloon on Saturdays, and spend it every bit! I could have been a rich man, a millionaire right now." He is a scrawny fellow, and would have looked funny in one of those long, slooping limousines; he is a banty rooster of a man. "I had the money once in my pocket. I was working on that telephone line. A fellow in a saloon tried to sell me a house with five acres of land. It was a big house, four rooms, sixteen by sixteen. He wanted to sell the house—out there in Texas—for forty-five dollars, and I had the money, sewed right here." Shanks marked off the place on his thigh where the money had been sewn; he marked it off on cheap, dollar pants, faded with washing. He drew out his sack of tobacco, rolled a smoke with his lean, mutilated hand. "Well, I wasn't thinking about nothing like that, buying land; I wasn't married then and wasn't thinking about settling down. Well, I come back by that saloon and house when I was working on the postal telegraph lines, and that house was worth $4500, and it wasn't more'n a year after that. I was there in July, July the Fourth—it was a legal holiday—and I was in the same saloon, and it was just one year later that same parcel of land and house was $4500! I could have been a rich man, but I'm a pauper."

"That wasn't all. My brother-in-law—he's in Texas—Davidson is his name, bought a bunch of land for $1500, and he's got something; he's been offered $15,000!" The regret and chagrin in his voice was real; his tone of voice was as angry as if he had just stumped his toe.

"But I've made money. I didn't know there was going to be a panic or anything. It was that panic and trucks that ruined me. Trucks are like gambling; you think if you spend just one more dollar on a truck you won't have to spend anymore. Trucks was my downfall. I was up there in Belgreen, working that timber. I'm up there now, but it ain't hardly worth a damn, but it's all I can get. It's worked to hell and back. I bought a bunch of trucks before the panic. I thought it would be better to have a truck, and then I could come home at night. I bought a truck, up here at Russellville, one Saturday. I bought the best tires I could buy—them Goodyear—worth $57.50 apiece. Well sir, I started home, and when I got to Bear Hill, my rear left tire hit a strip of iron." Shanks measured with his multilated hand a strip about ¼ x 1 x 6 inches. "It sliced a hole in the tire, ruining $57.50." He could taste the sound of that money. "Well I come on down here to Red Bay, and put on another just like it, and I went on toward the Ridge where I lived, and there was a horseshoe in the road, and that horseshoe carved a half-moon out of the other tire. Another tire, another $57.50. I guess it was partly because of the heavy load of timber I had on the truck."

"But that wasn't all! A feller out at the mill tore the back end out of a truck for me. Then them big heavy loads ruined the brakes. The brakes was on the outside, remember? I ruined them things right and left, and I'd have to have them relined, and that cost like the devil! Yeah, trucks ruined me, and I didn't have sense enough to stop. I've got some checks—cancelled checks over at the house—twelve thousand dollars worth, I lost on trucks."

He was asked about his stay in Jacksonville to cool his frustrations. "I run a show over there, showed movies and them travelling show-people would come and show for me. The movies wasn't no good is right, but they were new then. I was there in 1903, I think—three years there. I taught Edwin all I knew about the show business—that's how he got started being an operator, and Carl too." Edwin is out in Texas, and Carl operates a moving picture machine in Corinth, Mississippi. Of course, the old man didn't have anything to do with the boys, as he was sawmilling and getting drunk his off days. He would be put in jail there in Red Bay, and you could hear him cuss a mile. But he says he never was a drunkard!

"I ought to have stayed there in Jacksonville. I was making money. I was contracting, too. I built more houses than anybody." He will show you pictures of those houses, and himself standing before the house, standing proudly, the huge, box-like affair in the background. "Jacksonville was the biggest place in the county then. Anniston wasn't anything. Jacksonville was county seat. A company came in and wanted to manufacture in Jacksonville, but them old fogies wouldn't stand for it; they made them stop, even after the company had dug a big place for a spur line to a railroad. The plant went to Anniston, and purty soon Anniston was biggest, and voted the county seat to themselves. I sawmilled the lumber that they built the courthouse with."

In the pause, Mr. Shanks was asked how so much of his hand had been sliced off—the forefinger and thumb were cut off close. Yet he skillfully rolled his own smoke, and pulled the yellow drawstring of his tobacco sack with the few remaining teeth in his mouth. The teeth, he explained, were all right, except they didn't match. "My wife is having her teeth pulled out, and she's a-grunting, because she won't be able to eat right for three months. I told her she'd have to to hire somebody to chew for her," he grinned.

He told about the missing digits. "I was working out in Gladewater, Texas, when I got them cut off. It was in a hardwood mill, making shingles." He told of the enormous volume of shingles they produced. "I got them sliced off when I was feeding a rip-saw." He didn't tell then, but when the hand was cut, he took a needle and thread, and sewed the skin over the protruding bones, washed with whiskey, without calling in a doctor.

"My family? Half my family was big: my two sisters weighed three hundred pounds or nearly that apiece. There was two of my brothers little as me. There was seven of us all; some of us is dead. I am the oldest." He stopped and said with pleasure, "We generally live to be old." He said he was told, "A fellow as lean, flatbellied as yourself will live to be a hundred twenty-five."

"We're all long-lived. I'm healthy." But sometimes he gets to coughing while he drinks whiskey, cough-medicine, and cusses. He lies on the bed moaning and hacking away in his throat. Now he looked lithe and young and tough—perhaps he is healthy. His belly is flat, his hips narrow, his feet small, his neck and jaws a clean, fried red.

Walking down the street, he said, "I'm right proud of my boys—all of them. I let them do as they please. I did all I could for them. Carl, he's got a good job, and Edwin has done pretty nigh what he wants to. Two of my kids are dead." There was no sorrow in his voice. B. H. was killed a year or two ago; he was travelling with a show that put on moving pictures in schools, and he hurled his car head-on into another car, and the top of his skull was clipped from his head. He had been a reckless driver, was crazy about cars. "Trucks ruined me," said his dad again.

The boys are all, except Roy who married a prostitute and hobos, born mechanics. They are wizards with pliers, screwdrivers, wrenches. They can do things with copper wire, screws, armatures, magnets. They talk and blow, and tell jokes that aren't funny. Carl reads joke books in order to be funny. Roy married a prostitute, as said; Carl married a woman who fools him and Edwin never will marry. "I'm right proud of my boys," said Mr. Shanks, leaving the postoffice. "I never could educate them like I wanted to, though," he said.

Part Two

In and Around the New Industrial Cities at the Appalachians' Tail End

Nettie S. McDonald worked out of the editorial department in Birmingham. Most of her seven life histories are from the mining communities in and around that city, apparently written in response to W. T. Couch's specific request for such material. "Green Fields Far Away" was one of three Alabama accounts to appear in the Terrill and Hirsch edition, Such As Us. *In this part, three others by McDonald are included. "Mary Worked in the Mines in Belgium" and "I'm Crazy 'Bout Rats" have considerable detail on life in the mining communities, with a whole glossary of occupational terms. "Coal shooting," for example, was when a seam of coal was undercut and explosives were detonated in holes drilled on top of the coal to "set" it or drop it down to the floor, broken into pieces.*

Mary Worked in the Mines in Belgium

by Nettie S. McDonald

" 'Come over to America and you can make a fortune,' is what my father-in-law wrote back to us in Belgium," said Mary Lecomte.

Mary Lecomte is a large, dignified woman, still proudly erect, though seventy-three years old. Her soft, white hair was combed straight back from her forehead and fell in deep, natural waves. A little curl nestled beside her widow's peak. Her clear brown eyes nearly closed when she laughed. She wore a clean, faded percale dress and her apron was tied around her large waist.

Mary and Charles Lecomte keep house in two rooms, but in their kitchen is where they really live. It's a large, comfortable room painted cream color and it is very, very clean. The floor is completely covered with bright flowered linoleum. A three-burner oil stove, two cupboards full of pans and dishes, a table with red and white oil cloth, a few kitchen chairs, a sewing machine and three large rockers with soft cushions on the seat and on the backs, furnish the kitchen. Crisp red and white curtains make the room very gay.

Mary Lecomte got her big, black pipe, filled it, placed a large bowl beside her chair, lit her pipe and started puffing away. The smoke seemed to carry her back to her early life in the old country.

"Let me see, now," she began. "It's been nearly thirty-five years since we got that letter from Charles' father. We sold everything as quick as we could and me and Charles and the two children (the other two died the year before) set out for America the 'promised land,' and from that day to this, we never have had enough money to take us back there. My old father and mother told me that they would never see us again if we went so far away. I couldn't believe it, but they sure were right, for they died twenty years ago without ever seeing us any more." A slow tear coursed down her broad cheek as she looked away. Then she shook her head and went bravely on.

"Since I came over here, my life has been different. When I was just a slip of a girl, I started to work in the mines in Belgium. Oh, sure girls worked in the Belgium mines![1] Young girls and pretty, too. We all worked in pants. God knows we couldn't do a thing with skirts swishing around our legs. When we went into the mines, we had to take two safety lamps along. These lamps are just like the ones the fire bosses use in this country.[2] I could carry both of mine on two fingers on the same hand."

"We'd go down, down, down seventeen hundred yards in a cage. Then after we got out of the cage we had to walk at least a mile before we'd get to work. I'd put one lamp on one post and

---

[1]It long has been a superstition in the United States that women in a mine are bad luck; Wayland D. Hand, ed., in *Popular Beliefs and Superstitions from North Carolina*, vol. 6 of *The Frank C. Brown Collection of North Carolina Folklore*, ed. Newman Ivey White (Durham, N.C.: Duke University Press, 1952–64; hereafter cited as *North Carolina Folklore*), cites examples from North Carolina to California on p. 460. At one time this belief apparently was elevated to Alabama state law; see an undated pamphlet from the Alabama Coal Operators Association, *Mining Laws of the State of Alabama* (n.p.).

[2]Safety lamps used in the coal mines were covered with a cylinder of wire gauze that kept the flame from spreading to any surrounding gas. When "fire damp" (mostly methane) entered the lamp it burned as a bluish "cap" over the flame, warning the carrier; see Albert H. Fay, *A Glossary of the Mining and Mineral Industry*, Bulletin 95 (Washington: Department of Interior, Bureau of Mines, 1920), p. 586.

the other one on a post close by. That would give me plenty of light to work by."

"Oh, they'd give us girls 'most any king of work to do—pushing cars, stopping cars and turning the wheel that pulled the cars onto the cage. Turning that wheel was the hardest job I had. I used to brace myself against the post and push for dear life. It took a real woman to do that job. I sure was proud for not many of the women could do it; and besides that, it paid fifteen cents a day more than any other job."

"Sometimes other girls would try and try, but they couldn't turn it. They wanted to make the extra money and because they couldn't, they'd turn up their noses at me, because I could. I remember the worst fight I ever had in the mine was when a girl sent me word that she would slap my face for taking her job at the wheel. I waited for that girl, and when she saw me, she started in to beg me to wait till her sister got there to help her, but I didn't wait. I got her up against a post and I gave her one good beatin'! I always said, 'don't start a fight you can't finish.' "

"I kept on working in that mine until I married. When my first baby was five months old, my brother asked me to come back to the mine and help him out for awhile. I paid my mother-in-law to keep the baby and I started back to work. I did fine until my breasts filled up with milk and hurt so bad I couldn't use my arms. Then I'd stop and draw out the milk with a pipe. That used to make me feel awful bad. There I was, wasting the milk that my baby was at home crying for."

"I kept that work up for a year—until my brother didn't need me any more. Then I opened up a little store and I carried everything to eat, but not a thing in cans. Salt, pepper, tea, bluing, starch—everything was loose in jars and had to be weighed. I kept paper sacks of all sizes. Oh, I was a real business woman alright. I peddled, too. At first, I had a great big Belgian dog to pull my cart, but he was too fast, so Charles sold him and bought me a jackass. He was lots better."

"I had all kinds of fruit—apples, peaches, plums, grapes, and I had potatoes and oysters in the shell. I made up a song about my fruit and as I'd ride along, I'd sing it. Those were happy days. They could hear my song for a mile and when my customers heard that song, it was too bad for the other peddlers for they

Birmingham, 1936. Evans, FSA.

couldn't sell a thing. I made jokes with my customers and that kept them in a good humor and then they'd buy more."

"After I got through with my store peddling, I used to go home and make sandwiches to sell that night. As I think back, I can't help laughing about some sandwiches I sold once. It was at night and there was a big dance under the tents. I made lovely horse liver sandwiches with plenty of onions. The boys and girls would come over and buy sandwiches between dances like the boys and girls nowadays buy a Tom Collins. Well, that night my sandwiches tasted better than ever. A real pretty girl came over to me and said, 'Now, you're sure these are cow liver sandwiches and not horse liver?' 'Oh,' said I, 'you know I wouldn't sell you something I wouldn't eat myself.' She smiled and bought another one. But I don't mind telling you those were horse liver sandwiches."

"I believe that's one thing that makes the Belgian people so strong. Horse meat really makes you strong. Sure, it's good. You can't tell the difference between horse meat and cow meat to save your soul. A nice steak from a horse leg is good eating. I just can't eat this meat they sell in tins. You know yourself they don't can the best of the meat and I wouldn't doubt that half the canned meat they're all fussin' about from that foreign country, is canned horse meat."

"Belgian people eat lots of fish and oysters, too. When the peddlers brought fish around every Friday, all the bones were taken out and it was clean enough to eat without washing it, if you wanted to."

"When we first came to America, we moved to French Town in Pratt City. I had plenty of friends that went to the same church and spoke French. You see there isn't very much difference between the Belgian and the French language. If you can understand one, you don't have any trouble with the other. I think French is softer and sweeter than Belgian. When we first moved to French Town, there were 104 families there, and we all belonged to the French lodge. Once a year, we would all get together and have a big picnic with lemonade and sandwiches, and we'd dance till way late. Now, nearly all our friends have either died or moved away, and it makes me too sad to go over there, now."

"After we had lived there in French Town for five years, our house caught on fire and burned up everything we had—even all the pretty pictures and lace—not one thing did we save. But the worst of all, we didn't have a place to go. Not one single house was to be had for love or money. Pratt was on the boom then. We looked and looked and finally we found an old house Negroes had occupied. Negroes are dirty people and this house was filthy. I scrubbed it from top to bottom. After I had finished scrubbing the walls and the floors, I went out and borrowed a step ladder to get to the ceiling. I was getting on just fine, when I looked around and saw the doctor. He gave one look and yelled out at me, 'don't you know you'll kill yourself if you don't get down off of that ladder?' Well, he scared me so bad that I fell from the top to the floor. My twin boys were born that night, two months too soon. They lived just four hours."

"I had plenty of milk and to spare, but not for long. A friend of mine heard about my babies and brought her little poor, sickly month-old baby to me and offered me fifteen dollars a month if I would nurse and take care of that pitiful baby. I just couldn't refuse and I liked to make money, anyhow. Well, those days were plenty good. She bought me everything that was good to eat. She bought beer, and the best fruit and candy. The chocolates came from France. She wanted my milk to be extra good and it was. In no time at all, that baby didn't look like himself. Its own father and mother would have to look at him twice to make sure he was their baby. They couldn't get to see him but once or twice a month. I kept him for fifteen months and I got to feeling he was mine. Believe me, I sure hated to give that baby up. He's grown and married now, but every time he sees me, he throws his arms around me and kisses me—he's that glad to see me." Mary Lecomte leaned back in her chair with a faraway look in her eyes.

"Women can't make business over here like they can in the old country," she went on. "About the only business I could get here was taking washes, nursing babies and tending mothers when they had babies. Of course women have a much easier time here. They have electric irons, oil stoves, electric stoves and washing machines. Speed's the thing. Everything's faster. For instance, in Belgium I had four babies, one at a time, but here in America I had four babies, two at the time. Yes, speed's the thing."

"I think women have too much idle time here. We used to go in the mines at five in the morning and come out at ten at night. Of course, we had Sundays to ourselves. Then, too, they eat here too much out of cans. If they'd cook right and work more, they wouldn't have such poor health. Good, hard work never did kill anybody."

"Women complain too much. You can't get where there's a bunch of women, that they don't start talkin' about how bad they've been feeling. Then they'll tell you what one doctor said and what the other one said. Of course, no woman wants to be beat even in sickness, so the next one starts in to tell about her operation and when that starts, she's good for an hour if she's not stopped by somebody else that can't wait to tell about hers.

They can't be half as bad off as they make out or they couldn't run around as much as they do. I never heard of an operation till I came to America and Belgian women never complain."

"You know one thing, I've heard so much talk about sickness and operations that I even got to thinking that the pain in my legs and back wasn't rheumatism, maybe, so I decided to go to a doctor, myself, but not to one of those doctors that work at a hospital, where it's so handy just to step in and operate. I heard about a fine Negro doctor up in the country that just tells what's the matter with you. Well I got my daughter to take me and when we got there, we found cars from five different states. Finally, my turn came. I went in and he stood there and looked at me. Then he looked at my fingernails and then at my eyeballs. Then he told me I didn't have rheumatism like I thought I did, but I had female trouble—whatever that is, I don't know. This doctor gave me four quarts of terrible smellin' herb medicine and it tasted as bad as it smelled.[3] He told me to come back when all my medicine was gone and that'll be next Saturday. I feel fine already and I sleep lots better."

About that time Charles Lecomte finished his fence and came in to sit awhile in the kitchen. He's a little square faced man with thin sandy hair, and straggly mustache. His face is rough but kind. His hands are calloused and he walks a little stiff.

"I was just saying when you came in, that I'm about well," she said. "And when I do get well," she went on, "I'm going to get me another man. Don't you think forty-three years is long enough to keep one man? And Charles, wouldn't you like to have another wife?"

Charles smiled indulgently and nodded, agreeing with her. "For shame, Charles, and only yesterday you told me that you couldn't live without me," said Mary, her brown eyes twinkling with mischief.

"I bet you never could guess what my daughter gave me for a birthday present—a walking cane, of all things. I don't mean to

---

[3]Female trouble, the vernacular for irregular or painful menstruation, has a great variety of folk treatment, including, in Alabama, tea from the black-haw root; see Ray B. Browne, *Popular Beliefs and Practices from Alabama,* University of California Publications, Folklore Studies 9 (Berkeley and Los Angeles: University of California Press, 1958), p. 65.

have people asking me how I feel today and when did I get hurt—no, indeed. For just a minute, the other day, I thought I'd try it out and go to the store. I got to the front porch and then I knew what I'd hear the minute I stepped my foot in the store, so I threw that stick just as far as I could. When I get old enough and weak enough, I'll use a cane and not before. My daughter thought she was buying me the very thing I wanted, but she just didn't know her mama. I'm young yet and if this pain would only stop in my knees, I could do as much work as I ever did."

"Now Charles here, could work in the mine as well as he ever did, if he could get the work to do, over at Republic.[4] Of course, he's too old to start in with a new company and get a job. You never would believe it, but he's seventy-eight years old. I believe the work in the mines here is easier than it was in the old country, don't you, Charles?"

"It sure is," he said. Charles was glad to get a chance to talk about the work he loved. "It's a fact that the work is easier here but it's safer in the old country. Now, for instance, take the roof of the mine. You hardly ever hear of a rock fall there. The mines all have fine roofs. But here at Hamilton Slope[5] for example, a week don't go by without at least one man being killed or crippled. In some of the mines here, I've seen dust boot-high, and that's something unheard of over there. I'm tellin' you, a dust explosion is every bit as bad as a gas explosion. Just yesterday John Loni, a neighbor across the road, was brought home with a broken leg. My son works at Hamilton Slope and all these accidents keep me and the old woman stirred up all the time."

"In the mines here, the miners do a lot of their own coal shooting, but in the old country, the night shift does all the shooting and the miners dig and load it the next day. Here

---

[4]Republic Steel Corporation, one of the biggest firms active in the Birmingham area, had a series of coal and iron mines. The one referred to in the narrative is probably the Sayreton mine north and a bit west of Birmingham; see H. H. Chapman et al., *The Iron and Steel Industries of the South* (University, Ala.: University of Alabama Press, 1953), p. 150, Map 18, "Location of Principal Properties of Alabama Iron and Steel Companies, 1948."

[5]Hamilton Slope was owned by TCI (Tennessee Coal, Iron & Railroad Co., later U.S. Steel) southwest of the Sayreton mine and just north of the Birmingham city limits; see ibid.

you're paid by the ton but there you're paid by the square yard. The boss comes around and measures where you've dug and pays you. And if you don't clean your place clean of rock, then you have to do it over for nothing. Belgian coal is extra good— great big lumps that shines like it's been oiled. They don't sell the slack coal and the best lumps sell for a dollar ten a ton— that's about two forty here. What do they do with the slack? Oh, they put it to good use alright. They take the slack and put it into a machine and mix it with something that sticks it together and press it into brickettes, just the size of an ordinary brick. They sell for two cents apiece, and they burn fine."

"Lots of men that work here, couldn't get a job in Belgium. They don't know enough about mining. Why, over there, you have to go to school until you're twenty-one and study minin'. Then when you go inside, you know how to take care of yourself. Oh, no, women don't have to go to school because they don't dig or load coal. All they did was to push cars and such as that. They always said that the men had the easiest jobs and got the most money, but I don't think so."

"Oh, yes, they do have unions there. In fact, if anything, unions are stronger over there. Workers are not allowed in mines in Belgium, if they don't have a union card. Every Monday that card has to be shown, and if the dues are not paid up, then it's out you go till you're caught up."

"Oh, sometimes, the owner of the mines gets a raise in the price of his coal, and then he don't want to raise the miners' pay for diggin' it. Now that's when the trouble starts, for they all come out on strike until he decides to pay accordin' to what he gets. It never takes long, because other miners won't come and work until it's settled. As long as the strike lasts the union pays the strikers the interest on the dues paid in."

"Yes, all the workers have to go down in cages; twelve cars at the time. As the coal is loaded on the cages, it is brought out and twelve empty one go down—then when they're filled, the empty ones come back. They keep that up all day and lots at night. Sometimes the rope that pulls the cages gets out of fix and that means we've got to stay down there till it's fixed. That's when an hour seems like a day. When you're seventeen hundred yards down in the ground it's bad enough even if you know you can get out, but when you can't get out, that's the devil!"

"No, I never did do anything in Belgium or here except follow mining. That's all I know. Over here just like back in the old country, work gets slack in one place and whenever that happened I'd go to another mine. I was livin' over at Pratts when work gave out and I had to go off and look for work. We never have been able to save much, so I'd have to go to the old woman and get some of hers. I remember I sure made her mad. It was back when she was nursin' that baby for Mrs. Vines. She had saved up some money and she gave it to me to go off and look for work. The first two times I came home without the money and without work, it wasn't so bad, but, my God, the third time! When I told her I could have got work in Virginia Mine, but didn't, I thought she'd blow the roof off."

"Four days later when they had that terrible dust explosion and squeeze, she cooled off a little, but not enough to let me go off on another trip. After that, I had to know where, when, and how I was to work before I left to go off again. More than two hundred men got killed in that Virginia Mine explosion[6] and I missed it by just four days. Me and the old woman both knew that our good mother Mary was lookin' after me. Oh, yes, we're Catholics. All Belgians are Catholics. But I say there's not one God for the Methodists, one for the Baptists and still another one for the Catholics. There's just one God for us all. It makes no difference which way you travel so long as you're headed in the right direction."

"But I will say, I think the Catholics are stronger than the Protestants in one thing, and that's about divorce. We can't get used to the way children marry over here. I've seen girls twelve, marry boys not over sixteen. And the funny thing about it is, the mamas and papas don't seem to care. If you ask them if they're not afraid they'll be sorry for marryin' so young, they'll all tell you just about the same thing—and laugh—they'll tell you that they'll try this one and if they can't get along, they'll get a divorce and try it again. I think it's awful."

---

[6]The state mine inspector's report says 112 dead, "every man who went to work"; see H. B. Humphrey, *Historical Summary of Coal-Mine Explosions in the United States, 1810–1958,* Bulletin 586 (Washington: Department of Interior, Bureau of Mines, 1960), p. 25.

"Back in Belgium, the girl has to be at last eighteen and the boy at least twenty-one before they can marry. Besides that, they have to have the written permission of all four parents. When me and Mary got ready to marry, my father was in America, and we had to write for the papers to come all the way back. Then when a baby's born, they give you just twenty-four hours to post the birth certificate. A divorce over there is not heard of. I sure do wish it was stricter here. It'd be better in every way. And another thing, you never hear of a suicide in Belgium. About the only crime you ever hear of is a real good fist fight, and there's plenty of them. All the quarrels are settled that way. The law is mighty strict about owning a gun, a knife, or any kind of weapon. And that's a fine thing. If you can't get hold of a weapon you sure can't use it."

"I don't believe half I read in the papers here about people killin' each other. Paper can't get up and walk off. It has to stay still and let you write on it. These writers get paid to write whatever people read, so you can't blame them, but I don't take heed of half of it."

"Oh, you don't have to go just because I have to go back and finish my work in the yard. I want to have all my work caught up, if they call me back to work at Republic mine. They promised to let me know when they're ready with some more work. My garden's all caught up and the fences are fixed and when I finish the ditch around the house I'll be ready. I haven't had a day's work in the last three months. I sure hope it won't be that long again."

Mary Lecomte went into the next room and came back with grape wine as clear as crystal and perfectly aged. "When Charles was talking about those brickettes a while ago, my mind went back years and years ago," said Mary, as we drank the delicious wine. "I was stacking brickettes on my wheelbarrow just as high as they would go and wheeling them down to the river to load them on the boat. Well, this day I'm talking about, the board walk was as slick as glass and it was awful cold. Just as I got to the boat, my wheelbarrow slipped, and into the river went brickettes, wheelbarrow and all. I stood there with my hands on my hips. The boss came up and wanted to know why I wasn't workin'. 'Well,' I said, 'you don't think I'm riskin' my life for a durned wheelbarrow, do you?' He gave me a new one."

"I always said that me and Charles could work in the mine and around the mines, but I didn't mean for one of the children to do it. Well, I'll tell you how it turned out. Both of my daughters married coal miners. One of my boys works at Hamilton Slope—one of the worst. I always say that's where all these gray hairs came from. Every time I see a crowd or anything unusual out in the road my heart turns over. I know then and there that they've come to tell me Johnny has been killed or hurt."

"Now the other boy, Bob, started in the mine to help Charles when he was fourteen. Well, Charles wanted to teach him and make a real good miner out of him, so he fussed and he cussed when Bob did anything wrong. The more he complained, the better I liked it, for Bob got to where he was scared to death of the mine. He'd come home and cry and tell me how scared he was. I couldn't stand that, so I put on my best dress and went over to Pratt to see one of our rich French friends. I asked him to take Bob into his machine shop and let him learn a trade. He took him right in and started off payin' him twenty-five cents a day while he was learnin'. He kept on raisin' him and raisin' him until he got to making five dollars a day and now he makes eight dollars a day as a boilermaker. I sure made that man and his wife some fine dinners for helpin' my boy. I'm still thanking God that my boy got out of that mine before somethin' terrible happened to him. I believe when you're scared of a mine, you're being warned. The other boy, I guess, will work in the mines as long as he lives. He loves it like me and Charles and he's not scared."

As I started to leave, Mary Lecomte walked toward the porch with me. She insisted that I take care when I got to the yard and started up the road. "That road," she said, "was on the level with the yard before the Government tore it up. Now the road's high and the yard's low. I can't see they've done it any good—just spent a lot of good money. When you start up that road, you take your life in your hands. They tell me I can get some steps built up to the road, if I'll go in town and tell them what they've done. But I say let the people that buy this house worry about how they'll get to the road."

"I'm sellin' this house and the one next to it. My daughter that lives here with us has bought some ground up the road a piece, and me and the old man will move when they do. I can't stand to have the air cut off from me, like that road has done."

"Oh, yes, I like America fine, but I do wish with all my heart that I could go back to Belgium for a visit. Just the thought of a trip to the old country makes me choke up with a sort of a longin' and then I get trembly all over. Don't you see, when I was in Belgium, I was a real woman—no pains—and stronger than any other woman around where I was. I guess I've sorta worshipped that part of my life. You know you can start back rememberin' and after awhile all the bad things have a way of slippin' away, and things that used to be bad get to be wonderful instead. That's what your heart does for you. Right now my heart's speakin' and sayin', 'Mary Lecomte, if you could only go back to Belgium and get one of those good horse liver sand-wiches with plenty of onions, you could dance again and you could sing as you've never sung before.' "

I'm Crazy 'Bout Rats

by Nettie S. McDonald

"It was just before daylight when the timbers started crackin'. You could hear 'em way down there in the dark, like firecrackers poppin' in a croker sack. The men stopped diggin' all of a sudden; they didn't say nothin'—just cocked their ears and listened. A rock plopped down some'ers close by. At first, nobody moved a step—just listenin' with their mouths hangin' open. Then, when th' poppin' still seemed a good piece off, somebody yelled, 'Here they come! Let's get th' hell out!' "

"And they *was* comin', ma'am. You've heard of skeered mice. Well, these was big rats—but they was skeered, too. They knew as well as any man there that the roof was startin' to cave. I've always watched 'em mighty close, for they can spot danger a mile off. They're th' best friends a coal digger ever had, and I wouldn't kill one for anything in th' world. Folks outside cuss 'em for the trouble they cause, but I tell you, they've saved a flock of lives. When th' crackin' starts th' rats hear it first and come scurryin' out like hell fire. And they usually come runnin' in plenty of time for the men to get out. Me, I'm crazy 'bout 'em!"[7]

Jimmie Evans chuckled, and shoved his cap back on his graying head. He is a wiry, slouch-shouldered little man, with a face made pasty by long hours underground. But corded muscles on his forearm, revealed by rolled up shirt sleeves, show that his thin body has strength. He says, "I've been sinkin' picks in coal a mighty long time." He stood near the begrimed mouth of a long-used mine, running his fingers idly along the surface of weathered timbers. A few hundred yards away, over by the commissary, was the drab, gray house where he lived with his wife, Rachel, and the two boys. Other houses, similarly built and just as drab, lined the side of a hill made rough by blackened outcroppings of rock. At the foot of the hill, the railroad curved off into more distant hills. Deep ruts, left by trucks and autos,

---

[7]See Browne, *Popular Beliefs from Alabama*, p. 165, no. 2871: "If gopher rats leave a mine, it is a sign there will be a cave-in."

marred the beauty of roses and tulips planted by some of the community's women in their front yards.

Jimmie Evans reached down for a rock and tossed it away aimlessly. "Mine accidents are terrible things," he said. "You've always got to watch for cavin' timbers, and you've got to watch for gas. An explosion can kill men like they was flies. Now, in this mine, we don't have much gas. I'm happy 'bout that, because th' rats can't help out much when th' gas starts risin' and formin' in pockets. They're like us men—sometimes they feel danger, and then ag'in, they don't."

"There ain't as many terrible accidents now as in the old days. That's because men have learned better how to keep off the tragedies of nature. You take this mine; we've got air courses runnin' on a parallel with th' headin's and th' entry, and fresh air is fanned in through them all the time.[8] That wasn't th' case away back yonder. Why, I remember as if 'twas yesterday when the convict mine over at Banner blew up several years back. Th' explosion was so awful that it shook th' top of our coal stove. There was 125 convicts and eight guards killed in that one."[9]

"You know, ma'am, time sure does fly. I've been diggin' coal ever since I was seventeen, and now I'm gettin' along in years. You can go up th' road a piece and find th' first openin' I ever worked in, but they quit diggin' there a long time ago. After I'd come here to Republic and worked about fifteen years, my boss went over to Walker County and opened up a new mine. He took me with him as a partner, and paid me a pretty good salary besides. I cleaned up a thousand dollars over there, but th' lease played out and he brought me back here and made me a foreman. But I never liked runnin' things so much, because they's a lot of things to worry about. These payrolls have got to

---

[8]One entry would have been enough to haul coal out, but for ventilation there were usually several others. The side passages, or headings, also had ventilation passages parallel to them; see Chapman, *Iron and Steel Industries,* pp. 176–78, for a nontechnical description of coal-mining methods in the Southeast.

[9]There was more than one explosion at the Banner mine at Littleton in the twentieth century, but this undoubtedly refers to the April 8, 1911, explosion that, according to official reports, killed 128 men. The report reads in part: "About 6:00 a.m. the convicts (about 90% Negroes) entered the slope as they entered and left earlier than usual on Saturday than any other day." Thirty men survived the explosion that came twenty minutes later; see Humphrey, *Coal-Mine Explosions,* p. 38.

Coal miners. Birmingham, 1937. Rothstein, FSA.

be met, even if th' foreman don't eat. Then, I'm always uneasy 'bout havin' some sort of accident."

He extended his hands, palms outward, toward the mouth of the mine. "Just feel how cool that air is that's comin' out of there. The temperature stays at 'bout 65 all the year around. That's th' way it is with all mines that's got natural air for ventilation purposes, but when a mine's got th' artificial sort of air, a body nearly freezes. This here mine is what you call a slope, because it goes in on a gentle downward drag. Th' track's laid all th' way down through th' main entrance, and then into th' headin's. Inside there, th' rooms are so low that mules can't get in, so we use little tram cars that hold 'bout a ton of coal. No'm, you can't even stand up to dig. You've got to stoop over real low, and lots of times you've got to dig while you're layin' flat down. Sometimes rocks falls, and they hurt pretty bad. Three years ago I was hurt when one of 'em fell smack on my back, but I've been mighty lucky, all told. A man's got to be mighty careful all th' time. Course, props of pine timber are supposed to be placed every four feet in a room to keep the roof steady. They's a law requirin' that,[10] but lots of times it ain't carried out. Another thing that helps hold th' roof is th' coal that's left for pillars, and th' rock and slate that's thrown back or 'gobbed.' Sometimes when you go back in th' mines to pull th' pillars there ain't enough support, and then you have a 'squeeze.' "

"As I say, I've been might lucky. I'm lucky even 'bout my boss. He's fair to every one of his workers. In some mines where a man loads too much slate or rock in th' coal, they dock him a good amount; but Mr. Abbott don't never do that. When a man gets to loadin' slate and rock here, Mr. Abbott calls him out and warns him friendly like. Then, if th' man does it ag'in, he loses his job. That's fair as it can be, because a miner knows damned well when he's loadin' slate; it's a lot heavier than coal. In a good many mines, they're tough on a man who loads rock and slate. He has to lay off a full day if he loads twelve carbide cans full. For every other can he fills out of three tons of coal, he has to lay off for three days. You see, men'd get careless if you didn't watch 'em. They'd just load everything as they come to it—slate, rock and all."

"To watch a lot of miners, you'd think they're as ignorant of their jobs as the folks outside. It's right funny the ideas some people get 'bout this work. We've got lots of water here, and we pump out plenty of it to run th' washer. That washer washes all th' coal that we get out of this mine, but you don't wash coal to get th' dust off it, like some people think, but to clean it of slate and rock. The other day a man come down here to buy some coal for his furnace, and we told him we couldn't sell him any, because th' washer was out of order. Then he skinned his ignorance by sayin', 'Ah, that don't make any difference. Send it on out, and I'll wash it off with th' hose before it's unloaded!' But we won't be sendin' much more coal away from here. This mine's just 'bout through. That's why we still use mules to draw th' coal out, instead of puttin' in modern machinery. We're workin' now for th' reason that we ain't called a commercial mine. Th' big mines are all shut down 'til they sign a new contract, and most of the fellows are out on strike."

[10]See *The Code of Alabama, adopted by Act of the Legislature of Alabama approved July 2, 1940, recompiled* (Charlottesville, Va.: Michie Co., 1958), vol. 7, p. 70.

"What do I think 'bout unions? Well, ma'am, I believe that every miner has th' right to join one if he wants to. Th' operators have got a union, you know, and they really stand together for everything that's comin' to 'em. Th' main trouble that I can see with th' unions is that they need some real, honest-to-God leaders. Plenty of money was bet on whether th' CIO or th' AF of L would do th' negotiatin' for th' United Mine Workers of America. Th' CIO was the bunch that won out,[11] but I don't think it would've made much difference which way things went. Th' big bugs at th' top got all th' money anyways. But it's a good thing it was settled, because in Alabama th' boys who was strikin' couldn't go on relief, and couldn't draw no compensation, either; and didn't many of 'em draw union benefits."

"A whole lot of folks think that to join th' United Mine Workers, you've got to work inside a mine, or around it. But there ain't a word of truth in that. When th' chapter here was organized, half of th' charter members never had worked 'round a mine, and never even expected to use pick or shovel. All they had to do was join, pay their dues, and be initiated. The benefits they pay now is a whole lot better than th' way it used to be. Way back yonder when miners'd go on strikes, they'd hand out what they called 'Esau' instead of benefits. This 'Esau' was navy beans, side meat, potatoes, flour, sugar, coffee, meal, and compound lard. It was handed out accordin' to the size of the families, and if my memory serves me right, th' last 'Esau' was passed around during th' strike of 1922."

"I guess I love a coal mine better'n any place on earth. It sort of gets a fellow when he follows it awhile. Over at Westfield, a T.C.I. place, they won't give you a job if they find out you've worked in a coal mine. They know as good as anything that after they've fretted away time and money trainin' you, you'll go back to th' mines sooner or later. And I wouldn't deny that they've got us down 'bout right." Jimmie chuckled again, and looked up toward the house, where two young boys dressed in overalls were playing catch in the narrow front yard. "Le's go up there and see my old woman," he said. "I'll bet she's beginnin' to think we've forgotten all about her."

---

[11]This was John L. Lewis's successful challenge to the American Federation of Labor, beginning in 1936; see Bernstein, *Turbulent Years,* p. 431.

When we were almost to the porch, he paused. "Be careful here," he warned. "That middle step is off at one end, and if you don't watch yourself, you'll get your neck broke. All of us know where th' dangerous places are, but we have to tell our visitors how to get around 'em." He glanced up at the slanting roof. "This old place ain't so much anymore," he said solemnly. "Th' screens are all out, and when it rains outside, it pours inside. I would fix up that roof, but I never seem to get enough time. You can't blame th' owners for not wantin' to fix it, because th' mine's nearly worked out."

Inside the house, there was a sound of chairs scraping the floor. A moment later, a woman was framed in the doorway, the lines of her heavy body emphasized by a close-fitting cotton dress. She said, "Well do come in. I'd begun to think that Jimmie was goin' to keep you down there at th' mine. He ain't got any hospitality at all when you start him talkin' about that place." She shoved a chair forward for her guest, and then walked over to a quilt that swung on a frame in the center of the room. She pushed a needle into its cottony depths, and then drew up a chair for herself. "I've been wishin' somebody would come and stop me from workin' on this quilt," she said. "My back's so tired now it's about to break." She smiled, and tiny wrinkles played around her brown eyes. Rachel Evans is a strong woman, straight-shouldered, and with a determined lift to her chin. Her face is tanned by sun and wind; her hands look as strong and as capable as those of a man. Wisps of gray are beginning to show in her dark brown hair, but her slow smile is contagious, and her eyes are youthful behind thick lashes.

Jimmie said, "I'm goin' back to th' mine while you women-folks give us men the devil. I catch enough of it with just one woman around, let alone two." He laughed softly at his joke, and then walked out the door. Rachel Evans smiled and shook her head. "It'd take a block and tackle to keep him away from that mine," she said. "He stays down there whether he's supposed to be working or not. I don't know what he'd do without a coal diggin' to puddle about, and I guess I'm about as bad. We've lived here twenty-five years, and you get to feelin' close akin to a place after that long a time."

"I don't ever go to the mine now, but I remember a time when they had trouble keeping me out of one. Why, many a time I've woke in the dead of night and gone down there. I always had to sneak down, because if any of the miners saw me, they'd come scootin' out. You see, a woman's bad luck—else the men say they are.[12] I don't believe a word of it. Women always do more good than harm. But the miners say that if one of 'em enters the mouth of a diggin', there'll be an accident. They'll just pick up their tools and get out of that shaft. Some of 'em won't ever go back in the hole again."

"When I first married, I just couldn't seem to stay away from the mines. He was down there—Jimmie, I mean—and he was on the night shift. You know, when you love a man you're always worryin' about him. Sometimes I guess them that don't love get by easier. Anyway, I'd wake up, and when I'd get to thinkin' about him, I'd get so lonesome I wouldn't know which way to turn. Then I'd fix up some sandwiches to give me an excuse for goin', and go down there to him. Oh, he'd scold me sometimes, but then he'd laugh and tell me I was the beatenest woman he ever saw. There ain't a mean bone in Jimmie's body, and he'd be the best man in the world if it wasn't for old liquor. That's his chief trouble. When he puts whiskey in his insides, the devil goes in with it. Bad as I hate to tell you, he's just now gettin' over a three-day spree."

"That old stuff's caused all the fallin's out we've ever had. I wasn't goin' to tell you this, but I'd as well go ahead. One day several years ago I saw a bunch of men with guns at their hips pass by the house. They was headed toward the mine, and at first I didn't know what to think. Then it hit my brain that Jimmie'd been smellin' mighty loud of old wildcat the last few days, and my suspicions got up. I just threw down everything I was doin', got down my shotgun, and started runnin'. I followed a little path to the side of the hill and run right into a brush heap. Well, I stopped just a second to kick the limbs to one side, and what do you think I found? Some boards that covered a hole leadin' into the mine! I jerked those boards off like fightin' fire, and then I slid down through that hole. I landed right in front of Jimmie, almost in some of that slop he was stirrin'. Sure, that's what he was doin'—makin' whiskey! There wasn't any time for

---

[12]See note 1 in this part.

words. I yelled at him that the Law was on its way, and we got everything hid before the officers got there. They sniffed around a little, and the place must have smelled mighty rank, but they never found any of the whiskey. When they left I gave Jimmie a piece of my mind that he'll remember to the Judgment day. It must have done some good, too, because he buys all his liquor now."

She turned for a moment to her quilting, her tanned fingers resting upon the frame. "I think I'm goin' to have a mighty pretty quilt here," she smiled. "There's nothing in this world that I'd rather do, because a body can't have too many of 'em. But this one belongs to my girl, Joanie; she pieced it herself. That's one thing I taught my girls to do—make quilts. In summer when school was out, I had my girls workin' instead of runnin' about Lord knows where. Joanie had four finished when she got married, and she keeps wantin' more and more. Joanie's a might young thing to be keepin' house, but at that, she waited longer than the other girls. She's nineteen, and she's got a head full of good sense. Mr. Abbott, the man Jimmie works for, said he'd give her a set of silver if she'd finish high school before she married. Well, she got it. She got a good man, too—a miner over at Hamilton Slope, about six miles from here. They're goin' to have their first baby in June."

"It makes me sad and happy at the same time to think about my girls havin' babies. My oldest girl, Julie, was just fifteen when she was married, and she died when her first baby was born. She was gettin' on just fine when all of a sudden she took a high fever. They never did know just what was the matter— else they never would tell me—but I always believed it was childbed fever. I guess we waited too long about callin' the doctor. I never did have any trouble bearin' children, and somehow or other, I didn't expect Julie to have any. We took the baby, and kept him until his daddy married some other woman."

"I worry a lot about my girl Marilyn. She was just fifteen when her first baby came, and he's almost a year old now and full of life as a coon. It's her man that gives me my trouble. He's nineteen—old enough to know how to behave—but he's already started to run around with girls. He ought to have listened closer to his marriage vows, because they're mighty sacred. I believe

he tells the girls that he's not married, for they're nice-lookin'—
not the painted up kind that get in automobiles with married
men. I guess the old saying is true that 'when children are small
they step on your feet, but when they grow up they step on your
heart.' "

"Everywhere I turn these days, it seems that I run into babies.
My second oldest son married last July when he was seventeen
and his wife was just fourteen, and they're expectin' their first
baby in June. Joanie's will come about the same time, and I just
don't know how I'll manage to be with both of them at once. I'll
have to manage somehow, though, because my boy's mother-in-
law is blind and can't do anything helpful."

"Of all my children that got married, Faye hurt me worse. She
was the smartest child I had, and she's just fourteen now. I
didn't know that she cared a thing about boys, because she
never even mentioned goin' with anybody. I guess that's why it
was such a shock. She always said that she was goin' to finish
high school, and then go on to college; but she let the love bug
bite her. She was double-promoted twice, and could make
circles around every other young'n in her class. She told me
about lovin' this boy just two weeks before she married him, but
hurt as I was, I didn't raise a hand. It just seemed to be a case of
'marry she must, or die she would.' When she was a little thing,
she'd talk about bein' a school teacher, and I'd always hoped
she'd do that. I suppose I was tryin' to live my life over in her, for
I was always sorry that I didn't teach. I went through the tenth
grade, and back then I could have got a third-grade teachin'
license with that much learnin'. But I did what I wanted to
do—I married Jimmie Evans. And I know my girls are doin'
what they want to do when they get married. Jimmie and me
just have two little boys left at home with us now, but the
married children can come home any time they want to, because they don't live far away. Our smallest boy is ten, and the
other is twelve; and I know it won't be many years before they'll
up and fly the coop like the others."

"I can sit and look back over my life and know that I raised
good children—thank the Lord for that. Not a one of the boys
drinks or gambles, and none of the girls 'went wrong.' But I'll
have to say that not a one of them belong to the church. That

won't seem so strange when I tell you that we've never had a regular preacher out here, though it's only a fifteen-minute drive into Birmingham. There ain't no preacher that's goin' to preach without money, and I, for one, don't believe in payin' anybody to preach the gospel. I belong to the Hard Shell Baptists,[13] and lots of my beliefs are taken from that teachin' of my church, 'What is to be, will be.' One of the girls did talk a little once about joinin' up with the Missionary Baptists, but she was only ten years old. I told her it was scripture that Christ said to 'let the little children come unto me,' but then I told her that I wished she'd wait till she knew her mind better. That was a mistake, I guess, because she never has even so much as mentioned joinin' up with any church ag'in. Jimmie don't belong to any church either. I hate it, but he don't like to talk about it."

"If we'd a had a good live church here, I don't reckon we'd a been so hell bent on keepin' our school. For a long time the county board has been tryin' to consolidate our school with some others, and send the children on buses. They said they could do better by the children that way, but we don't think so. Sometimes it seems the board is goin' to win out despite us, but we always come back at 'em with enough arguments to be good for another year. Why, I don't see how we'd get along without our school. We'd never get together in a bunch if it weren't for the P.T.A. and school meetin's. You've just got to have somethin' to work together on if you ever feel at home in a place. We just got two teachers for six grades, but we got the best P.T.A. in the county, with thirty-five members. I won't have a single child in school after this year, but I won't stop fightin' for the others. I promised if they stuck by me, I'd stick by them. My religion comes in right here about the school business. I say that if a young'n wants to learn, he'll learn no matter how many grades are in one room. If he don't want to learn they could have a hundred teachers, and still he wouldn't know a blessed thing."

---

[13]The Primitive Baptists, an antimission group, emerged around the 1830s. Nicknamed Hardshell Baptists, they were (and are) particularly strong in eastern Tennessee and northern Alabama; see Lawrence Edwards, "The Primitive Baptists" (Master's thesis, University of Tennessee, 1940), p. 34.

There was a sudden sound of noisy footsteps on the porch outside. The two boys, who had been playing catch with an old baseball in the front yard, filed into the room, caps in dust-stained hands. For a moment they stood in silence, glancing in uncertainty first at their mother and then at the visitor. But at last, the youngest of them took a deep breath. He said, "Ma, ain't we ever gonna have any supper?"

The Flowers

by Nettie S. McDonald

Mrs. Flowers opened her door. She is a neat, pleasant-faced woman. "Do come right in," she said. "I've been looking for you a long time, but then I always forget there are fourteen blocks to walk after getting off the car. When you phoned you were coming, I stood in the middle of the floor and wondered what in the world to do first, for the whole house was such a mess. If I had known a little earlier, I would have been nearer ready. Oh, let's forget about the house. You sit over where the light is best."

"Yes, we like this place," she said happily. "Look right through that window and you can see the county line. If we were just one block over, we would have escaped the city taxes, but then we would have been forced to send the children to the county schools and I don't think they are as good as the city schools. I am convinced that Birmingham public schools are the very best in the entire south. There you see is an example of the law of compensation. We live in the country, but we have all the privileges of the city and so our inconveniences and comforts balance. We just can't stand the noise of the city."

"Oh, no, we never get lonesome a minute. I listen to all the stories on the radio, and my housekeeping chores make it seem just a little while from the time the children go to school in the morning until they come home again in the afternoon. Charles, who is sixteen, will finish just as Mary Rose, who is fourteen, enters Woodlawn High School next year. I do wish you could see them. They are both grand looking children and they are so congenial." Then Mrs. Flowers made an odd comment. "My girl is really too beautiful for her own good, I am afraid. Sometimes a girl's beauty works to hurt her. We are planning to send both through college, although I'm sorry to say that Joe isn't as interested in the children's education as I am. There's a reason for that difference," she added thoughtfully.

"When I was a little girl there was nothing in the world I wanted as I wanted an education. My mother couldn't even write her own name and I never knew anything about my father except that he came from very fine people. That's a sad part of my life that I don't like to talk about. Anyway I am not as resentful as I was when I was younger and had to use my mother's maiden name for mine. Some of that bitterness is gone."

"When I was just a little girl I told my mother that I intended to go to school and later to college; so when I was thirteen years old, my mother asked my aunt to let me live in her house and work so that I could go to school. I remember it just as if it were yesterday. My aunt said, 'Yes, Ginny, just send her down any time and I'll send her to school.' I put on my red plaid dress, tied all my clothes in a flour sack and started out. Aunt Nancy was kind to me and in return I worked hard to keep the house clean before and after school. My uncle was the Christian minister at Morris and he lived a true Christian life."

"I was in the fourth grade when I started but I studied very hard and made several grades in one year. One of the teachers took a great interest in me and offered to help me go to college after I had gone as far as I could in Morris. I never went back to my mother's house except to spend one day, because my step-father was unkind to me. He seemed to hate me because my mother loved me so much."

"The only money I required was twenty-five dollars for my first year at college. My mother brought it to me all wrapped up in a sack, for it was all in nickels and dimes and pennies. She is a grand woman, is my mother, and good, through and through. She saved all that money from her sale of milk, butter and eggs. She had a hard time hiding it from my stepfather."

"Well, with that twenty-five dollars and the help of my teacher I went to college and finished the Home Economics course. That course is a help to me every day of my life. It enables me to give my family the food they need at the lowest possible cost. My meals are always well balanced even when I don't try to think about it; proper selection of foods is perfectly natural to me. Throughout my college course I worked all winter and during the summer vacations I was dietician at a summer resort hotel in Tennessee."

"Oh, I almost forgot to tell you where the college was. It was at Maryville, Tennessee, a Presbyterian college. No, I'm not a Presbyterian. My children and I belong to the Christian church, and Joe would join that church too, if he joined any. Joe never discusses religion, but he lives a Christian life. We don't live near a Christian church, so the children go to the Baptist Sunday School. We feel that it doesn't make much difference, so long as you live honestly with your fellowman."

"No, none of us go around at night. We are all satisfied with each other, the radio and our work. When things get too monotonous, we go to a movie, but even then we all go together. About the only real extravagance that we indulge in is baseball. No amusement is half as thrilling to this family as a good baseball game! Even if I tried to argue about the expense, it wouldn't do a bit of good. Joe would go without me. So I dress and we all go right along and don't even think about how much it costs. Later I just cut a corner somewhere in my household expense."

"Yes, you're right—it will be a little far out here for the boys to come to see Mary Rose, but that suits me just fine. The fewer boys come to see her, the better I'll like it," she said with an anxious frown.

"What kind of work was Joe doing when we first married? He was working in the oil fields. We were married in Birmingham in 1921, and went immediately to Byar, Oklahoma. At that time there was a big dispute about which state really owned the oil wells, because it was right on the border between Oklahoma and Texas. Oklahoma won. Joe operated the engine that pumped the oil from the wells. The engine was run by natural gas. Joe took care of the engine for three years. Yes, we did well out there. We had outhouse, fuel, lights and water furnished and his salary was $175 a month. I'll admit that it seems strange that we should have left all that and come back to Alabama, but there was nothing else to do. It will take right much explaining, but if you really want to know, I'll tell you."

"You remember that I told you Aunt Nancy kept me and sent me to school for four years? Well, it so happened that when Joe was a little boy, his father and mother separated and their children were parceled out and the Hudson family got Joe. They sent him to school just as my aunt sent me. Well, one day we received a letter saying that my uncle had died and Aunt Nancy wanted us to come back to Morris to look after her. In return, she would leave her property to us at her death, since she had no children of her own. You see we both felt indebted to her, and we just couldn't refuse to help her in her old age."

"So back we came to Morris. We had saved about seventy-five dollars each month, and with our savings Joe bought some trucks and did contract hauling. He hauled all that heavy material for the big bridges around Morris. We call the biggest one the Flowers Bridge for Joe. He hauled every single piece that went into it. We are thrilled every time we pass over it."

"Well, we stayed at Morris and Aunt Nancy who was seventy years old married again. Then we looked after both her and her husband until Aunt Nancy died. Did we really get the property? No, we didn't. You know what that old man did? While Aunt Nancy was very sick, he and his children tricked her into signing some kind of paper giving the property to them. Joe and I decided against a law-suit. It wasn't much of a place anyway. Maybe we could have had it, but his children would have given us trouble about it as long as we lived, so we just let it go. Then we moved to Birmingham and he started to work at the Continental Gin Company. When the plant shut down, we couldn't pay our rent, so Joe learned the trade of installing weatherstripping."

"There's Joe now. He's come home for his dinner, so while I'm in the kitchen, he'll be glad to tell you all about his work. He knows more about it in a minute than I do in a whole week. He can tell you all about how weather-stripping keeps the dirt from coming in but I can tell you that you still have trouble with dirt accumulating in the house! Nothing seems to cure that."

Joe sat down and said, "Now, let me see just where I should start. I want you to know how I make my living. One of the first and most important arguments for weatherstripped doors and windows is that twenty to forty percent, depending on the weather conditions, of the heating expense of a house can be saved by weatherstripping the doors and windows. Engineering tests have shown that. To weatherstrip a five-roomed house like mine costs about seventy-five dollars. This whole side of my house is weatherstripped, but the other side isn't. You see we have just this one fire in the grate going and it's perfectly comfortable, isn't it? Now come with me and I'll let you see the difference in the rooms."

In the other rooms the temperature was uncomfortably lower. Then he began again with renewed enthusiasm. "You have seen for yourself what it will do to the temperature. Well, it keeps out the dust, drafts, soot, rain and snow just as well. It's a great help to a housewife because it helps her to keep the curtains and the wall coverings clean. You've seen windows that were fitted so close that you could hardly open them and when you finally got them opened, you had just as much trouble getting them back down? Well, weatherstripping corrects that fault. It's mighty hard to leave a window that is weather-tight, loose enough for easy opening and shutting. Weather-stripping the windows and doors keeps the outside noises on the outside."

"I'm sure you can see why I'm sold on weatherstripping. There are still many other reasons, but none is more important that the prevention of heat loss. People are always wondering why on earth they have to buy so much coal and are still uncomfortable much of the time. Just figure a little and you can see for yourself. Cracks between the frames and the sashes of double-hung windows vary in width from a very small one to one-fourth inch. Multiply the crack by the distance around the window, which is usually 216 inches. That will give you about thirteen and a half square inches. If you should see a hole that big in your wall you couldn't cover it up quickly enough and yet that is the average space around each window."

"Then there's the question of wind. In the living room of the poorly-built house, the leakage through this one window we were talking about would change the air every eleven minutes. In this type of house, there is a constant drafty circulation of air that keeps expensive warmed air flowing from the house. A wind blowing on the north side of the house causes cold air to come in and then the warm air goes out the other side. Now you can see that if three sides of the room are weatherstripped, the leakage on the fourth side won't be much."

"When windows warp, swell, or shrink from dampness, weatherstripping takes care of the space left and stops that nerve-racking sound of rattling windows. It will easily pay for itself in the saving of fuel, and of laundry and paint work, but there is one thing to be remembered and that is, that the best type of material, if applied wrong, will help very little. Fully eighty percent of the efficiency of weatherstripping is in the skill of the mechanic that installs it. Good weatherstripping put in right should last as long as a house does. The weather-stripped house is more comfortable in summer too, so you see it's a good investment anyway you take it."

"If all this is so, you want to know why we don't hear more about it? Well, I hate to tell you, but the people in the south just haven't realized the savings to be made. Now in the north, it's different. They use some form of insulation in nearly all the houses and the idea is gradually spreading south. We weather-stripped the Comer building, the Farley building and many others. It was a job working on those high windows in the Comer building and we were as black as could be when we came home in the evening."

"No, I am not a partner in the company. A salesman goes around and gets the orders for jobs. He does all the contracting about prices and credit and all we have to do is to install them. My wife's brother has worked side by side with me ever since I started this work. He is really my right hand. He takes out the windows and strips them while I prepare the facings. I would be lost without him. We are called mechanics."

"I have been doing this work for about twelve years. There are about three months in the year that business is good and then I make from two hundred to three hundred dollars a month. During the other months we do odd repair jobs. Several rental agents give us all their work. I have a car and we put all our tools in the back seat and go wherever we can find work. Lately some of it has been out of Birmingham. Nora doesn't like that so much. When the children were small, she used to go with me and stay at tourist camps, but she can't do that now. We don't like to be separated so much, but we have to make a living."

"A living is about all we have made in the last few years, but we have managed to stay off relief. Sometimes it looked as though in spite of everything that we could do, we just couldn't make it, but along would come another job. The president has done some wonderful things, but I am glad that we haven't had to use any of that money."

"Yes, we own this house, or at least we are buying it. We were just saying the other day that we have been paying on it for twelve years and the mortgage is about the same as it was at first. But there's one good thing about buying a place—you don't have to worry about the rent going up and then too, they can't sell it from under you. Besides, the payments are less than rent would be.

"I am certainly glad that I have shown you that weatherstripping is not a kind of wood, as you thought it was. Maybe if more people knew what it was, my business would be better and we could pay off that mortgage. But we're doing pretty well anyway," he finished cheerfully. "Already we are beginning to feel an improvement in our business since the company started radio talks on the many benefits of weatherstripping."

"There's Nora now. Dinner's ready and she always has something good to eat. Stay with us and see if I'm not right about that."

Victoria Coleman was one of two university graduates added to the Alabama Writers' Project in December 1938 in an attempt to upgrade the staff.[14] This account, dated January 31, 1939, is the only life history by this author.

Soil Pipe Worker

by Victoria Coleman

On a bleak winter afternoon, I approached an attractive modern brick house with a well kept yard, and the lights from the windows shone out invitingly. I was met at the door by an elderly little woman with snowy hair who was becomingly clad in a house-dress and apron. "Come in," she said, "I am just starting to fix supper." The house was as attractive within as without. "Is it warm enough for you?" she inquired, adjusting the already warmly glowing gas heater. Presently an elderly man of medium height and with regular features and keen gray eyes appeared. He was clean shaven and neatly dressed. "This is my husband, Mr. Jones," the little woman said. Then a handsome young man entered the house, and was introduced as Mr. Thomas, Mr. Jones' son-in-law.

Mr. Jones told his story, his son-in-law frequently adding comments, while his wife came and went preparing the evening meal. "My wife and I used to live here by ourselves, but we now have my daughter, her husband and two small children with us. My daughter is right now upstairs sick with a cold, and I have just been up there sittin' with her."

"This here doesn't look to be sech a large house, just seein' it from the street, but it is. We have a nice apartment on the other side that we rent. It pays for our taxes, gas, and a few other expenses. The apartment has a bath, living room, bedroom and kitchen. We have two baths on our side, one upstairs and one downstairs. This is a ten-room house. Yes, I own it, but I don't own no car; they cost too much." From where I sat on the

---

[14]Miles to Couch, January 19, 1939, FWP—Couch Papers.

comfortable living room sofa, I could see into the kitchen. There, everything was clean, new-looking, modern and colorful.

"My father and mother left Ohio with me when I was seven years old," he continued. "They were poor. They stopped in Missouri and my mother died there. When I was eight years old my father came to Anniston and died here that year. I was left alone from that time on, to take care of myself and to make a living for myself. I lived with first one person and then the other. I worked hard and earned my own way. I can remember wearing old clothes the folks would give me, and painfully recall one pair of shoes that were too little for me and that rubbed bad blisters on my feet. But I always got along, and I will tell you one thing: no one ever took advantage of me; folks always treated me nice."

"I never went to school a day in my life." "Do you think an education pays?" I asked. "Yes, I know it does," he replied. "A man can't hardly get along without one these days. If I should get without a job now without an education, and at my age, I couldn't get one nowhere. It takes an education to get on these days. In fact, I wouldn't have no job, old as I am anyway, if it weren't for Tobe Hampton, my boss, and he is the best boss to work for in the world. I am now sixty-nine years old, and been workin' in the pipe shops[15] for forty-six years. I guess I am the oldest pipe shop worker in Anniston; maybe in the world. Well, Tobe says I am the oldest pipe shop worker in the world, and he ought to know."

"What do you think is the average number of years a man works in the pipe shops?" I interrogated. "About thirty-six years, I would say," he answered. "That is about right," remarked the son-in-law, Mr. Thomas. "Papa, you might explain to her about the wages and the nature of your work." Then he remarked to me, "Papa is a moulder."

"That is right," said Mr. Jones. "Every moulder has a helper, and the helper doesn't make as much as the moulder. They pay six, seven, eight, nine and ten dollars a day, and we get from three to four days a week. The shop has not run regular in about nine years. We used to get six days a week. In them days they

---

[15]The soil pipe under discussion is cast iron pipe, not any kind of ceramic as the name might imply. Anniston was, nationwide, its greatest producer; see Alabama Writers' Project, *Guide to the Deep South*, p. 160.

Concrete mixing plant. Birmingham, 1936. Evans, FSA.

urged you to work every day, six days a week, but now they don't care if you don't work. They got more men than they can work anyway. We made about five dollars a day in them days. I have made as high as four hundred dollars a month in my lifetime, but I have had to work hard for it. I have got up at two o'clock many a time and gone to work for my family. But they was worth it."

"I met this lady here," he proudly indicated his wife, "in Cherokee County. We been married close onto fifty years. Will be fifty years in a few months now. That's a long time to live with one bad woman," he laughed. "But I'll tell you what, if she ever was to die, I wouldn't marry any more. I don't believe in no second marriages. The Lord didn't intend you to marry but once."

"Oh go on, Bill," said his wife, slightly embarrassed. "Well, I mean it," he said. "We had eleven children and five of them died. We had a hard time with all those children. But they have all turned out well. I now have four girls and two boys, and your girls sure will do more for you than your boys. One of my boys works here at a drug company, and the other one is a mechanic at the CCC camp near here. I have a daughter who is in Austin, Texas. Her husband is manager of a big creamery there."

"He is going to get a new job; did you know, Papa?" Mrs. Jones said. "They wrote about it. He will get two hundred and fifty dollars a month." "Well, that's fine; he wasn't making but a hundred seventy-five at his present one," rejoined the father. "One of my daughters works for the Coca-Cola people in Virginia. She is a stenographer. My other daughter's husband, who was general manager of the Coca-Cola Bottling Company in Anniston, got her the job."

Mr. Thomas said, "He had a split-up here, but he is now general manager of a bottling company in Birmingham. You see there is only one general Coca-Cola syrup company, but there are any number of Coca-Cola bottling companies. Before my brother-in-law lost out with the Coca-Cola people here I worked as salesman for them for five years. The Coca-Cola company is a mighty fine company to work for. However, coca-colas are not as easy to sell as some people think, because the company sells on a strictly business-like basis, and some of the merchants object to the fifty cents a carton they have to 'put up' on each crate."

"Selling is my line, though, and even though I lost out when my brother-in-law did, on account of the politics of the thing, yet one of the men in the organization, who was his political enemy, said that I was one of the best salesmen in the organization. Selling is meeting the public, and that is what I like. It is like baseball. I played professional baseball for eight years before I sold for the Coca-Cola people. I played in several states and was at Anniston for a while. I am temporarily out of a job, but I don't think there is much doubt that I will get back my Coca-Cola selling job soon. There is no life like 'the road'." He left the room and came back carrying a child. "This is my ten-months-old daughter," he said. "How do you like her red hair?"

"I will tell you something else," said Mr. Jones. "When I was a young man I worked side by side with Mr. T. C. Hampton. Tobe, we called him. He is my boss now. We was pipe rammers then.[16] If you are going to write anything, say something about what a fine man and a fine boss he is. He is the finest boss in the world to work for, and he sure has made money, too. I don't get no easy work, I have had to work hard for everything I have gotten, but the pipe shop is a mighty fine place to work at. When I worked by Tobe Hampton we both were starting out, and we worked at the Central Foundry Company. I worked for twenty-six years there without stopping. Well, first thing I knowed Tobe Hampton come to me and said, 'Bill, I'm gettin' a job at Mr. Rudisill's Foundry. He is making me a foreman.' I said, 'Be careful now, Tobe, be sure you are gettin' a better job.' 'I will try to be,' he replied. Soon Tobe had started a pipe shop of his own."

"I hear that Mr. Hampton's business has prospered quite a bit," I said. "Yes, indeed it has," he replied. "Well, you know the price of iron went up," his wife said. "The whole white way of New York City was made at the shops right here in Anniston; also, the white way in many another large city was made here," he said. "Anniston makes more cast iron soil pipes than any other place in the world, they say."

---

[16]"Pipe rammer" was a specialized occupation in the pipe shops. According to James McIntyre Camp, *The Making, Shaping and Treating of Steel*, 7th ed. (Pittsburgh: U.S. Steel Corp., 1957), p. 384: "Greensand molds—made of moist sand which is rammed about a pattern (usually of wood) in a 'flask' of wood or iron, and the metal is poured with the mold in condition as rammed." Dry sand molds were a variation on the process.

"Once I had a chance to be made a foreman, but I figured that a man like me without no education had better not take it. I was afraid I couldn't handle it right, and that the men might cheat me on their time. All I wanted to be was a good honest work-man. I wanted to live right too. I am a Methodist, and I think that and the Presbyterian Church is the finest churches there are. But it is really how good you are that counts. I don't take much part in politics, I vote and that is all. I think it don't look so nice to see women smoking, but that is their own business—drinking too."

"Well, goodbye and good luck," he said as I told them I had to leave, "and if I can give you any more information, just you let me know." This ended a most pleasant visit, and I stepped from the warm air into the cold of the outside.

One of the earliest life histories written in Alabama, this account by Woodrow Hand of the editorial department in Birmingham was dated September 15, 1938. Hand's only other life history was of Gertha Couric, a fellow member of the Alabama Writers' Project.

Johnnie Fence, Truck Miner

by Woodrow Hand

Helena, lying seventeen and a half miles south of Birmingham on the main line of the L&N Railway, is the central point of what once was a great coal mining locality. Main Street, or the business section, has on one side two stores and a shoeshop. On the other side is a store and the Post Office. The Post Office is alone in its assurance of continued operation. The streets of Helena are rough and dusty, or muddy, depending upon the whim of the weather. They pass rambling houses that sag at the roofs and on the corners—shotgun houses that are even worse than their already questionable name. Helena, with one exception, fits any of numerous ghost town descriptions. The exception is that people live there. They are a varied group—living examples of what Helena has been and hopes to be again.

On a hill overlooking Helena lives Dr. White, dentist. "Leave Helena?" His fat teutonic face first registers surprise, then indulgence, such as that reserved for a questioning child. "Why should I leave? It's my home; I've made a fortune here. Those people down there need me. They still have the toothache—much oftener than they can afford to pay for relief."

Other illnesses fall upon the Irish shoulders of Dr. Kelley. "I wouldn't leave this place," he says, "because there's plenty of good fishing around here." Then with a twinkle in his eyes, "And you know how people *will* keep having babies. Why, I've got six kids myself. Believe you me, people will have babies and get sick regardless. Besides, I've been doctoring these people for twenty years; I know their troubles. Pay? Pshaw! These people can't pay! But they used to. The offices of six mines used to cut their men a buck out of every payday. I haven't spent all of that yet."

Wesley Miller, seemingly the busiest storekeeper in Helena, was next. "Business is bad," he says, "but we'll make out. I let out a lot of credit, but most of the bills are paid sometime or other." Suddenly Wesley laughed and pointed across the railroad tracks. "There comes Johnnie Fence with a case of snuff from the Paramount commissary. He brings it in as fast as I can sell it. You see, the commissary charges so high that the miners trade with me when they draw a payday; but their paydays don't come very regular. The miners have to trade checks. But Johnnie—he trades his check for snuff and it isn't above the popular price. The he swaps the snuff to me for groceries. Pretty smart that."

Johnnie's face bears the unmistakable mark of years underground. It is pockmarked and lined with blue scars—wounds that healed over coal dust. His hands are gnarled, with stubby fingers. Over all are the identifying blue marks. The introductory handshake was like rubbing a piece of oak bark.

"Shucks," Johnnie grinned, "I can tell you plenty 'bout minin' 'round here, and show you plenty, too. Only I'd better go home to do it. Hattie don't like to keep supper waitin'. I gotta get home with the baby's candy, too." Helena's main street becomes an ordinary road a few hundred feet west of Wesley Miller's store. Johnnie led the way past houses in every known state of disrepair, all facing the road.

"See how the porches are slap up a'gin' the road? I leave for work about five o'clock to walk the three miles to Paramount by work time. In hot weather, a lotta folks sleep on them porches in practically nothin'. Some of them oversleep. Some mornin's I'm late for work. Do you blame me?"

After nearly half a mile, the road suddenly tops a small rise. In a little valley below is a cluster of fairly new, unpainted houses, slightly weather-worn. The houses are bungalows of four and five rooms. One has a cracked-rock front. This is Johnnie's home. He explains: "A twister cleaned out what we owned three years ago, and the relief people helped us build back. I bought my place twenty years ago when things were hummin'.'"

Flowers of varied hue dot the front yard. To the side is a small vegetable garden. A chicken yard and a half acre of corn take up the rear of the lot. From the porch, the front door opens into the living room. Left is an open fireplace built of small white rocks. On each side of the fireplace are built-in bookcases—bare of books. The room is neither painted nor papered, but the floor is covered with a soft rug that matches the mohair furniture. In the corner is a radio of 1925 vintage. Johnnie says, "It don't play so good, but I like to tinker with it."

Through an arch from the living room is the dining room furnished with a second-hand suite of maple. Also in this room is a circulator heater that is expected to heat the entire house. Moving on toward the rear is the kitchen, which is as large as any of the other rooms (approximately fourteen by sixteen feet). A large coal stove takes up an entire side, with space reserved for a closet in which groceries and cooking utensils are kept. A table and kitchen cabinet dominate the rest of the space. Most of the eating is done in the kitchen. Hattie sees to that. Two bedrooms and a sleeping porch comprise the rest of the house.

Hattie has brown hair and eyes and a healthy, buxom figure. Her forty years are hidden by lines of laughter around her eyes. Hattie's yell, "come to supper," is immediately drowned out by a rush of feet, and out of nowhere appear a four-year-old girl and a twenty-year-old boy. "John Robert beats me to the table ev'y time," the little girl complains. "I wish he'd go back to college."

"Joan means Howard College,"[17] Johnnie explains, "but I doubt if she gets her wish. You see, I saved what I could while I was makin' it so's John Robert could be educated right, but you see (Johnnie waves his hand over the table, the gesture covering a bowl of lima beans, fresh garden lettuce, homemade jelly, fried white meat, and buttermilk) what we have to eat. Ain't no money in truck minin', and buildin' back the house, sending John Robert to Howard one year, and Joan—who we hadn't even figured on—just about took all I had and all I can make."

"We been tryin' to get it fixed so John Robert can work his way through college. That'll help a lot. A feller's got to have a

[17]Howard College, a Southern Baptist–related college in Birmingham, today Samford University.

good education these days. Take me for instance. I know as much about minin' as anybody and I ain't braggin'. It's all I ever done. But awhile back there was a fire-bossin' job open at Paramount. It pays a salary, and all I'd had to do would be to look for gas and anything that might cause explosions. I could do the work with my eyes shut and my lamp out, but you know what happened? And the boss was pullin' for me too. I had to go to Birmingham to stand examination and I couldn't answer a dang question that was on the paper. Another fellow took the test; said he was sure glad he knew triggermomity. What is trigger-momity anyhow? Anyway, that dude got the job. And I know as much about gas as anybody. So I still work by the day at Paramount, and ain't many days that Paramount works. That's why my two kids need educatin'."

Politically, Johnnie isn't sure how he stands. "I vote straight Republican," he said, " 'ceptin' when it comes to Roosevelt. Then I vote Democrat. If he hadn't stood behind us workin' men I don't know where we'd be now. Too bad we didn't have him in '20 and '22. That's the time us miners busted our hames. Come on out on the porch where it's cool and I'll tell you about it."

Briefly, here is the story. John Fence has worked the Cahaba Valley coal seam since he was old enough to swing a pick. He has seen coal mining communities grow from a shack at the prospector's hole to thriving colonies with up-to-date facilities; then with the fading of demand, sink into obscurity among impenetrable, blackberry briar-entwined undergrowth. This was the fate of Roebuck Numbers One, Two, Three and Four, Coalmont, Mossboro, Red Ash, and Falliston. Once these names stood for prosperous towns with electric lights, running water, recreation centers, schools, and fine people. Today, the concrete mouths of the mines have fallen into the dark slopes. Tons of dirt have closed the entrances. Water, once pressed from the mines with high-powered pumps, has crept upward to meet the dirt and shale of the slopes.

The railroad line from Birmingham to Centreville rushed hordes of sweating laborers to build spurs to these mines when they were in their heyday. Grades and trestles were built for permanency. They thought the coal would last forever. The coal is still there; but the mines and the railroad spurs are gone.

Labor trouble which culminated in the Alabama strike of 1920 and the national strike of 1922 started the industry in this locality on a jerky sleigh ride that was sometimes fast, sometimes momentarily halted, but always downhill. The sleigh eventually smashed.[18] Out of the pieces there arose the truck mining industry.

In Johnnie's words, "It's hard to say exactly when it started, but it musta' been about ten years ago. It took about six or eight years for the operators to decide that they'd never do anything else big with all the coal in this part of the country."

"Oscar Harrison was about the first to try truck mining around here. He'd made a pile and held on to it. He took his two boys and cleaned out the entrance of Number One Roebuck down to the first headin'. They cut pine poles and built a tipple and coal chute.[19] From the chute to the first room of the headin' they laid a track that threatened to fall apart every time it was touched. Instead of the usual boiler engine, they rigged up an old auto engine with a contraption that looked like the roller on homemade well pulleys. It worked, pullin' up two cars of coal at the time. The daily output depended upon the trouble they had gettin' to the coal. Sometimes, they'd spend two or three days cleanin' out rock falls that, for the lack of workers, couldn't be propped right."

"From that, truck minin' spread all the way from the highway at the Jefferson and Shelby County line down the Cahaba River for thirty miles or more. Usually they didn't and don't last long, either foldin' up because all the available coal is taken or the operator goes broke. Truck mines are more or less like lightnin' bugs. They flash up and then fade out."

Paramount mine is a truck mine, but slightly different. The operators were well financed to begin with. The facilities are

---

[18]There were major strikes and accompanying violence among Birmingham area miners as early as 1882. The 1893 recession helped cause the formation of the UMW of Alabama, and by 1898 it merged with the UMW proper. A big strike in 1908 was defeated, and an even greater event came September 8, 1920, when 12,000 of Alabama's 27,000 miners struck. For seven months the UMW fed some 50,000 people, until it finally agreed to arbitration; see Marshall, *Labor in the South,* pp. 72–75.

[19]The tipple, usually at the mouth of the mine, is where coal cars are tipped and dumped so the coal can be screened and loaded; see Fay, *Glossary of the Mining Industry,* p. 689.

more modern. Five trucks usually operate between the mine and Birmingham. The miners as a whole have come to accept the laissez-faire philosophy. When there is work, they work. When there is none, they live as best as they can. Johnnie says, "Sometimes I go a week without hittin' a lick; then get called for Sunday, right when me'n Joan are all triggered up to go down to the Baptist church to Sunday school."

So at Helena, if a group of men sit beside the railroad track, it is safe to assume that they are either waiting for someone to go over the hill into a hollow and open a truck mine; or waiting for Paramount to resume work. All are not so fortunate as Johnnie Fence, who manages to keep a fairly even keel. He owns his home and is content.

*On September 16, 1938, Myrtle Miles wrote W. T. Couch that
Jack Kytle was leaving that morning "to spend the weekend
with fishermen who are living along the banks of the Coosa
River," according to plans Kytle and Couch had discussed
earlier.[20] The result was a series of seven life histories from the
Talladega Springs area. The longest of these was published in
Terrill and Hirsch,* Such As Us—*"A Woman's Like A Dumb
Animal." Two more follow here. Kytle had a touch of the jaun-
diced vision that marred R. V. Waldrep's work. It can be seen
even in his titles: "Jim Lauderdale: River Wreck"; "River
Widow: Portrait of Poverty"; and "Pattern of Ignorance." These
accounts are substantial in length, however, interestingly detailed, and for the most part in the words of the informants.
Kytle was thirty-one when they were written and had been
assistant director of the Alabama Writers' Project since October
1937. A native of Tallapoosa, Georgia, he had studied two years
at Mercer College and then worked on a series of newspapers.[21]*

A Dead Convict Don't Cost Nothin'

by Jack Kytle

"All my life I slaved an' made a good livin' for her. I give 'er a
place to live for goin' on forty-five year, an' she didn't never hurt
for nothin' to eat. I slunk aroun' like a hound, takin' things off 'n
her, when I ought'er've busted her with a hick'ry limb. Now look
what it got me. I'm here by myself, dyin' by th' graduals, an'
she's gone." Jim Saunders slouched there on the front porch of
his pine-board shanty in the straw-bottomed chair. His thick,
knotty fingers trembled as he placed his hands on thin, denim-
covered knees. His bald head glistened in the bright morning
sunlight, but his skin was a puffy, pasty yellow, seared by deep
furrows.

---

[20]Miles to Couch, September 16, 1938, FWP—Couch Papers.
[21]Miles to Alsberg, October 18, 1937, in "Alabama A–Miscellaneous," Administrative
Correspondence, FWP—Central Office. His full name was Elvyn J. Kytle.

He said, "Th' Ol' Man'll be comin' fer me any day now, an' I couldn't tell you who'll bury me. Doc says my heart's cuttin' up sump'un terrible. I'm a ol' man—I'm seventy-six—an' I ain't of no use to nobody. That woman took ever'thing I had, an' now she's gone to Sylacaugy to live with our girl. They work in th' mill up thar. They make twenty-two dollars a week between 'em, but they don't help me with none of it. They don't never come to see me." He raised a shaking hand to his stubbled cheek, as if shielding a secret. "Cora turned my girl an' my boy ag'in me. She done it. She told 'em a pack of dirty lies 'bout what I done, an' I ain't done half the things she said. She has throwed up to 'em a million times 'bout me bein' sent to Kilby,[22] an' she told 'em that I allus did run atter sorry women. Now, I ain't got nothin' to say 'bout Kilby—ever'body knows I had to go down thar—but th' other is a passel of goddam lies. She knows it is. She started p'isenin' their minds when they was little things. If it was a shame fer me to be in prison, she can thank herself fer it. I'd a never done it if it hadn't a been fer her. They's ways I coulda got by, but it's diff'runt whar thar's somebody else. I was pushed to it. When I quit work at th' mines I had enough to come off down here an' live by careful savin'. My heart was bad, an' I knowed I couldn't do no heavy work ag'in."

"When I got here I had a little better'n three thousand dollars in cold cash, an' I wanted to find a place to put it. I allus did think that Ol' Man Mitchell was a good friend of mine; he had a head full of sense, so I knowed he was keepin' his money whar it was safe. I went an' asked him whar to put mine, an' he told me th' safest place he knowed of was th' bank at Sylacaugy. I trusted him, an' I done what he told me. He oughta knowed 'bout th' bank, fer he was mixed up with runnin' it in some sort of way. Well, it seemed I hadn't no mor'n got my money in thar than it went busted. Course, th' first thing I done was to go to Ol' Mitchell; I don't know why. I should've knowed he didn't give a damn 'bout what become of me, but when I seen him, he looked all down in th' dumps. He said he'd lost most of his money, too, an' that he was worse s'prised than anybody in th' world could be. He said he wasn't up on what was goin' on at th' bank, an'

---

[22]The Alabama state penitentiary near Montgomery, in operation since 1923.

that he didn't know they was a thing wrong. He was a goddam liar. He knowed that bank was goin' under, an' I bet he didn't lose one red penny in it. I thought he was my friend, but I tell you, they ain't nobody yo'r friend when it comes to money. Anybody'll beat you. What happened was that Ol' Mitchell an' th' other big wigs in that bank took th' folks money an' then lived high an' wide on it. They ain't a way to prove it, but that's what they done. Atter I was busted flat, I'd see that ol' man sittin' on th' porch up thar at th' Springs in his big brick house, livin' on some of my three thousand; an' it was all I could do to keep from goin' up thar an' stompin' him. I never did speak to him ag'in, an' I wasn't sorry when he died. It was good riddance."

"If you ain't lost no money in a bank, you don't know what it does to you. They wasn't nothin' I could do 'bout it but r'ar an' cuss, but I knowed I had to make some more to live on, an' I couldn't do no hard work. It all ended up with me goin' to Jessie Staley an' j'inin' up sorter as partners with him. He was makin' popskull down on Peckerwood Creek, an' we fixed it so I'd sell it at th' Springs. I gived him what little money I had left to buy sugar an' shorts, an' th' way we had things worked out, I stood to make a little profit."

"I oughter've knowed they was trouble comin'. Cora is one of these damn holy roller kind—crazy religion, an' 'fore th' third customer had come by th' house she was raisin' hell. She said so help her God that she was go'nter report me. I knowed she was th' meanest woman that ever lived, but I didn't think she'd take bread out'n her own mouth. Well, I's wrong. I was sittin' on my front porch one Sunday evenin' when a automobile driv up, an' out hopped a bunch of depitys from Talladega. They come runnin' in th' yard like they was somebody bein' killed, an' some of 'em started pokin' aroun' in th' weeds out at th' side of th' house. Th' chief depity was with 'em, an' he come up to whar I was sittin' on th' porch. He says, 'We're sorry 'bout this, Jim, but we got a report you're sellin' likker.' "

"It was all as clear as water to me. I didn't move one inch, but I looked out t'ward th' weeds whar th' others was searchin', an' they was makin' out like they was havin' trouble findin' th' stuff. I told him, 'Go on an' git it; you know whar it is. They ain't no use makin' out you don't know 'bout it when you done been told.' He laughed a little, an' then he walked out thar an' picked up th' jug. Nobody but Cora could have told 'em, fer she was th' only one 'sides me that knowed whar it was. She was in th' house when they come, but I never even said howdy to 'er. I jes' went with 'em to Talladega, an' stayed in jail till I got Mayford Jones to go my bond. My case come up at th' next term of court, an' that's why I had to go to prison. She sent me thar, an' now she is p'isened my children's min's ag'in me."

"Why I ever got married to her, I don't know. I'd knowed her ever since she was a strip of a gal, but I never knowed she was a devil. I ain't got no excuse, though. Her daddy come to me 'fore we was married, an' he says, 'Jim, they's sump'un you ought'er know. Cora's mighty nervous-like, an' sometimes she does things that make me b'lieve she ain't got good sense. She's got a good face 'round you, but she can raise more hell'n a mean mule. I don't like to talk 'bout my own flesh an' blood, but I jes' want you to go in this thing with yo'r eyes open.' That ol' man was tellin' me th' God's truth, but I didn't b'lieve him. I thought he was jes' wantin' to keep his gal at home, but I know now he was a good friend tryin' to save me. He tol' me that when she had one of her spells she'd take a dress an' rip it to pieces. That tickled me, fer I thought Cora was th' best hearted woman in th' world. Well, I've seen her tear up dresses. I've seen her tear up a lot of 'em."

"It wasn't a week atter we married, 'fore she was r'arin'. They wasn't nothin' that'd suit her. I was workin' at the quarry then, makin' thirty-five dollars a month, an' that was purty fair money in them times. We didn't pay no rent, an' I'd bought up a little furniture. We had plenty fer our bellies an' backs, but that wasn't enough fer her. She got atter me right off to go to Mr. Bob an' tell him he'd have to pay me more. She got to talkin' 'bout him an' his folks ridin' in their fine buggies an' wearin' their fine clo's, while we was makin' out with nothin'. Well, you know a man can't go to his boss an' ask a raise right off'n th' bat. He'd git fired quicker'n you can bat yo'r eye; but Cora didn't give a damn 'bout that. She was jes' full of ol' hell, an' she didn't like fer things to be quiet. When she seen they wasn't go'nter be no more money, she started waggin' her tongue. She tol' ever'body that come to see us how hard it was to be married to a po'r man, an' she said she wouldn't never marry me ag'in. That got next to me, but I stood it till she started carryin' tales 'bout Mister Bob. She went aroun' tellin' that she seen him fall off 'n his horse, he's so drunk. That wasn't nothin' but a lie, fer Mister Bob never drunk none; but th' tale didn't do me no good with other men at th' quarry. Course their wives tol' 'em about it, an' I guess they couldn't understan' why I didn't put a stop to it."

"I knowed I'd hav'to git Cora away from thar. Didn't nobody come to see us no more, an' it was gon'ter be jes' a matter of time till Mister Bob got hold of one of them tales. He liked me, but I knowed he couldn't put up with nothin' like that. I started castin' out my lines, an' one day I got a chance to go to th' Red Diamond mine close to Birmingham.[23] I'd never fooled none with coal, but I's ready to try anything. Well, sir, it looked like that move was a good'un. I's makin' sixty dollars when I first went thar, but it wasn't long 'fore they put me to guardin' the convicts an' give me sixty-five. Cora seemed to be th' gal I'd courted fer a while, an' she was havin' a good time with th' extra money. It didn't cost much more to live in Birmingham then, fer it was jes' a little town, 'bout th' size that Sylacaugy is now. It wasn't long 'fore Cora was go'nter have a baby, an' I thought my troubles was over."

"I got my first trainin' at handlin' men when I's watchin' them convicts. They was a bad crowd, an' I had to be bad with 'em. I hadn't been thar two weeks when I got atter a buck nigger 'bout how he was buildin' a scaffold that keeps th' roof from fallin' in; an' he sassed me. They'd done told me never to take nothin' off them bastards, so I jes' went over to him an' nearly beat his brains out with my club. That nigger wasn't able to dig no more coal fer a long time."

---

[23]Red Diamond was a coal mine worked with convict labor, and judging by the speaker's subsequent identification of Birmingham as "jes' a little town," the time was before 1900. Convict lease lasted until 1928 in Alabama, longer than in any other state. George Korson, in *Coal Dust on the Fiddle: Songs and Stories of the Bituminous Industry* (Hatboro, Pa.: Folklore Associates, 1965, reprinted from 1943), has an interesting sketch of the convict lease system in the mines in Alabama, pp. 164–74. See also George Washington Cable's description of convict miners encountered in Alabama, in Archie Green, *Only a Miner: Studies in Recorded Coal-Mining Songs* (Urbana: University of Illinois Press, 1972), p. 158.

"They was a lot of people back then who was causin' trouble 'bout th' convicts. They said it wasn't right fer th' State to hire 'em out to th' operators, an' they kept on till they put a stop to it. But I don't know if they was right or not. A man wouldn't be so ready to rob or kill somebody if he knowed he was goin' to th' mines. When he was hired out back then, they wasn't no pamperin'. I remember they told us to shoot quick as hell if anybody got rough, or tried runnin' off. They said they was lots more whar these come from, an' that when you knocked one of 'em off it was no worse'n killin' a hog or a cow. I never did have to kill nobody. A white man started runnin' off one day an' I let him have a load of buckshot in th' legs, but he got well. We had one guard, though, that'd killed a flock of 'em. He was a big, raw-boned man name of Giles, an' he had th' convicts so skeered of him that they'd start tremblin' when he was aroun'. He told me one day that when he leveled down on one, he aimed to kill him. He said th' company'd rather have a guard do that than to jes' wound one, fer a dead convict didn't cost nothin' fer medicine."

"We done some things that wasn't right, I know. When I was bein' watched by th' law myself, I thought about that, an' I was thankful I waited till I was a ol' man to git in trouble. We useta keep a big barr'l out back of a shed at th' mines, an' when I think back on it now, I know we whooped niggers jes' to have fun. We'd pull their britches off an' strop 'em across th' barr'l by their hands an' feet so they couldn't move, an' then we'd lay it on 'em with a leather strop. I've seen niggers with their rumps lookin' like a piece of raw beef. Some of 'em would pass out like a light, but they'd all put up a awful howl, beggin' us to stop. It wasn't right fer us to do that."

"Th' company had lots of ways to make a bad convict work, but us guards didn't follow 'em much. Didn't nobody want to put a convict in th' sweat box, or feed him on bread an' water, fer they wasn't no fun in watchin' that. We had one white man that was servin' a term fer robbery, an' he was one of th' stubbornest devils I ever seen. He was put in th' sweat box, an' he was whooped a time or two, but still he loafed aroun' lookin' like he was wantin' trouble. Well, one day 'long 'bout quittin' time, he got it. They'd put him in Giles' gang—that's whar they put most of th' bad 'uns. Giles kept tellin' him that he was go'nter make him work if he had to kill him, but th' convict either didn't b'lieve him or he didn't care. Well, it kept up like that fer a good while, an' then Giles got some handcuffs an' had 'em bring th' con to whar he was. He handcuffed th' man's hands from behin', an' then he took him back of a shed. I won't never see nothin' like that ag'in, fer I couldn't watch it now. Giles backed the con up to th' shed, an' when he started hittin' him, th' blood splattered ever'where. Giles was jes' usin' his fists, but he was strong as a bull, an' he hit a awful lick. He beat this con's face till it was a mess of blood, an' he wouldn't let him fall. When th' feller's legs give 'way, Giles caught him by th' throat with one han', an' kept on beatin' him with th' other. In jes' a few licks, th' con's nose was broke an' it looked like his teeth was all knocked out. Somebody asked Giles to stop 'fore he killed him, so he hit him one or two more good licks an' let him fall. They tried to make that feller work next day, but he couldn't do it. He couldn't see. His eyes were as blue as a pair of new overalls, an' they was swelled tight. It wasn't right to beat him so bad, fer they was other ways of makin' him do th' work. I don't know what ever become of him."

"Things ain't like that now. Course they still beat 'em in some of th' gangs, I guess, but th' big prisons don't do it. When I was at Kilby, ever'body treated me nice. They took it fer a big joke when a man was sent thar fer makin' likker, fer they all drunk it when they was off'n duty. One guard told me he was comin' down to Talladega County some day, an' he wanted me to have five gallon ready fer him."

"As I said, I was gettin' along fine with Cora th' first month or so at Red Diamond. But all of a sudden she started buyin' up new things fer th' house—sofas, tables, an' th' like—an' I knowed I'd never pay fer 'em if she kept it up. Th' baby was on its way, an' that was go'nter be a good bit of expense. I stood her buyin' spree long as I could, an' then I asked her one day to kinder ease up so we could cool off. Well, sir, she went into a fit, teared up a coupla dresses, an' took a hammer an' beat th' new sofa till it was nearly ruined. Lots of folks would've thought she was gone crazy, but I knowed it was jes' th' ol' hell poppin' out'n her. I put a stop to that buyin'. I done it by jes' not givin' her th' money to buy with, an' refusin' to pay fer anything she got on a credit. I hated to do it while she was carryin' my baby, but I guess it was one of the best things I ever done. It was th' only way fer me to save any money. She took a lot of tales to th' neighbors, an' she tol' enough lies to damn my soul forever, but it didn't hurt me none. Th' people livin' 'round us got onto how she was, an' they didn't pay no 'tention to her atter awhile."

"Our first baby was our girl, an' Cora was hog-crazy 'bout it. She started pettin' her from th' very first, an' when th' boy come three year later, she was th' same way 'bout him. She never did want me to git close to either one of 'em. Lots of times when they was little, I'd bring candy or some toys home to 'em, but Cora'd take th' presents an' tell th' children she bought 'em. I never had sense enough to know then how she was workin' in with 'em. I wouldn't raise no sand 'bout how she acted, fer I wanted to keep her temper down if I could. But I know now that she started p'isenin' 'em ag'in me from th' time they was able to walk. A man ought'er pay more 'tention to what's goin' on in his own family. I'd like to go over them days ag'in, fer I'd run my place diff'runt an' git in better with my children. But I was too busy makin' a livin' to think of much else. Things was lookin' up in coal an' iron then, an' Alabama was boomin'. I scratched ev'ry nickel I could an' I saved some of 'em. We was workin' at th' mines in twelve-hour shifts, an' they wasn't no such thing as a union. We kept them convicts humpin', an' we got things done."

"They ain't much I know 'bout unions. They may be all right, fer they've got th' hours down to nothin', an' th' wages is better. But back in my day, it was diff'runt. You didn't ask no boss fer more pay then, fer if you got unsatisfied they'd jes' throw you out. I was lucky to have a good bossman. I never did ask Mr. John fer more money, but he paid me fair. He kept me on th' payroll when I's too sick to do much work, an' they don't do that these days. I know one thing fer sure. We couldn't a done sump'un back then that I seen at th' mill up at Talladega a few months ago. They was havin' a strike thar, an' they wouldn't let nobody go in th' mill to work. If anybody'd tried that on Mister John, they'd a been plenty of shootin', fer he didn't monkey 'round 'bout nothin'. I remember they tried to git up a union at Red Diamond once, an' they sent soldiers in thar to break it up.

A few heads was cracked then, but it wasn't nothin' as bad as I've heard of since.[24] Unions wouldn't a ever suited me, I don't reckon. I allus tried to be on th' boss' side in ever'thing, an' maybe that's why I was allus treated good. That's why I kept gittin' better money, till I was makin' a hundred fifty dollars 'fore my heart got too bad fer me to work. I guess it was a good thing that I was happy on my job, fer I wasn't havin' no peace at home. It was hell ever'whar I turned, an' even when I's makin' good money, Cora was still complainin' 'bout havin' to marry a po'r man."

"I jes' let her rave till th' children was growed up a little, but then sump'un happened that got her turned ag'in me from that time on. She was goin' to a church whar they got down on th' floor an' cut up—whooped an hollered an' jabbered—an' jes' acted crazy in ev'ry way. I was worried 'bout her mind, but I didn't say nothin' till she started tryin' to take th' kids down thar. Now, I figgered they was as much mine as her'n, an' I made up my mind that she wasn't go'nter take 'em into that mess. I don't go to no church—I never did—but I b'lieve thar's a God an' a life beyond this'un. I jes' don't think a body has to go crazy to git to heaven; th' Lord don't want a gang of fools up thar."

"Well, when she tried to take th' kids to them meetin's, I took a stand ag'in her. It was on a Sunday night an' she was dressin' 'em up, goin' on crazy-like while she was doin' it. I went in to whar they was, an' I told her she wasn't go'nter take 'em outa th' house. When I said that, she jumped up an' run up to me shakin' all over. She says, 'You mean yo'r go'nter 'pose th' Lord?', an' I told her th' Lord didn't have no toleration fer this sort of thing. I said I didn't aim fer my own little children to git mixed up with a bunch of crazy people. 'Fore we finished th' row, ever'body but me was a cryin', an' she was huggin' th' kids an' takin' on over 'em. Po'r little things, it wasn't their fault. I ought'er 've knowed right then that their minds was bein' sot ag'in me, but I jes' let things rock on till they was gone too fer. That sort of thing kept up long as I lived with her. She got th' children to b'lievin' that I wouldn't give 'em no money, but that I

---

[24]Possibly the use of convicts as strikebreakers in the Pratt mines in 1882; see Marshall, *Labor in the South,* p. 72.

was spendin' it all on sorry women. She told 'em that I'd allus been mean to her—that I'd beat her when they was little—an' all them sort of lies. Now, I never laid a hand on her in my life, but I should a done it. When she first started carryin' on I should a got a stick to her."

"I never will fergit th' day when I's laid off at th' mine. I'd been pokin' about fer a long spell. My heart was bad, an' I's coughin' purty awful. I guess that coal dust gits in a man's throat an' makes him cough that way. Anyway, I's past doin' my part of work, an' when Mister John come up to me one mornin', I knowed what it was all about. He was mighty nice, but he told me how things was. He said th' company was go'nter give me a month's pay, 'sides what I had comin' to me, an' that I could stay on in th' house till I got myself settled ag'in. No sir, I don't think he could a done me no better. A laborin' man is jes' like a horse—when he gits wore out an' so old that he gits in th' way, they ought'er take him out an' shoot him. I'd been drawin' my paycheck thar better'n thirty-five year, an' some of th' checks was mighty good. No, sir, it ain't Mister John's fault that I'm what I am today. It ain't nobody's fault but Cora's an' Ol' Man Mitchell's. If I could a kept my three thousand dollars to go on, I'd be all right. I'd still have my family, I guess, fer long as th' money was flowin', Cora stuck aroun'. She wasn't go'nter leave no good thing, but soon as I was broke, she got out'n here fast as her legs'd carry her. Our girl was already workin' in Sylacaugy, so Cora went up thar an' housed up with her. Th' boy is stayin' with 'em an' doin' odd jobs aroun' in garages an' things like that. No, sir, they didn't git much schoolin'. They done like I did—fell out 'fore they was finished. Ain't neither one of 'em married, an' I don't guess they will long as Cora lives. I guess they's seen so much hell in bein' married that they think ever'body is like that."

"You know, a man's a goddam fool. I know that, fer I helped Cora stack up a good case ag'in me. Now, like I told you, I ain't never had nothin' to do with sorry women—I jes' don't like 'em, an' I never would have no part of 'em. But I've hit th' likker bottle pretty hard, an' when a man is seen full a couple times, people's ready to b'lieve anything that's said 'bout him. Children ain't no diff'runt from other folks; so it was easy fer Cora to make 'em b'lieve that I was bad in a lot of other ways. I wouldn't tell you this, but I jes' want to show you how she could make a thing look awful. Th' children wasn't here when it come up, but they's seen other things like it. I was fishin' down on Cedar, and Jess Holmes come by with a jug of syrup likker. We hit it up a little, an' you know how that kind of stuff gits you. Weren't no time 'fore we was pretty full. Well, sir, I come in quiet-like that night. It was right atter I got out of prison, and I didn't want to git no 'tention. I was in my right head—I wasn't even staggerin' much—an' I figgered I'd git in th' house an' lie down awhile. I might a knowed better. I ought'er 've jes' stayed on with Jess till I was cold sober, fer I hadn't no mor'n hit th' door when Cora started carryin' on. She yelled as bad as if I's beatin' her, an' maybe I rose my voice a little; but they wasn't nothin' callin' fer so much noise. She run out on th' porch, takin' on an' wringin' her han's, so ever'body in hearin' distance knowed 'bout it. She wanted 'em to know."

"Ever'thing would a been all right if it hadn't a been like that. But first thing I knowed, that damned preacher that lives over thar crost th' road was here, an' he took a han' in it. He didn't even try to fin' out what was causin' it, but he come bouncin' up to me, yellin', 'You better be on yo'r knees beggin' fergiv'ness 'stid of sittin' thar in that cheer.' Well, that runned all over me, an' I told him to git th' hell out; that it wasn't none of his damned business. They might as well of called out th' fire wagon at th' Springs to make it a good show. It wasn't no time 'fore that ragged-tailed p'liceman from over thar come runnin' up with a squirr'l gun. He asked Cora what I'd been doin' an' she says I was cuttin' up so bad she was skeered to stay 'round me. Now mind you, I was purty sober by that time, but he wanted to ac' smart. He took me into th' Springs an' locked me up in th' callaboose. Nex' mornin' in that little two-by-four mayor's court over thar Ol' Man Winley fined me five dollars an' give me a good talkin' to, while ever'body in town packed in to lis'en. When I come home, Cora'd done gone, an' she's been gone ever since. They sent a truck down here 'bout a month ago an' took nearly ever'thing I had in th' house—Cora said th' stuff b'longed to her, though I paid fer it. I didn't raise my hand ag'in 'em, fer a ol' man like me don't need nothin' but a bed to sleep on. I reckon all th' folks 'round here blame me fer none of my family livin' with me, but it's got to whar I don't care. I don't have nothin' to do with nobody, an' it ain't go'nter be long 'fore th' Ol' Man is comin' atter me. I'm 'bout ready to go, too, but I'd like to git things fixed up so's they'd bury me good."

"One of th' things I wish fer mos' is a chanct to git even with that goddamned p'liceman. I'd like to give him a bellyful of hot lead, but I can't 'ford to do that. He thinks he's smart as hell goin' aroun' puttin' people in th' callaboose; but he'd run like a black snake if you ever jumped at him in th' dark. I had a chanct a few days ago at Ol' Burkhead, that preacher over thar crost th' road. I was sittin' right whar I am now, an' he was out on his porch tryin' to read. Well, they was a little ol' dog over thar, too, an' he was sick or sump'un, fer he kept howlin' an' wailin'. The more he went on like that, th' madder Ol' Burkhead got. His face turned so red that I could see it shinin' from over here. Well, sir, he slapped at th' dog a coupla times, but that didn't do no good. It jes' kept up its howlin'. Then all at onct, Ol' Burkhead got a hammer from some'rs thar on the porch, an' he went over an' beat th' dog to death. He didn't kill it at th' first lick, so he jes' kept chasin' it an' hittin' it ag'in, an' he was ragin' mad. Atter it was all over an' he'd sot down again, I jes' went out in my yard an' yelled at him. I says, 'Don't you git on yo'r knees an' ask fergiv'ness when you kill a po'r little dog like that?' He started out'n his cheer like he was go'nter do sump'un big, but he ain't done it yet. He knowed he'd done a worse thing than take a few drinks of likker, an' I hope he roasts in hell fer it."

"I'm sorry 'bout you havin' to go, fer I don't reckon I'll live to see you ag'in, 'thout you come back mighty quick. Doc says I'm liable to go out any time 'less I stop hittin' my bottle, an' I'm too ol' to be stoppin' that. It's got to whar it takes some fer me ever' day—I think it does my heart good. Won't you come in an' have one? It ain't th' bes' in th' world, but it's good shinny."

"I wish when you git back that you'd ask them Gover'mint folks 'bout what they go'nter do fer th' ol' people. I keep hearin' talk of it, but if they don't rush up, it ain't go'nter do me no good. These welfare women'll have me starved to death 'fore my pension gits to me."

I'm Allus Hongry

by Jack Kytle

Willie Bass said, "It'd kill me to go thar—to th' big jail, I mean. I was in th' one over at Rockford goin' on a month, an' I nearly died. Why, I'd git up in th' night an' beat th' or'n bars with my han's so hard that my fingers'd swell an' turn blue. I guess I wouldn't never git useta bein' hemmed up thataway." He lounged in the ruffled red sand of the river bank, propping his cadaverous torso with an elbow that rested on a pillow of brown pine straw. A slim fishing cane was in his free hand, and his dull, gray eyes were intent upon the bottle stopper he was using for a cork. His voice was nasal, so high pitched that he seemed to whine as he talked.

"They got me red-handed," he said without looking up. "I was over thar on Hatchet Creek, near whar th' ol' Williams' place is, an' I thought that I was hid so good that a ha'nt couldn't fin' me. I was juggin' up th' stuff, gittin' ready to carrry it up th' river soon as night come. But when night come I's locked up tighter'n a coon trap, an' I guess ev'ry damned depity in Coosa County was a-wollerin' in my likker. It ain't above 'em. They says they pour it out, but they ain't never poured none out when I was watchin'. I know that bastard of a Tom Hart ain't never poured none out, an' he was headin' th' gang that kotched me. They tear'd up th' still, but I seen that they put most of th' likker in a bresh pile—th' little that 'as left atter they'd all took a jug fer evidence."

"If I'd seed 'em 'fore they was clos't enough to've shuk han's with me, I'd a got away. They ain't no fat-bellied depity go'nter outrun me in a fair race; but when a man's got th' diff'rence in his han's, they ain't no use bein' a fool. Ol' Hart'll shoot if you bat yo'r eye. He's th' son-of-a-bitch that shot that Morton boy down on Paint Creek, an' they ain't nothin' never done about it. Th' boy's folks tried to raise a stink—he didn't never fool in no likker—but they couldn't git in th' back door. Ever'thing was squshed up. But when things come out th' way they done, I'se glad I didn' run er try nothin' brash. If I'd a had doodle bug brains I'd a knowed that maybe Judge Hammet'd treat me good as he could, fer I've knowed 'im a good while, an' I've done some

favors fer 'im. He useta come down hyar to fish 'fore he got
down with rheumatism, an' I'd row th' boat fer 'im an' dig bait."

Willie sat up as suddenly as if he had been stung by a wasp,
his eyes hard upon the tiny cork. It bobbled, hesitated, and then
plunged under the yellow water. Willie lifted the slender cane
with a snap, and a moment later a small greenish bream was
leaping in the sand. He picked it up and deposited it in a large
bucket of water that stood nearby. "Them's th' best bait you can
git fer yaller cats," he said when he had run his hook through a
worm and placed it in the water. "It's ag'in th' law to use 'em an'
if th' game warden kotched me I'd be in a hell'uva fix,[25] but he
don' never come down this way. I've got nearly a hundert of 'em
in that bucket, an' I'm go'nter put 'em on my trotline. I bet I git a
good cat; th' water's jes' right." He slouched down into the sand
again, crossing his thin legs Indian fashion. His shoes were held
together by wrappings of twine; he wore no socks. His overalls
were caked with grayish river mud, and they were heavily
patched at the knees.

"Now, I got down to whar I's goin' up 'fore Judge Hammet,"
he went on in his whining tone. "I knowed they wasn't nothin'
fer me to do but plead guilty, an' I felt lower'n a moccasin's belly.
I felt like I wouldn't a keered if lightnin' had struck me dead, fer
I didn't see how I'd stan' goin' to Kilby. Jim Sherlock was thar
once, an' he'd tol' me all about it. He said they treated you
wors'n a bare-footed nigger boy; said they whooped him fer not
sayin' 'Yes-sir' to a guard."

"When I's took in th' courtroom they was a nigger up 'fore th'
ol' man, an' I heard what was said. They'd kotched him stillin',
same as me, an' when he got a year an' a day my heart sunk. I
knowed I's a goner. But what you think happened? When I
stepped up in front th' Judge peered at me over his spec's, an' he
looked s'prised enough to jump out-a his britches. He says,
'What you done?,' an' I tol' him how I'd been kotched with th'
likker. Well, sir, he looked at me fer a minnet, an' then he
beckoned fer one of th' depitys that was on th' raid. They locked
their horns an' whispered awhile. I thought they was hell to pay
then, but atter awhile Judge Hammet says, 'You ain't never

---

[25]Bream were classified as game fish, to be fished for and not with, according to
Alabama state law.

been in no trouble 'fore now?,' an' I says, 'No, sir, God knows I ain't.' He writ down sump'un then, an' he says atter awhile, 'I'm go'nter let you go home, but I'm warnin' y'u. If you ever come in hyar ag'in it's go'nter be two years in th' pen. Don't you go back over thar an' make no more likker. If y'u do, they ain't nothin' I can do ag'in.' "

"I never was as happy as when I heerd them words, an' I ain't never seed nothin' as purty as this ol' river when I sot eyes on it ag'in. I made up my min' then that I wasn't never go'nter make no more likker, an' I ain't. It's hard as hell to git enough to eat by jes' fishin' an' piddlin' with that ol' pore land of our'n, but it's better'n bein' in jail. I don't want-a go to Kilby. I'd die down thar. I reckon a man gits to likin' his own stompin' groun's better'n any he'd fin'. I reckon you'd like a town best, but me, I wouldn't have no callin' to be thar. I was borned in these woods—right over thar by Hogan's Cliff—an' I been hyar goin' on forty-one year. I reckon th' ol' sayin's right that you can't git away from yo'r raisin'."

"Course my raisin' ain't been nothin' to do no jig about. When I was younger'n I am now, I had a idea once an' awhile to git outa hyar an' go some'rs else, but I jes' never did. I didn't wanta leave my folks. We ain't got nothin' but a shirt tail an' a pray'r, but we ain't low-down. We ain't like them Bartletts over at th' Kingdom. They ain't never tried to do nothin' but beat people outa ever'thing they could, an' they'd steal th' handles off'n a coffin."

"Ever since I's knee-high to a grasshopper I ain't knowed nothin' but hard times. Me an' Pa has been th' only menfolks, an' he never was much stout. My two sisters an' my Ma helped all they could—chopped cotton, pulled fodder an' that sort of thing—but woman jes' ain't built fer hard work. They shouldn't ought'er have to do it. Things are worse right now than they ever was, fer th' ol' people is gittin' too ol' to do any work atall. They ain't go'nter live much longer, an' then it'll jes' leave me an' my sisters. I useta hope they'd git 'em a man apiece so as to ease things up, but I don' reckon they ever will. It's purty hard on a gal to live out like this. They ain't many men, an' them that is aroun' ain't worth havin'."

"You seed my oldes' sister, Pearl, when you come by th' house, an' I guess you seed how her han' was tied up. It worries

me a lots, fer it's jes' rottin' off. It's been goin' on that-a-way
since las' fall, an' they don' seem to be nothin' to do about it. We
tuk her to th' doctor in Sylacaugy right after it happened, but he
didn't he'p her. We ain't been back since. We was pullin' fodder,
an' she was tiein' up a bundle when a rattlesnake bit her right
on top of th' hand. Didn't nobody kill it—it crawled right off—so
that's what made it so bad. If you kill th' snake, some of th'
p'isen is killed, too; but if it gits away, then you better start
prayin'. We thought Pearl was go'nter die. We kilt a good layin'
hen, cut it open, and stuck her han' inside it to suck out th'
p'isen.[26] That allus does good, but her arm swelled up 'till it was
twice its size. By th' time we got to th' doctor she was out a her
head, breathin' gaspy, like somebody dyin'. Th' doctor said we'd
waited too long an' that they wasn't much he could do. An' he
didn't do much. They ain't nothin' I hate wors'n a snake. I ain't
never been bit by one, but it's because I got good eyes fer 'em.
They's moccasins on this river so old they walk on crutches.
One of Ed Hope's little boys was bit by one las' spring. They
gived him all th' likker they could pour down 'im, but it didn'
help a bit. He was stone dead inside two hour."

Willie took his hook from the water, baited it again, and spat
on it. "That'll make 'em bite," he explained. He moved down the
bank a few yards, paused in front of a half-submerged snag, and
began fishing beside it. Almost immediately, he jerked out a
fingerling catfish. "Ain't worth a good damn," he cursed. "A big
fish has got to be hongry as hell to bite one o' these. I reckon it's
on account of their sharp fins. See how this'un bristles 'em out,
like he wanted to fight?" He removed his small catch gingerly,
glared at it, and then flung it far up into the woods.

"No, sir, a man can't do no fancy eatin' when he hasta git his
grub fishin'. He can eat a bellyful o' fish, but he'll git tard as hell
eatin' 'em. Sometimes when they's nothin' else in the house, I
jes' go hongry. But that ain't nothin', fer as that matters. I'm
allus hongry. Atter we split up what's on th' table 'mongst four of
us, they ain't enough lef' to feed a kitten. I git to feelin'

---

[26]Folk remedies involving killing the snake and the use of a chicken to draw the poison
are common in Alabama; see Jack Solomon and Olivia Solomon, *Cracklin Bread and
Asfidity: Folk Recipes and Remedies* (University, Ala.: University of Alabama Press,
1979), p. 161, and Browne, *Popular Beliefs from Alabama*, p. 94, nos. 1602–06.

sometimes like ol' man Crosby. Ever' time he hears 'bout some-body dyin', he'll say, 'I'm glad to hear it.' An' if you ax him what he means talkin' that-a-way, he'll tell you, 'They's better off'n we'uns; they's in Heaven playin' on gold harps, an' we'uns is pore as ever.' "

"Maybe he ain't sech a ol' fool as people think. I feel that-a-way when I fish my lines hard all week, an' still ain't got a damned thing. I feel that-a-way when we'uns raise a little sump'un, an' then haveta give it to Ol' Man Mac. He owns that crop of our'n, an' we work it on shares; but thank God A'mighty, he don't own th' shack. We'uns built it, an' its on Alabama Power Company lan'. They's supposed to charge three dollars a year fer it, but they don't never come 'round to git any money. They jes' axes us to take keer of th' lan' an' watch out fer fores' fires. If they come, I don' know whar we'd ever git three dollars at one time. Atter we settle up with Jay Smithers, at th' Springs, we ain't got a thing. I don' know what we'd do if it wasn't fer Jay, so I don't 'grudge him nothin'. He's let us have sump'un to eat when they wasn't a penny he could hope to git. I owe him a coupl'a dollars now—I've owed it a smart while—but he don't never dun me. I'd do a lot fer him if I ever got th' chanct."

"I remember back when I was a boy that fishin' was good on this river. Seems to me that ever'thing was better then. They was a feller named Hosey who had his lines out right whar I got mine now, an' he made good catches all th' time. But that was 'fore th' dam was built,[27] an' 'fore th' river was full of mud. Fish jes' don't like mud. I got a notion they ain't many of 'em left in hyar. They goes up th' river whar th' bottom is sandy. Them that's left is kept skeered to death. Ever' Thursday, th' power company starts openin' th' gates, an' th' river starts down. You know that skeers th' fishes. It'd skeer us if we was a fish an' th' water started down all aroun' us. We'd do jes' like they does; we'd head fer th' middle an' our min's wouldn't be on nothin' to eat. When anything gits skeered its belly ain't cravin' no vittles. Most of my good catches is made on Saturdays an' Sundays. You see, the gates is closed then, an' th' water starts backin' up. That sends the fishes closer to th' banks, an' they got their min's on

---

[27]Lay Dam on the Coosa was built in 1914; see Kitty Sutherland's article "The Coosa," in *Rivers of Alabama* (Huntsville: Strode Publishers, 1968), p. 93.

feedin' ag'in. Sometimes I git cats that weigh upward of forty pound, but they's hard to sell. Fo'ks says that th' meat is too strong and coarse. Fo'ks want these little old squealer cats that weigh 'bout a pound an' that ain't worth keepin'. It ain't no fun to take a little ol' fish all th' way to Sylacauga an' not git mor'n 'bout fifteen cent fer it. An' you'd be s'prised to know how they try to beat a man outa what he's got comin'.'"

"Maybe they's honesty lef', but you don' find much of it. Las' spring I got up a good catch of little 'uns—clost to fifty pound—an' I figgered out whar I could ease off some bills with what I'd get. Th' price is s'posed to be fifteen cent a pound—and fishes is worth ever' bit of it. But when I got to th' market at Sylacaugy, Ol' Man James started pokin' his nose 'bout th' fish, an' he tol' me, 'They's nearly sp'iled; they ain't worth havin'.' Well, I knowed they wasn't sp'iled. It was cold that day, an' fish don't sp'il in that kind of weather. But they wouldn't a kept if I'd a had to drag 'em back twenty mile down hyar. I knowed what Ol' James was up to, an' I wasn't wrong. He sniffed aroun' awhile, an' then he says, 'Tell you what I'll do; I'll take a chanct on 'em an' give you six cent a pound.' I tol' him that they smelled a'right to me, an' that I'd worked mighty hard to catch 'em. But he wouldn't give no more. I had to sell 'em to 'im fer that, an' he turned right aroun' an' got twenty or twenty-five cent fer 'em."

"It ain't fair to treat a man like that. Folks says that a bootlegger ain't to be trusted, but I'd take my chances with 'im ever' time. When me an' Son Capp was makin' likker down on Hatchet Creek, we got th' fairest dealin's you ever seed. Ever' Saturday night we'd load up a motor boat with likker an' run it up th' river clost to Wilsonville. A truck from Birmingham would be waitin' thar, an' we'd dump th' stuff on th' banks fer 'em. Well, sir, we done that goin' on a year, an' we never did lose nothin'. Lots a times, we'uns an' th' men in th' truck wouldn't say a word. Me an' Son'd unload th' likker, an' then one of th' men'd stick some bills in one of our han's. It'd be dark, an' we wouldn't count it till we was back in th' river, but we never was beat. We got two dollar a gallon, an' they never did try to beat our price down."

"It looks like I oughta made me some money when I was foolin' with that stuff; but you know, I ain't knowed many that made much outa it. Pa useta tell me that they wasn't no money

in it, fer it was ag'in th' Lord's way. He said them that did make
a little allus ended up losin' it, and it looks to me like he was
right. You take Ol' Guy Haywood over on Paint Creek. He made
a passel o' money an' he bought hisself a fine car and clothes.
Then, all a sudden, ever'thing beginned happenin' to that ol'
man. First thing, he was kotched, an' that cost 'im a purty pile.
Then all his folks come down with sickness, two of 'em died, an'
he spent all he had. He ain't got a plate to eat off'n now, an' Pa
says th' Lord seed that he was punished."

"When I come back from jail, Pa said, 'Well, Willie, you ended
up like all th' rest of 'em. You're worse off'n you was when you
started.' I knowed he is right. But sump'un happened to me 'fore
that to show me they ain't no way of enjoyin' likker money. Me
an' Son made up our min's we'd save us a stake an' go to town
fer some fun. We worked hard, an' when it come time to go I
had thirty-seven dollar in my pocket. I was eatin' in high clover,
an' I was ready to throw a big'un. First thing we done was to fill
us a coupl'a quart bottles, an' that's whar we made a big
mistake. Time we got up to Talladega we was feelin' good as
hell, but we didn't stop hittin' them bottles. Son knowed a
coupl'a women, so we got 'em with us an' drunk some more.
Then we went outa town to a place that Son knowed an' got us a
room apiece. Well, sir, they ain't much I remember atter that.
Th' ol' gal that was with me was as ugly as hell, an' I knowed I'd
either have to be drunk to play with 'er, or else put a sack over 'er
head. We sot aroun' in th' room awhile drinkin', an' she kep'
climbin' up in my lap till I beginned gittin' tard of 'er. Atter
awhile, I got so sleepy I couldn't hardly hold my head up, so I
dumped 'er in a cheer an' stretched out crost th' bed."

"That's all I knowed till 'bout daylight th' next day. When I
woke up I was lyin' thar with my clo'es on. My head felt like it
was go'nter bust any minute, an' my mouth tasted like I'd been
kissin' a hound dog. At first, I thought I'd jes' took a nap, so I
laid thar quiet a minute or two. Then I sot up an' looked over at
th' cheer, an' I seed that th' gal wasn't thar. It takes things a
while to soak in my brain, but all of a sudden I jerked up in th'
bed. I felt in my back pocket, an' then I nearly jumped outa my
pants. My money was gone. I runned around the room crazy as
a bat fer a minute; then I got outa thar an' went to fin' Son. His

gal was still with 'im, but mine wasn't nowheres to be found. We went huntin' her, but I knowed I'd never git my money back. You know damn well that th' gal with Son knowed whar th' other'n was, but she made out like she didn't. Anyways, we didn't find 'er, my cash was lost, and I didn't git nothin' fer it. It wouldn't a been so bad if she hadn't a been so damned ugly. They wasn't nothin' she had that I wanted. I'd a lot rather it'd been a purty gal, fer that wouldn't a galled so bad. But when I thought of that gumpheaded heifer spendin' my thirty-seven dollar, it made me madder'n a stuck bull."

"I coulda bought lots fer that money, an' it got nex' to me when I seed how my sisters an' Ma needed clo'es. That was th' Lord punishin' me, I tell you straight; th' best thing fer a man is to git hell skeered. Pa says that. He says that when a man gits skeered enough of roastin' his damned skin on the devil's red hot coals, he ain't go'nter do nothin' much bad. That's like I am now. I ain't makin' no more likker an' I ain't runnin' with no women. They ain't nothin' closter to th' Lord than a good woman, an' they ain't nothin' as awful as a bad 'un. If I was back whar I was once, I might marry somebody. I thought a lot of Mr. Hancock's oldes' gal when I was comin' on a young man, but I never did let her know nothin' about it. I useta go over thar to help the ol' man chop his cotton jes' so I'd be whar I could look at her. It's funny what a fool a man is. She never did pay me no min', but I still think she's a fine woman. She married Ike Harris, an' they got a house full of kids now."

"It wouldn't be right fer me to marry nobody. They's lots a people that ain't able to keep up theirse'fs that git married, but I ain't go'nter treat nobody that way. I ain't never had but one job whar I knowed what I was makin', an' that was when I's on some road work over at Marble Valley. You take like it is with me; my Pa an' Ma ain't go'nter be hyar much longer, an' then somebody's got to look atter th' two gals. Jean might fin' her a man some day, but you know Pearl ain't never go'nter git well of that han'. It might be a year an' it might be ten, but that rottin' is go'nter keep up till it kills her."

"Ain't none of us much healthy. Ever' since th' power company backed this river up mor'n twenty years ago, they's been chills an' fever hyar. It ain't bad as it was right atter they built th' dam, but it'll still kill you. I b'lieve that th' fever come when th' water was backed up over th' trees. The trees beginned rottin' an' that put th' fever in th' air."

"It ain't funny to be sick, but they's funny things happen. When they first built th' dam, Ol' Man Mac come down with chills so hard that he shuk th' bed posts, an' he liked to died. It was a long spell 'fore he was able to be up, but when he got outa bed, th' first thing he done was to go hell bent fer Rockford. He got a lawyer thar an' sued th' power company fer th' biggest figger of money he could think of. Well, that lawyer had a slick tongue. He had Ol' Mac thinkin' that th' money was as good as his already, an' they wasn't nothin' left to do but cash th' check. That ol' man went looney crazy. He run aroun' tellin' people he was go'nter be rich, an' he bought up as much as he could on a-credit. He even tol' Pa that he was go'nter give him th' land we farm on, an' th' biggest mistake Pa ever made was by not gittin' him to sign th' papers right thar. He'd a done it. He didn't have th' brains of a peckerwood. Course he didn't git nothin'. He went to court lookin' like he was already dead, an' he had a chill or two sittin' right up in thar. But th' jury didn't pity 'im. He might a knowed that they ain't no pore man can win nothin' off'n th' power company. They look at us folks hyar on th' river like we'uns was no better'n a dog. A pore man don' stand no more chanct than a June bug in January."

"They was lots of people died when that dam was built. Ol' Man Weston useta have a purty place over by th' Kingdom, and didn't nobody live thar with him. That ol' man was mean as hell. He stirred up trouble on this river long as he lived, an' he was past seventy when his number went up. That was a awful thing. Didn't nobody see 'im fer nearly a week, so some of th' women-folks got to thinkin' he might be sick up thar by himself. A bunch of 'em went up to th' place one mornin', but he didn't answer when they hollered. They peeped in th' winder then, an' it was a awful sight. He was lyin' on th' floor naked as a jaybird. He'd fell off th' bed an' died without ever gittin' back. If you've ever seed that ol' house he lived in you know how skeery it is. They ain't nobody ever lived in it since he died, an' it's all growed up with honeysuckle vines. Atter he'd been buried 'bout a year they was some people come hyar who said they's kin to him. They took his furniture an' things, but they didn't even go to whar he was buried. They ain't nothin' on his grave to tell who he is."

"I had sumpin' happen to me clost to that grave one night that I don't like to think about. I'd been 'coon huntin' with a bunch from Fayetteville, but I left 'em long 'bout midnight an' started home by myself. I didn't think about ol' Weston, or I wouldn't a went thar. He never did like me. Anyways, I was right clost to th' place when sump'un riz up an' begin moanin'. Didn't nobody have to tell me what it was. I nearly run outa my shoes. That ain't the last time I've seed 'im. Jes' let me git 'round that ol' house of his'n, an' sump'un'll happen to let me know he's thar. We'uns never had any use fer each other, an' that's jes' his way of tormentin' me. You know, I never could understand why it's jest th' bad folks that stays to ha'nt th' earth. I guess th' good'uns is done gone to Heaven."

Willie pulled in his line, winding it slowly about the slim cane. He walked over to the bucket, ran his hand into it, and sloshed around in the dingy water. "I mus' have plenty of 'em in hyar," he said. "That's enough to bait my lines anyway, an' I ought'er git some yallers with these baby breams." He shielded his eyes with a brown, gaunt hand, and looked toward the sun, which was now a flaming crescent in the great elbow of the river. "We got time to bait out 'fore night," he said. "Come on, I want-a show you a little island out thar. If I ever do hav'ta make any more likker, it's th' finest place fer a still that you ever seed."

Part Three

From the Cotton Farms, Cotton Cities, and Mill Villages of the Black Belt

Mrs. Pratt Tartt was a native of Livingston, Alabama, a graduate of Alabama Normal College (now Livingston University), and later a student in portraiture and photography at the New York School of Arts.[1] Her work with the Alabama Writers' Project, signed Ruby Pickens Tartt, is most visible in the ex-slave narrative collection; Ben Botkin virtually featured her work in Lay My Burden Down.[2] This and other information about Tartt, such as her social status in the community, is revealed in this note from Myrtle Miles to Henry Alsberg, dated October 13, 1938:

> With this story is a paper on a Negro funeral that came to hand this morning. I was personally so impressed that I want to submit it in the hope that some use may be made of it. The writer, Ruby Pickens Tartt, is a specialist in work of this type. It is wholly impossible to get her to do any other type of writing whatsoever. She has a fixed conviction that she cannot write. She knows and likes the Negroes who have known her and her family (one of the proudest in that part of the State) all her life. She was genuinely distressed over the death of Amy Chapman and knowing that we have stories of Amy in our files, she added this, her best contribution.[3]

Ruby Pickens Tartt was then fifty-eight years old. The Writers' Project apparently convinced her that she could indeed write, because her short stories eventually appeared in eight anthologies, including the 1945 O'Henry Collection of "Best Short Stories of the Year."[4] More important for the cultural history of Alabama may have been the black folksongs collected as a result of her contacts, beginning with John Lomax's recordings for the Library of Congress.[5] Ruby Pickens Tartt wrote four life histories, two of which are presented here.

---

[1] December 1, 1974, obituary from unidentified newspaper, in the vertical (Alabama authors) file, Southern Collection, Birmingham Public Library.

[2] See Introduction.

[3] Miles to Alsberg, October 13, 1938, FWP—Couch Papers.

[4] See Birmingham News article on Mrs. Tartt, March 6, 1966.

[5] Alan Lomax, who accompanied his father on some of these recording trips, remarked on a recent visit to Alabama that Mrs. Tartt was a remarkable hostess and facilitator for any fieldworker.

Jupie Wall, Midwife

by Ruby Pickens Tartt

Jupie's house is a dilapidated affair; the roof leaks in bad weather, the gallery needs patching in a dozen places, and the rickety front steps give under the slightest weight, but her yard is aglow with flowers. She has done her best to make the place cheerful with zinnias, marigolds, perennial sunflowers and verbena; and their bright pattern somehow reflects her attitude toward life.

Jupie was a child when she first went to work, and from childhood work is all she has ever known. Now, at sixty-eight she finds herself with a "house full of chillun" and an old Negro woman (no relative of hers, but simply a helpless old woman she has taken in) to provide for. And, somehow, she manages to wring a living of sorts from wornout acres which have been planted to cotton since slavery times, meanwhile pursuing her days in contentment and finding in them apparently more enjoyment than many of us in happier circumstances.

Jupie was born at Belmont, about ten miles from Coatopa, and has never moved far from the "white folks" that raised her. She is very proud of the fact that she grew up in her white folks' house, for as a little girl she came to stay with Mrs. H. G. McCullough whose sister, Miss Ryan, was an invalid to whom Jupie made herself generally useful, waiting on her and at night sleeping on a cot in the same room. Her mother, who had been a slave belonging to John Worley, and Aunt Creasy, her grandmother, worked in the same household and lived nearby, so she was never lonesome and homesick. The McCulloughs were good to her and she remembers them with affection and her childhood with happiness, especially the dolls they gave her. "I always had plenty of dolls to play with," she smiled.

Miss Minnie Ryan was unable to walk, and every morning she took the air sitting in a wheelbarrow which Jupie's father pulled through the gardens and perhaps a short distance down the road. "Now I'll tell you sumpin funny on Miss Minnie," said Jupie, laughing with anticipatory relish. "One afternoon she wuz settin' on de gallery en I wuz settin' on de floor right beside her playing with my dolls. . . . I 'members it jes' as good! Miss

Agnes en Miss Jennie come callin'. Miss Agnes wuz kinda po'ly herself. She had spells. En dat afternoon she *had* er spell, right on de gallery. She screamed en screamed en de hair—she had pretty long hair down to here" (she indicated her waist) "switch on her haid. Lack dis," and shook her woolly mop. "When Miss Agnes screamed, now, everybody run off en lef' po' Miss Minnie. En she so skeered she jump up en run in de house en lock de door! En she never walked a step fo' dat long ez I'd knowed her, but when Miss Agnes screamed hit skeered dat sumpin offen her, en she wuz all right from den on!"

After Miss Minnie's recovery and her services as nurse were no longer needed, Jupie was given other tasks and she continued to stay with the McCulloughs. During this time she attended school, finishing up to the seventh grade, and this elementary education was doubtless of great use to her later. When she married she moved a short distance from her "white folks" and she and her husband farmed for them. Some years later, Aunt Susan, who now lives with her and who goes with her on her rounds [the last of this sentence is missing; it was probably to the effect that Aunt Susan was already a practicing midwife]. Thus acquiring experience, Jupie also became a midwife after a time.

She says that she has brought some fifty or sixty babies into the world and that she used to have more white than colored patients. In fact, one white lady relied on her so that "she say she gotta send atter me don't keer whar she go!" beamed Jupie. Sometimes she would arrive before the doctor and bring the baby herself, and she says that she's seen "some swift boys, but not many girls is fast." Now the local nurse comes once a month to hold meetings and "explain the new rules," but Jupie has been unable to attend lately and has given up her practice, if such it may be termed, for this reason. She says she "ain't worthy of de job ef she can't do whut she sought to."

At this point in our conversation, Jupie paused to deny any ability to foretell before birth whether the baby would be a boy or girl. But she added, "I don't know with peoples, but I *do* know with beasts. If you gonna breed a mare en you turns her haid to de east, de colt'll be like de mare. Ef you turns her haid to de west, de colt be er horse. Poppa tole me dat, an tole me always breed a mare nine days atter de last colt come, en I ain't knowed hit ter fail. Day's a colt in de pastur' now what'll prove whut I say!"

The high point in Jupie's life seems to be a storm which struck the neighborhood some years ago. "Hit wuz de frightenest thing I ever knowed," she said. "Hit blew down four houses, en all de time hit wuz blowing I jes' walked up en down slapping my han's en praying 'Lord hab mercy, save us Jesus!' My sister-in-law run out of her house, en I doan see how she made hit ter my place, de wind wuz blowing so bad. I seen her run out de door, en jes' den er big tree blew down ercross her house— she'd er been kilt so ef she hadn't er lef'! Aunt Susan wuz here wid me too en de storm blew a tree down on her roof, but hit didn't knock de roof in. En de wind tuck her hat whut wuz hanging on a peg en carried hit up on de hill, pretty ez you please. We foun' hit dar later, but my house didn't git hurt a-tall."

"You know," she continued, "you can't see de wind, but looked lack I seed a somepin dat day! Spirits is imagination, is whut I always say. You hear folks talking about spirits en den you see sumpin whut skeers you en you say dat's spirits! I been skeered plenty er times, but I always come ter find out hit's sumpin I knowed. Dat's why I say spirits is nothin' but imagination. One night I seed a sumpin switch de willow branches right in front er me. En I stop en say, 'whut dat!' Den hit switch de willow branches ergain. I jes' stopped still en commence ter holler. Needn't worry 'bout whut I'm gonna do when *I'm* skeered; oh I jes' stand still en holler till somebody come git me!" The play of emotions over Jupie's expressive face as her narrative turned from fear of the supernatural to comedy at this point, was worthy of an actress. Never have I seen a better portrayal of dubiety and horror, followed by relief in such swift succession. "Den my husban' come up ter see whut ailed me," she continued, "en tweren't nuthin' but a little steer yearlin' wid horns switchin' down branches!"

"En one time when I wuz little, I wuz out wid my mother, en hit wuz a moonlight night. We wuz goin' home cross de lot, en dey wuz a mule name' Mary jes' standin' dere wid her years bucked lack she wuz lookin' at a sumpin'. En in a minute she snort, 'Urrunh.' Dat skeered us en we stopped, en erbout dat time she snort ergain, 'Urrunh!' En mother grabbed me en run. She say de mule see a sumpin ter make her snort lack dat. En de mule wuz lookin' right towards dat hill, en dey says dey is spirits up dar. But I always do say ain't nuthin' ever skeered me but come ter find out hit twuz sumpin' I knowed."

"My husban' believed in spirits, en I used to tease him—make him so mad! He say one night he out huntin' wid some men, en he had a ole dog named Bootee. En he see a spirit walkin' long side er Bootee wid a switch in its han'. Didn't none uv de others see de spirit, but he swore hit wuz er sumpin' tall en white. 'Bout time he wuz fixing ter call ole Bootee, de spirit hit him side de haid, en you know dat dog carried his haid ter one side till he died! He always said twuz on account uv de lick de spirit give him, but I useter laugh at him en say, 'How come you think hit wuz a spirit? Dat ole dog jes' got sumpin' in his year ter make him cock his haid dataway,' en he get so mad! But whutever hit twuz, dat dog sho carried his haid ter one side from den on!"

Once embarked on a topic which obviously fascinated her in spite of her professed disbelief in the supernatural, the flow of talk went on without interruption. "No *ma'am*, I doan believe in conju'.[6] I wouldn't give a nickel to have nobody workin' on me! All I know about conju' is whut Aunt Susan tole me. She useter tell me lots about hit, but she so now she doan like to mention it."

"She say one night she dream she walkin' along de road en she thought she step on a needle en hit hurt her severe. She got hit out. She chewed hit up." Jupie's voice became sing-song intonation. "Whut she represented, hit wuz planted dere fer her. En she got hit." Here her voice returned to normal and she continued, "De next mornin' atter she dreamed dis, she went down de road, personally, en got hit. En de day atter dat, she couldn't walk!"

"I had a conju' woman working me wunst. God knows I don't believe in hit, but I had a sumpin' in my ankle, en I doan keer

---

[6]Carl Carmer, in *Stars Fell On Alabama* (New York: Farrar & Rinehart, 1934), written a few years earlier than this life history, has a section on what he called "Conjure Country," pp. 195–229. A few of the individual chapters, such as "Two-Toe Tom," look much like the Writers' Project life histories.

whur I walked when I come back home I'd be lame fer two days. So I went to de conju' woman's house. She warn't dere, so I waited in de yard en pretty soon she come er-skippin' erlong. She had straight hair lack a witch er de pictures in de funny books. She come th'oo de gate en say, 'Hmmmm, somebody been here today, drawed my coffin.' En sho 'nuff, dere wuz de marks on de side uv de house! Cou'se she could er fixed dat up fo' I got dere, I doan know about dat." Jupie's struggle to preserve her attitude of skepticism toward a cult bred into her race centuries before was amusing. "Den she went in de house en fixed up sumpin; I didn't see whut she got, but she rubbed off de marks."

"I tole her about my ankle how hit would hurt me when I walked any piece on hit en she say, 'Hmmmm, somebody throwed at you. Grudge whut you got.' But she says she could uphand anything brought befo' her so I asked her to work on me. She took my foot in her lap en rubbed hit. Den she went in de house en got three things, I doan know whut they wuz, but they wuz three things she put on my ankle en rubbed hit. En dat ankle wuz jes' ez well ez de other one, en hit ain't bothered me a bit sence!"

"Dis conju' woman didn't charge me much 'cause hit wuz de fust time I'd had anything ter do wid her en she wanted ter persuade me, but she sho charge other folks mighty high. A dress er five, six, seven dollars right back on up. Ef you had a hoss stolen, hit wuz more, but she tell you right now whar ter look fer hit!"

"A 'oman I knew, whut wuz ailing, went to her, en she say, 'Dis here a little ole brown-skinned woman. Short hair. Small feet. Small hands.' " Again Jupie's voice was almost a chant. " 'She had a girl. She come up wrong. She laughed at her!' Den she said twuz a sumpin in de water de woman wuz drinking en tole jes' where ter find de spring. En I could witness dat, 'cause I wuz lookin' fer ducks en saw hit. I didn't know whut wuz happening den, but twuz jes' like de conju' woman said hit wuz. I seen her at de spring, standin' over de water lack dis, talkin' to hit. En she put a sumpin in de water bucket, look lack a green pepper. So I could witness dat, 'cause I seen hit all, jes' lack de conju' woman said hit wuz. But how *she* knowed, I couldn't say. She went in de house a couple uv times whilst we wuz talking, so er co'se she *could* er cut hit in de cards." To Jupie this seemed to constitute a perfectly legitimate means of obtaining information entirely disassociated with occult powers of any sort! "But whether she cut hit in de cards or how she knowed hit I couldn't say."

"Wish Aunt Susan would talk ter yawl about conju'." (Aunt Susan had replied to all insistence with a stubborn, "I doan know nothin' about hit.") "All I knows is jes' whut I'se heered from her en she could tell you *plenty*. She could sho tell you 'bout slave'y time, too, she's talked ter me about hit a lot. Make her tell you about when she wuz pulling corn en they leave de quarter ter go down ter de fiel' in de mawning dey take er thick plank en pile dirt on hit en put a fire on top en put de hoe cake on, en make'em carry hit on dey haids. En by de time dey be done get ter de fiel's whar dey 'sposed ter work, de bread ud be cooked en done, ready ter eat. Lawsy, you ain't never heered er dat? Lots er times we do dat en parch peanuts whilst us walking along wherever we'ze goin'; en reach up on de way en pull de peanuts outen de fire en eat 'em. No'm, hit doan never burn our haids, de dirt en de plank be'ze too thick fer dat."

I hated to leave, but saying good-bye all around I walked down through the front yard gay with fall flowers, followed by Jupie and the children, who formed a semi-circle around the car and stared silently with bright little animal eyes at a respectful distance. In the middle of voluble invitations to be coming back, she suddenly remembered some information she could get from me. "You know de County Nurse over in Livingston?" she asked. "When you gits back ter town, I wish you'd call on her en tell her my health ain't so good en when kin I come in fer treatmint? She got plenty er postal cards, ain't she?" Poor Jupie, so anxious not to impose on anyone's kindness. "Ask her to write me one, please ma'am."

I backed the car around, sending the "young 'uns" scurrying and at the bend of the road a glimpse in the rear vision mirror showed Jupie and her "house full of chillun" still waving a silent good-bye. I felt that my visit had been a great event in the quietness of her usual life, and knew with certainty that for some time to come she would enjoy dramatizing it for the edification of her colored neighbors.

No Lawd, I Ain't Ready

by Ruby Pickens Tartt

The old house was set back from the dirt road. Where the lawn had been only dog fennel was growing. The low picket fence was almost down. A back chimney had fallen, and part of the roof was open to the sky. There were no steps at the front. A tangle of wisteria gripped the rotting gallery. No one answered my "hello." I pulled myself up by one of the rickety pillars and picked my way over sagging boards to the door. I knocked but no one answered. Wandering around the gallery to the back, I met an old Negro man who invited me to walk in and "res" my hat.

Through a side door I entered a room with drawn and torn shades. As my eyes became accustomed to the dimness, they picked out an old rosewood piano. On its top were several daguerreotypes, a family album, and copies of old songs with mildewed pages. On the wall above were two hollow-cut silhouettes, one a man and the other a pretty woman. On the mantel was a small figurine, perhaps of Derby Bisque, whose companion no doubt had shared the fate of other treasures. To the right stood an old wing chair, its needlepoint cushion soiled and frayed. There was an old blue perfume bottle holding a bunch of faded artificial flowers. On a small marble-topped table nearby was an etched hurricane glass of great beauty.

In turning, I faced, though it was partly hidden now by the open door, a tall bookcase filled with books. Crossing the room, I read several titles on the shelf level with my eyes. There was Darwin's *Origin of Species, The Descent of Man* and various works of philosophy. Suddenly I heard the sound of shuffling feet and a voice broke into the silence.

"You better git outa here, 'cause Mr. Frankie ain't go' lack nobody rummagin' 'round 'mongst his things." Turning around I saw standing across the room an aged Negro woman, barefooted, and dressed in a loose, soiled blue homespun dress and faded blue head handkerchief.

"I'm looking for Ellen Tucker," I answered.

"This here is Ellie."

"I heard you lived on the old Williamson place and thought this was the house, until I saw these books. Now I wonder if I might buy some of them."

"Hit too late now," she said, "but I wish to de Lawd you had er got 'em a long time ago, for they ain't never done Mr. Frankie no good, nor nobody else, ef you ax me." She walked slowly into the room, through the door I had entered, and out the back. "De front door done been boa'ded up," she added, "caze don't nobody never come here no mo'," putting into that cryptic sentence all that one somehow felt.

I followed her down the back steps and across the narrow plank walk to a small cabin which I had somehow not seen on the far side of the house. "If this is your house," I said, "won't you let me come in and talk with you awhile, and tell me something of your family, and what you do and where you came from?" Her dialect, I had noticed, was different from that of the usual Alabama black belt Negro.

With an apparent distrust, not only of me, but of life in general, she sat down on the steps, and in that same haunting voice said, "Tain't no use to come in caze I ain't got nothin' ter tell, caze I don't know nothin'. My name is Ellen; jes' lack I said, Ellie Tucker is what I goes by. I ain't never been married ter nobody, that is I ain't had whut *you* might call no reg'lar husband. En all I does is jes' stay here and look after Mr. Frankie. I ain't never been no fiel' hand. Jes' stays in de house. I ain't got no folks, dey's all gone too long ago. My mammy's name was Lucy Tucker. She came out here in slav'y time wid Marse Bob, frum Char'ston, South Ca'lina in a wagin. Didn't none uv her folks come wid her, jes' her by herself, en she say she didn't never see none uv 'em no mo'. Den I wuz born here, right here in dis yard, and didn't never know no pappy, but I wuz here 'fore Marse Bob died, en 'fore his two boys, Mr. Joe and Mr. Johnny died too, en once dey's gone ain't no comin' back. I can't recollec' Miss Ca'line much, caze my 'membrance is shaller, but she wuz us old Mistess. I knows she had er heap er troubles; I hear Mammy say dat. I used to wash and iron de shirts en look atter de house in dem days, jes' lack Marse Bob lef' hit, dat's jes' lack he found hit. But ain't nothin' lef' now to look atter.

Ev'ything done drunk up an' in ruination. Mr. Frankie mos' done come to de end uv de row, en my tiredness done come down on me too. I don't 'zactly know how ole I is, but I knows I is gettin' on, but you better go 'long now, Miss," she said, "caze I'se got plenty ter do 'fore dark en hits mighty nigh fust dust now."

I apologized for having taken up so much of her time, and then remembered to say that I had been invited into the "gre't house," as she called it, by an old Negro man. "Must er been 'Bokay,' " she said, "but he don't b'long here no more en you does, he jes' roams about caze he ain't got no place ter stay at, en he's sorter franzy-minded too. He can't do nothin' much 'cept chop a little wood now en den."

A straight mulatto girl came up the path carrying a battered oil can and a small bundle of broom straw. "Here's the kerosene, ma," she said to Ellen. "Mr. Frankie say fill up de lamp 'fore he get here, but he say he specks ter be late caze he gwine to de chicken fight over in Green."

Encouraged by this, I decided to find out more if possible about this pathetic old Negro. "Doan take dat green broom straw in de house, Violet," said Ellen. "De fros' ain't fell on hit yet en I'se done had 'nough bad luck 'thout that. Us can make de broom outside, I reckon. Don't reckon Mr. Frankie give you no money did he, Violet?" asked Ellen. The girl untied the corner of a large smudged handkerchief and displayed a twenty-five cent piece. "This all he gimme for de church supper." I recalled the Negro church that I had passed in the woods near the big road.

So I asked if she were a member of Good Hope Church, and if she was going to the supper with Violet. If she had heard some bad news she could not have looked more bleak. She sat motionless for a few seconds, then slowly raised her head, and looking not at me but far beyond said, "No'm I ain't goin' to *no* church wid *no*body. I ain't j'ined no church, caze I ain't never had no b'lief an' no 'sperience, and you can't jine 'thout you is got 'ligion. Hit's too late now I reckon. I used ter want ter jine, but Mr. Frankie say 'ligion wuz jes' a pack er foolishness, en dat all dat shoutin' en whoopin' en hollerin' whut folks did, wa'n't nothin' but foolishness neither." She paused a moment, then added, "En I thought he knowed. No'm I didn't never jine en hits too late now I reckon. I b'lieves Heaven's a good place to go though, but I can't tell you how come, caze I doan know nothin' 'bout hit. I ain't never 'fessed no hope in Christ, ain't never sung none uv dem old songs lack I hear 'em sing:

'De folks keep a-crowdin' on de gospel ship
There's no use a-waitin' fer de 'scursion trip.' "[7]

"En I know dere ain't, dere sho' ain't, but I feels de need ter be baptized caze hit soon be time fer me ter ride on de Jordan tide en I ain't ready, no Lawd I ain't ready! I been settin' here thinkin' 'bout dat en I b'lieves my time is mos' out. I sneezed las' night wid my mouth full of vittles en dat's a sho' sign er death, hit doan never fail hardly,[8] en whut is I gonner do? I hear folks say Christians kin view God-er-mighty, en git happy if dey jus' 'fesses Christ. Some folks tells me dey kin hear little moans en kin walk 'cross hell on a spider web, but *I* ain't never seen hit done. 'Fore Mammy lef' she tole all us chillun on de plantation ter live fer Christ, caze she said hit wuz de onliest way, but I didn't pay her no mind."

"You see, Miss, Marse Bob didn't 'low none uv his colored folks to go ter no church in dem days, er to no meetin', en didn't 'low 'em to have no books er no schoolin' caze they say he wuz feared uv a uprisin' 'mongst 'em. Dem wuz sad times, en Marse Bob said 'ligion wuz a lot er trash jes' lack Mr. Frankie do now, en both them got book larnin', Mr. Frankie en dem is, an' Mr. Frankie he know dem books by heart. I ain't never been ter no school. I doan know whut de Bible say 'bout hit, caze I can't read no printin'. I used to try to pray sometimes when I got lonesome lack, en I'd shut de door en put my head down in de wash pot so hit could kech de soun', den pray easy lack so Mr. Frankie wouldn't hear me an' fuss. I reckon ef I could er prayed out loud I could er got 'ligion but hit's too late now; hit look lack I jes' can't hardly b'lieve somehow." She dropped her hands between her knees and said no more.

---

[7] Perhaps a variation of "The Gospel Train" or "I Do Wonder Is My Mother On That Train"; see *North Carolina Folklore*, vol. 3, pp. 588, 633.

[8] See Browne, *Popular Beliefs from Alabama*, p. 189, nos. 3210, 3214; and *North Carolina Folklore*, vol. 7, p. 12, nos. 4935–36 for other examples of this common belief.

In Myrtle Miles's plans, Montgomery was to be a district writers' headquarters. Not only did this fail, but it proved surprisingly difficult to recruit responsible and capable writers there. Beginning in January 1939, Adelaide Rogers wrote the only three life histories from the area. "Never No More," like "No Lawd, I Ain't Ready," deals primarily with black-white relations. Again, the interviewer is white.

Never No More

by Adelaide Rogers

An ex-farmer who loves the Bible, an ex-preacher who loves the farm, is James Little, the Negro janitor at a synagogue in Montgomery. Seventy-one years old, James has been married five times. He maintains, however, that he has never had but *one* wife—and that *one* was Matilda, the mother of his eight children.

James' first and "only real wife" died forty years ago, the nineteenth of last December. But he can see Matilda as plainly now, he says wistfully, as though they parted only yesterday. He and Matilda had been married thirteen years when she died of child-birth pneumonia, in Russell County near Hurtsboro, Alabama. Something went out of him when she died, James remarked simply, and he has never felt the same since about anything. "But you can't give up," the old man opined, "as long as others weaker than yourself is looking to you for help. Hearts break—but they keep on beating. And we can't quit until they does. Of course I had my children. After Matilda died I lived for them and my farm. I had never done anything else then but farm. I love a farm."

"The happiest and best life a man is ever to know in this world waits on a farm. From the time the birds begin twittering at the break of dawn, until the first shadows of night fall in the evening, there is something to do on a farm. That's why lazy people never likes to farm. It's not the place for them that wants to set and think. Or even just to set. No ma'am. You got to be up and doing from morning to night, hour to hour, season to season, if you make a success of your farm. When I lived on a farm I was always up by three in the morning. After breakfast— and I always had a good breakfast on the farm—I'd go out to my barns. Sometimes it wouldn't be good daylight and I'd carry a lantern. I'd hitch up my plowin' pardners—if I didn't have no mules I'd plow steers—an' we'd be in the field by dawn."

"If I didn't take the plow to the field, I'd take myself irregardless. I've always thought that old sayin', 'Don't let the grass grow under your feet,' was meant for farmers. Grass in your field amongst the furrows will choke out a crop worse'n diphtheria will choke a baby. So when I wasn't plowin' I was hoein'; an' when I wasn't reapin' I was sowin'."

"St. Valentine's Day on the fourteenth of February is the best time to sow tender plants. If you put them out any earlier they are sho' to be killed by a cold spell. And in the spring, it's always best to plant just before the full of the moon. The moon plays an

Coal miners' homes. Birmingham, 1937. Rothstein, FSA.

important part in farming, just like everything else. All sun-plants, like cotton and corn, grow faster under light rays, whether of the sun or moon. The dark o' the moon must also be took into account if you are trying to turn all of nature's tricks to your advantage. For some reason frost is not as killing on a dark night as it is when the moon is bright. And even on the coldest night, if freshly killed meat is put out under a bright moon, the meat will spoil. Yes, ma'am, the moon has some strange powers and it just don't like freshly killed meat."[9]

"The weather, of course, next to energy, can be a farmer's best friend. And it pays every farmer to watch the weather signs. When the wind shifts to the west, or northwest, and stays for forty-eight hours, look out for cold weather. Then if it is too cold to plow, the thrifty farmer will not spend his time by the fireside talking about how cold it is. That neither makes it any warmer nor chops out the Johnson grass. Solomon says, 'By reason of cold, the sluggard will not plow, but will beg bread in the harvest.'[10] Now I am not a sluggard. So when the cold had made the ground too hard to be broken by the plow, I knew I should use that time to cut down the grass and undergrowth which if left to itself will strangle a young crop. But speaking of weather signs: if the wind in this latitude goes south and stays twenty-four hours, then you can expect continuous showers. Yes, ma'am, there's a lot of sense sometimes in those little rhymes. They are easy to remember and mighty, mighty useful. I know another one that says, 'Rainbow in the morning, sailors take warning; rainbow at night, sailor's delight.' 'Lightning in the north in summer or spring, a hard soaking rain the evening will bring.' "[11]

"I don't believe I ever prayed for rain, even when my crops were burning up with drouth. I always felt I was too insignificant for the good Lord to drench his earth just to accommodate me. The good Lord sends the rains and the seasons according to

[9]Browne, in *Popular Beliefs from Alabama,* pp. 247–50, nos. 4166–4239, lists similar beliefs dealing with planting by the phase of the moon and the signs of the zodiac.

[10]Proverbs 20:4.

[11]See *North Carolina Folklore,* vol. 7, p. 226, nos. 6124–29, and Browne, *Popular Beliefs from Alabama,* p. 211, nos. 3528–31, on rainbows and lightning respectively as weather indicators.

his own pleasure, and we can't return any of them to be done over like a shirt, or a dress that hasn't been washed and ironed proper. I know when the seasons or the weather is due for a change. But I can't neither make, nor hinder their operations through no kind of prayers or supplications."

"Everybody that has ever lived in the country—with his eyes open—knows that fig trees never put out their tiny green buds until summer is really on the way. Of all the plants, the fig tree is the wisest, and most truthful. It has never forgotten that our Lord cursed it once for deceiving Him. For its falseness, that particular tree was withered overnight. So from that time until the present, fig trees have been truthful as well as wise."

"I have noticed too, that when termites or flying ants come out from their bed in rotten wood, winter has really gone. And it will not be long before we have our annual feast of fresh fruits and vegetables. All these signs a farmer must read and apply— along with hard work—or he will not succeed in his endeavors. Folks will tell you nowadays that a man cannot make a living on a farm. Well if a man can't make a living on a farm, he can't make a living *anywhere*. I loved and understood my farm like a mother loves and understands her children—because I watched it, and thought about it all the time. But then, I came into this world on a farm, and if I had my way, I'd go out of it on a farm."

James was born on the Borum plantation at Creek-stand, Alabama, three miles from Hurtsboro, an old township in Russell County. He spent his childhood roaming the woods—fishing and hunting, playing hide and seek, blind man, and all the games in which boys regardless of creed or color have throughout the ages found their diversion. Then one day young Mr. George Brown, a relative of the Borums, came to visit his cousins, and the whole course of James' life was altered. For between him and Mr. George there developed one of those rare friendships that sometimes bind a white man and a black man with indissoluble ties of affection.

"We were just like brothers," James' voice dwelt proudly on the word 'brothers.' "Whatever he had, I had. And what I had belonged to him, if I thought he had even halfway took a shine to it. We roamed the woods all day, and at night we sat on the door steps lookin' at the stars, and dreamin' and talkin' about the big things we'd do in the world when we grow'd up to be men. Sometimes we'd scare each other with tales about ha'nts or ghosts we had heard of. Then again we'd plan to go off to a war together, like white gentlemens and colored boys had done before. But mostly we just played, and talked, and had fun."

"When the summer was over and he went back home to Hurtsboro, I went with him. We stayed in the same room then, and wore the same, or nearly the same kind of clothes. We ate the same things—at a different table, and we often carried our meals upstairs so we could eat together. I toted his books to school for him, and waited around outside until he was ready to come home. As soon as he'd get out Mr. George would say something like this: 'Come on now, James. Let's get busy. I'm going to learn you what they learned me today.' So laying down on our stummicks in the grass, he would learn me, out of the same book they had learned him."

"Because Mr. George wanted me to have some of everything he had, my learning had to come before we played any games. And that night after supper when we had gone to our room, we had learning again. We'd put the lamp on the floor and lay down beside it to read out of our book. One night his pa came in unexpectedly and caught us. 'Why James,' he says, all surprised, 'I didn't know you could read.' 'He can read just as good as me,' Mr. George spoke up real proud. 'Just as good as me.' Nothing would do then but I had to read for his pa. Afterwards *he* read for his pa. And when they all decided I read a little the best, the happiest and proudest one was Mr. George. He was the best man what ever lived in the world. There never was no other man like Mr. George. Just like there never was no other woman like Matilda."

"I married her young. And we went to live on a farm not far from Hurtsboro. I didn't want to be too great a distance from Mr. George. So I went to live on his farm, while he run a store in Hurtsboro and I looked after the place in the country. He came out twice a week to the farm. And I went in town every Saturday to buy my supplies. Of course I traded with Mr. George. I wouldn't of thought to buy nothing from nobody else while he was operating a store. We still went hunting together too, in the fall. And we always spent some time fishin' in the spring."

"Then he married Miss Leila. And we didn't see each other so often as time went on. But years a-passing don't make no difference to folks like me and Mr. George. He had his store, and his wife and children to keep him hustling. I had Matilda, and six children, and my farm that was really Mr. George's. Though I couldn't have had more interest in the place if I'd owned every stick and stone of it."

"Daylight found me in the field a-plowin'. At first I plowed with oxen. Then after Mr. George saw what a good farmer I was, he bought me a pair of mules. And about that time, I hired a nigger boy to help me in the field. We made fine crops too. I raised cotton on shares with Mr. George, and while he got most of the money that come from our cotton, I got a part of it. And I had all the sweet potatoes, black-eyed peas, corn, onions, cabbage, turnip greens, chickens, eggs, squash and tomatoes that I could raise. In those days white gentlemen wouldn't stoop to raisin' pigs. Cotton, old King Cotton, was the white folks' crop in Alabama. So I had all the pigs on the farm. I kept three cows too. And all the milk and butter I didn't want I sold in town. I sold all my surplus vegetables, eggs, and fruit too. Yet people say you can't make a living on a farm."

"Why, Miss, if I had been working in town, and had had to pay rent, and buy everything my family and I ate, and buy it with the wages a workman gets in this latitude, we would all have starved to death. As it was, my children had plenty of milk to drink, plenty of good food to eat, and I had thick, sweet cream on some kind of pie every night with my supper. That was the meal that we all ate together. When I went to the fields in the morning, the little folks were asleep. I carried my lunch along with me, so I didn't come home to dinner. But at night we ate together—cracklin' bread, simmered peas, turnips, sweet potatoes, pork shoulder, ribs, sausage, or just plain ham, and pie. We had eggs whenever we wanted them, fried, scrambled, boiled, or in sweet custards. Sundays we had fried chicken, rice and cream gravy, flour biscuits and honey, and old-fashioned sweet potato pudding."

"Twice a week I went fishin'. And I never came back without a nice string of fish for supper. I had noticed that if white children ate pork too steady, they broke out in boils. Now, if pork meals ain't good for white children every day, they ain't good for colored children either. So twice a week I went fishin'. I got to the place where I didn't specially care about fishin' as a pastime. In fact I didn't like to lose a whole afternoon out of the fields. But I didn't want my children to get sick. White children what ate pork all the time were never well. I wanted my six to be healthy, fine set-up children. There would have been eight of them, but the last two were stillborn."

"I was crazy about my children. After I lost Matilda, I don't believe I would have married again except for them. You can't leave little children in the country without somebody to look out for them. Ida, my second wife, was a good woman and a good cook. I reckon you might say I married her as a convenience. Ida didn't live so long. But I disrecollects of just which particular sickness she died. She use to grumble, I remember, because I made her help in the field. I wouldn't let Matilda work in the field. But Matilda was my wife. And Ida was just a woman I married."

"After Ida's death, I married Emma. She was a good cook too. But like Ida, she was jealous of Matilda being my wife, and they just the wimmins I would happen to marry. Wimmins are always going to be jealous, though, about one thing or another. And a man is lucky if he can give them something *real* to be jealous about, instead of them making his life a burden on account of something they have thought up for themselves."

"Soon after I married Emma, Mr. George left Hurtsboro and come to Montgomery to be a bookkeeper in a store. I didn't want to stay in Russell County and Mr. George in Montgomery. So I come to Montgomery too. Mr. George got me a job as a porter, in the furniture store where he kept books. And once more we was together again—almost like when we was boys. Then Mr. George died. And I couldn't stand Montgomery no longer."

"I went to Birmingham and got a job as a car greaser for the T.C.&I. Railroad. I didn't like Birmingham at all. Not in no ways. But I couldn't come back for a while, to Montgomery without Mr. George. And I couldn't live happy in Hurtsboro without Matilda. So I stayed on in Birmingham. Since I was going to be miserable anyhow, I figured I might as well suffer in some place where I could draw good wages. My children had all grow'd up, and struck out for themselves. That left just me and Emma to get along on what I made out of the railroad."

"I had taken up preaching in the meantime. And I got considerable comfort out of religion. My father was a preacher too. He was a presiding elder in the Opelika district of the African Methodist Episcopal Zion Church. That's the one I belong to. I reckon there are other good churches, but I can't think of none that I would put along side of the Methodist. If a man is a good Methodist, he is a good Christian. And that is as much as anybody can ever hope for to be."

"During my stay in Birmingham, Emma died of being too frail, I suppose; and a short while later I met Mary. Mary was a widow well along near fifty. I should have knowed better than to give a serious thought in her direction. But she was so persistent in her pleasant widow-ways that I began going to her house for Sunday night supper. Now whenever a man starts eating Sunday dinner or supper in a widow's house, he has already hung out the white flag of surrender. And all that is needed is his final 'I does.' I didn't realize this at that time, but Mary did. So she kept asking me to eat in her house, and I kept going, until Mary married me, without my consent, so to speak. But I will say this for Mary. She could make the best chicken stew out of rabbit that ever set on a preacher's dinner plate. Yes ma'am, she could cook a rabbit with a little onion, and green pepper and raisin sauce, till that cottontail served on the table with dumplings, and apple salad, ice tea and banana pudding, wouldn't know itself from chicken. Mary was smart in them ways. And that chicken-into-rabbit dish was her own fifty-year-old game of widowish deceit. After me and Mary was married, our life was one long disagreement. Nothing I could do seemed to please Mary. And everything she did afflicted me the wrong way. She didn't even cook good no longer. So I divorced Mary right here in Montgomery."

"I had moved back here, thinking the change might help her disposition. But it made her worse. So I got shet of Mary for all time. After I got rid of her I went to Chicago on a visit to my daughter, Minnie. And I felt better when I came back than I had in years. But no matter how good a man feels on his own account, he has to eat. So I married Maria some twelve or fifteen years ago, I believe; and I have been eating well ever since."

"Maria is a good woman as well as a first class cook. She is twenty-one years younger than I am and has a job cooking for well-to-do white folks. Maria makes five dollars a week, and they let her tote. That means she can bring home her meals instead of eating them in the white folks' kitchen. If she eats in the white folks' house, I wouldn't get none. So I told her she would have to either tote or quit. Rather than be without a good cook, the white folks will let 'em tote their meals home. In that way, all the fine cooks usually has husbands. For if you'll notice, the good providers of either sect is never without a mate."

"I reckon I should be thankful to have Maria. I am too old now to preach. And I have just recently laid down my job as janitor at the synagogue. I do wish—since I am old and penniless, except for the meals and room that Maria donates toward my upkeep— I do wish, I say, with all my heart that I could get a pension."

"The Lord never intended a woman to be the head of a man's house. But if she makes the living, and is able to pinch down on the purse strings, then the Lord's will, as well as her husband, is made to look foolish. It takes very little to give a woman the idea that she is a man's equal. In fact they already think so anyhow. Then when they were allowed to vote, and plainly told they were our equals, it unsettled the woman's head. That's what is ruining our country today. Wimmins said they wanted equal *rights* with men. But they didn't. What they really wanted was equal *wrongs,* freedom to live their own lives—getting drunk, neglecting children, running around all hours of the night, and fussing with their husbands if the poor old fellow wants a dime for to buy himself a sack of smoking tobacco."

"This is a rich country. They give big jobs in Washington to white men who serve their party in some notorious fashion. Well, I have served the Democratic party in my small way just as well as Mr. Jim Farley or Mr. Senator Harrison.[12] I began voting in 1887. Since then, I've always been a Democrat. I have always cautioned the colored people not to vote Republican, but

[12]Probably James A. Farley (1824–88) of Montgomery, and George P. Harrison of Opelika, state senator 1878–1904; see Henry S. Marks, *Who Was Who in Alabama* (Huntsville: Strode Publishers, 1972), pp. 62, 81.

to vote Democratic along with the white gentlemen of the South. So it seems to me that a rich country like ours could give one little pension to a poor old darkey like me. If I could get a little pension money to spend now and then, Maria couldn't domineer over me on account of her being the financial head of the house, with I looking to her for all my necessities. As it is now, I am in her power. At those times when she can't get a job cooking for white folks, she works at the sewing room of the WPA. I believe they pay her ten dollars a week. But she won't allow me even ten cents a week. Anybody ought to know that is not right. The Lord did not give the man to the woman. He gave the woman to the man. Now the white folks have reversed the Lord's judgment, and given the man—along with all the money—to the woman. I have heard that 'every dog has his day, and every woman her hour.' If that is true, it explains why we are passing through one of the darkest hours of civilization."

"I am living now with only one hope. And that is the belief that in the life beyond the grave, I shall see Matilda again. Her, and my boy, Exton, who went away to the war in France, and didn't come back. I never knew if he died of some sickness or was killed in fighting, or just didn't return. If I wrote off to find out, and they told me he was dead, I'd *know* then, and I'd have no more hope. But this way, the door is always open. I can think maybe Exton will come home tonight. Maybe he will come tomorrow. Tomorrow, or the next day. But especially tomorrow. I loves that word. There is something wonderful about tomorrow. In that tomorrow toward which I am looking forward, Matilda and I shall be together again with our children. Reunited, we may forget the loneliness of the years we spent apart, and remember only that we are together again—to be separated no more. Never no more, Lord—never no more!"

Cotton mill workers made up a large occupational group all over the Southeast. Couch specifically mentioned this group in his initial life history suggestions, and five of the Alabama accounts deal directly with mill workers. Unfortunately they are all so brief as to be mere sketches. Two are printed here. The first, by Maude Cain of Alexander City, is about a family in Avondale Mill Village. The other is by Gertha Couric of Eufaula and is about a family in Cowikee Mill Village.

Susan Childs

by Maude Cain

I found Susan Childs in her kitchen preparing the midday meal. It was a bright September morning about 9:30. When I arrived she willingly transferred her culinary duties to her daughter, Myrtis, while she invited me into the front bedroom. This is the room which the Childs family uses as their living room, evidently because it is the best furnished. It is very small, but its one bed looks comfortable enough. At first Susan could hardly talk to me, but the difficulty proved to be only a mouthful of snuff. She had picked up the snuff-dipping habit from her playmates as a small child, she explained to me. She seemed to feel the need of some sort of apology. "I wished I didn't use it," she said, "but it's a whole lot of satisfaction." She did not wait for questions, but, without further preliminaries, launched on the story of her life.

Susan was born on a farm in Tallapoosa County thirty-five years ago. While she was still very young, her father brought the family to town, hoping to provide for them better by putting the two older girls in the mill. Susan was not old enough to work, so she did not go into the mill. She entered school. But she was "skeered of her teacher." She did not like school and her parents did not force her to go. She was still too young to work when she met Paul and they decided to get married. She was fifteen years old and he was twenty. Paul worked in the mill. Susan's first baby was born when was she was sixteen. After that a new one came every year or two. Now Susan is thirty-five and she and Paul have eight children, six boys and two girls.

Their home is on Peachtree Avenue in Avondale Mill Village. It is a dingy brown little four-room cottage on a hillside and it is surrounded by a grove of trees, most of them pines. Other similar cottages are dotted here and there on the hillside. Susan likes the place "right well" because the children can play in the back yard among the trees. Susan is proud of her children, every one of them, and wants them to get "some schoolin'." But her Paul finds it difficult to provide for eight children with only one

Migrant family. Near Birmingham, 1937. Rothstein, FSA.

of them old enough to work in the mill. He is a weaver[13] and "makes a right good salary—that is, when he can get regular work." But even so, their income is very inadequate.

Hugh, their oldest child, is nineteen. He plays football and is able to work in the mill mornings and attend school in the afternoon. His mother said Hugh used to have a terrible cough "from smokin' cigarettes." He could not sleep at night. Five months ago he gave up tobacco and now he can sleep almost all night without coughing, Susan explained. "Smokin' was sure bad for him," she remarked earnestly. I found the second child, Myrtis, a bright and intelligent girl and one who would be considered good looking in any walk of life. She had to give up school to look after her younger brothers and baby sister, so that her mother could work in the mill and help support the family. "Myrtis is ashamed to go to school, now that she's done got so far behind in her books," Susan told me. But Susan heard of a WPA teacher in a nearby community and she knew Myrtis wouldn't mind one person knowing how ignorant she was. So now Myrtis manages to have a few lessons at home each week from the WPA teacher.

The baby, when they showed her to me, was sleeping peacefully in her little bed, which had not a semblance of a sheet. The chubby little blue-eyed girl opened her eyes and smiled for a moment before snuggling back into the folds of the bedcover (this last nondescript object, which had evidently had only a speaking acquaintance with soap and water, seemed to be some grown person's outworn and discarded kimono). Susan is especially proud of the baby, because she is the first girl since Myrtis and Myrtis is seventeen. The second, third and fourth boys were at school when I called on the Childs family and the fifth and sixth, too young for school, were playing in the back yard.

Susan does not seem to have a single worry about the future, as the family has pretty good health and she is satisfied. She had to give up her job in the mill in April, 1938, but she expects to go back as soon as the baby is old enough for her to leave it.

---

[13]One who tends one or more weaving machines—one of the more skilled and better paid employees in the mill.

The Jim Bittingers—Cotton Mill Workers

by Gertha Couric

The Bittingers live in a five-room, screened house, painted white with green trimmings. White furniture, a swing, and pots of geraniums and ferns mark the front porch, which gives entrance into the living room. This social center of the Bittinger house has clean white curtains at the windows and is furnished with a sofa, chairs, a table with reading lamps on top, and a radio. Several vases filled with artificial flowers, crocheted mats on the table, "tidies" on the back of chairs, family pictures on the wall and a flowered rug on the floor, complete the cheerful living room. Three bedrooms each have plain oak furniture and clean white curtains at the windows. The dining room and kitchen are combined. An electric stove and refrigerator contribute to the ease of housekeeping.

Mrs. Bittinger answered my knock, and seemed quite willing to tell of the life in Cowikee Mill Village. "I worked in the mill thirty-five years," she said. "But I ain't worked for ten years now. My old man Jim has been workin' here forty-five years, but he's pretty old now, just sorta piddles around at the mill, odd jobs and 'sweeping.' He gets nine dollars a week. I was Missy McLauren, of Comer, and was visitin' here when me and Jim met. He started courtin' me and—well we got married. I was from good folks; was born near the old Comer plantation, so naturally, I wanted us to get ahead. But it was sho' hard in them days, workin' from six in the mornin' 'till six in the evenin'. We didn't have no electricity nor nothin' either. We had to draw the warps in by hand, and threadin' them looms by mouth was some pin terrible.[14] I'm 'shamed to tell it, but that's why I started dippin' snuff; to keep the lint out of my mouth. But, I dunno, the doctor says there's one good thing about snuff. It'll keep you from havin' hookworms."

---

[14]When one cotton thread on the warp ran out, the worker customarily wet his or her fingers and with one quick motion twisted another thread to it, making an effective splice.

"We got four children, all of them grown now. My oldest boy, Mark, has been livin' in Jacksonville, Florida, but he's here without a job now. We got twin boys. Arthur is a weaver at the mill; gets sixteen dollars a week. Walter is a-workin' at the printing office. I don't know what he makes. Jim, you know, is pensioned by Mr. Donald Comer. The boys didn't finish high school, but my girl, Sarah, got through and has a good business education. I sho' am worried about Sarah. She's taken up with them 'holy rollers'[15] and it's about to kill me and her pa, us bein' Baptists and not believin' in nothin' like that. But we can't do nothin' with her; she's a grown woman, you know."

"Aw, you've seen 'holy rollers.' Sarah's a preacher; she's preaching someplace up in Georgia now. All them 'holy rollers' is preachers. They all take turns preachin', standin' up there shoutin' 'till they lose their voice. When they sing, they jump up and down to the music, and the more excited they get, the faster they sing and jump. To see them, you'd think it was a barn dance. After they jump awhile, 'till they can't stand up, they fall down and roll around, and talk the 'unknown tongue.' How do I know what the 'unknown tongue' is? All I know is that it sounds like a lot of gibberin' and gurglin', like when somebody has a mouth full of mush; or like somebody that can't speak for stutterin'. The choir members are all preachers and the preachers are all choir members. After anybody stands up in the congregation and testifies to all their sins, and come up to the altar to be prayed for, then he's a preacher and a choir member too. Once at a protracted meetin', a woman kept standin' up and testifyin', and goin' up to the altar to be prayed for, and then goin' back to her seat. We all commenced to think she just wasn't goin' to get saved. Then, right on the last night, after she'd been prayed over, and talked to, and prayed some more, all to once she jumped straight up and began to shout: 'I got it! I got it! All the preachers slapped her on the back and she began to jump up and down and the singin' started, and all of them shouted 'amen.' On the way home, a friend asked the woman how come it took her so long to get saved and she answered: 'I forgot to spit out my snuff.' Now that's supposed to be the

---

[15]Derisive nickname for Pentecostals.

truth," said Mrs. Bittinger. "That's why I'm so worried about Sarah."

She resumed the affairs of her home life. "I have so much to do at home, it keeps me pretty busy. Cookin', washin', milkin'— we got a fine cow—all takes a lot of time. I don't go nowhere, because Jim works from two in the afternoon 'till ten at night. I crochet a lot when I have any spare time, and usually sell my extra pieces. Every little bit helps with expenses. House rent is twelve-fifty a month. Jim works in the garden mornin's. A garden cuts down grocery expenses a lot. Our chickens and cow help too. For instance, at a meal, we can have fried chicken, collard or turnip greens, rutabagas, beans, peas, and butter milk; that we don't have to bring home in a sack."

"The boys enjoy the Men's Club and the Community House. One of the boys, Arthur, is a member of the band. We all have a pretty good time, even if me and Jim are gettin' pretty old." Mrs. Bittinger, a regular anarchist and "Dame Van Winkle," knows all the gossip and scandal of the town. She views the young people in this light: "They're some'pin' scandalous and terrible, the gals smokin' and drinkin' liquor, just like the men. They're all goin' to Hell!"

Jim Bittinger, quiet and mousey in a hen-pecked way, has always been hard working, thrifty and uncomplaining. He is now quite feeble. In his reserved and unassuming manner, he has this to say of the younger generation: "Young folks will be young folks. They ain't so bad; could be worser." Their politics are strictly favorable to the Democratic party and it is a good bet that Mrs. Bittinger guides the Bittinger vote.

Mrs. Rhussus L. Perry was the only black writer of Alabama life histories. There was consistent pressure on Myrtle Miles from the regional and national levels of the FWP, including Sterling Brown's Negro Affairs section, to get some project work in Tuskegee Institute and vicinity. The latest of a long line of suggestions came from the Washington office in July 1938, and just over a month later, on August 28, Mrs. Perry was hired.[16] In the following year her project work included four life histories about people whose lives, like hers, had been influenced by Tuskegee Institute: a professor whose ceramics class she had taken, an elderly ex-slave who often visited the campus, and two self-sufficient women living in the countryside around the town of Tuskegee.[17] Perry's prose is simple but effective, as can be seen in the introduction to her story on Janey Leonard, "Janey Gets Her Desires":

> *(She) is a dark brown skin woman. She is about 4½ feet tall, weighing about 130. She has soft hair which she keeps dyed jet black. The gray hair close to the roots may be seen. Her almost round face carries a very pleasant smile. When she talks to you she looks straight into your eyes with her sharp, dark brown eyes. She holds herself quite erect and has a quick gait. Her speech is clear but quick. She is a good entertainer. She is a farmer and enjoys it. Most of the work is done on shares. The year round you can find hams and bacon which she kills and cures on her place.*

All four life histories are presented here. Mrs. Perry, now Mrs. Rhussus Saunders, as of this writing still lives in Tuskegee.

---

[16]See Office of Negro Affairs to Couch, October 19, 1938, FWP—Couch Papers, noting a July 23, 1938, letter; and also Miles to Couch, January 4, 1939, FWP—Couch Papers, a letter summarizing her activity in regard to hiring qualified black writers.

[17]Letter to editor dated April 29, 1981. Mrs. Saunders remembers being asked to write stories about "ex-slaves and black people who had made marked progress since slavery." She recalls that she made three trips to Father Timmons's home before she finished that life history. Father Timmons was a great admirer of President Roosevelt, and when the president visited Tuskegee Mrs. Perry (she was then) took Father Timmons up to his car to introduce her "subject" to him. In her words, the "President signaled to let him by. Father Timmons fondly threw his arms around his neck. The guards gently removed Father Timmons' arms. The President smiled a grateful smile."

A Day With Becky Clayton

by Rhussus L. Perry

I set out to spend the day out in the country on Green's plantation. It was a lovely day in January. The sun was shining warm and nothing seemed more inviting than a day's visit with some of the country folks. Out on Green's plantation live a number of interesting persons, but really Miss Becky is the central character in the community. The women gather at her house to hear the latest news and happenings. When they have a member of the family sick they set out to Miss Becky for advice. They bring her their family troubles, their trials and tribulations. On Fridays and Saturdays the men and boys come to her house for her son to cut their hair and shave their beards.

Going across the fields from the highway, I enjoyed looking at the sloping hills thick with pine saplings, every now and then a sturdy, bare oak, sweet gum, or black gum. The fields near the house were thick with broom sage which they all gather and make into brooms. I noticed a pine-pole square pen built by piling pole upon pole until it was about four feet high. In this pen were four large banks of sweet potatoes. The potatoes are banked by piling them up on pine straw, then laying straw all over them. Boards are stacked around them in tepee shape. Some use corn stalks or pine bark. More straw is piled on and then dirt piled up on all this. Just beyond this pen is a little smoke house built for the purpose of curing and storing meat.

My attention was drawn to the old dilapidated house in which Miss Becky lived. It was a large, old barn-looking house. The few windows were wooden, resembling doors. The house leaned forward and reminded one of an old man bent with age. As I neared the steps I noticed on the right of the house a barn and lot. In and around were several healthy-looking chickens, three pigs, a black dog, and two spotted puppies. A gray mule grazed lazily not far from the lot. A little calf was sleeping in the sun just beyond the large pile of wood and kindling. In the yard not far from the steps stood a huge chinaberry tree, the largest I have ever seen. This tree is not very tall but its trunk would measure almost four feet in diameter. Most of its roots seemed to be above the soil. There was another chinaberry tree, tall and slender, near the gate. Farther to the left was a large pecan tree. Here and there were beds of flowers.

As I started up the steps, I had to look close for a safe place to put my feet. I called, "Hello Miss Becky." "Come right on in iffen yo' can git in. Well suh! Come in and sit down by de fiyah." All the while she was busy moving things back out of the way and making the fire burn. "I brought you something," I informed her as I handed her a paper bag. "Much erblige ter yo'," she grinned as she took it, joyfully looking into it. She burst into a laugh as she remarked, "Now ain't de Lawd good? Now ain't He good? George Washington smoking tobacco; jes' whut I likes. De Lawd gwineter bless yo' honey," she assured me. She then introduced me to the others who were sitting there. "Dis yeah's my baby daughter. She married'n lives right 'cross de road there. Dis yeah's my sister; she lives a pretty good piece frum heah. She come ter see me terday."

After she finished telling me about her sister and daughter she said, "Lawd, chile, pull off yer coat'n hat an' make yerself at home. 'Scuse my manners. I ain't had real good sense since I come frum dat funeral yestiddy. O, 'twas a lovely meeting, but it sho' was sad. Jodie Gobson wuz her name, poor critter. She done groanin' in dis lan'. She had a hard time, her husband treated her so bad. Her folks tuk on so hard. De church was jes' packed. Rev. Reuben, he had to stop praying, de folks dey wuz carryin' on so bad."

She put another piece of wood on the fire as she said, "I like a good fire, an' den hit has ter be a good fire in heah, dis ol' shack, so open. Dis jes' ain't no house now; it useter be, but hit ain't good as a hoss barn now. Us begs Miss Green to fix hit but she jes' won't do it. She won't fix nary house on de place, on dis plantation. She got plenty money but she won't give us a nail ter fix nothin'." I looked up as directed and there were rotten boards overhead ready to fall, it seemed. She carried me across the hall into a large room to show me how decayed and open it was. The floor was still damp from the rain of two days before. Cracks large enough to see the sky through were in the roof of this room. I said to her, "It is a wonder the government allows people to live in such dilapidated houses. Why don't you move?" "Well," she said, "I jes' lak dis place. I hate ter leave. I axed Miss

Green ter tear dis house down 'n jes' buil' me a little two-room
and kitchen house but she won't do hit. Iffen she don't do
sumpin', we gwineter have ter leave 'cause dis house 'bout to fall
in on us."

We returned to the room where we were sitting. Nearly
everything in her house is very old. In the room where we sat
were two large wooden beds and one of those olden-time dress-
ers with three drawers and a dim mirror. There was a sewing
machine, and several chairs that had been rebottomed with
plaited shucks. On the mantel I noticed several liniment bottles,
a large bottle of castor oil and several salve boxes. At one end
was an oil lamp without a chimney. From this mantel hung a
scalloped blue oil cloth. Down by the open fireplace sat an old
iron skillet with legs, that they use to parch peanuts. All around
on the smutty planks of the walls hung hats and pieces of
clothing. A rusty horseshoe hung downward over the door. Old
coats stretched over the wooden windows to help keep some of
the cold wind out.

"Heah dat dawg howlin'?" she asked. "Dat's a sign o' death
sho' as yo' bawn in dis world.[18] Some people don't believe in
signs, but I does." Her sister said, "We had a dawg once;
'member, sister Becky? When dat dawg howled someone sho'
died. Dat's de truf. Yas, suah." Then Miss Becky interrupted,
"Yas suah, las' night my hands eetched an' I rubbed dem
tergether and see dis mawnin' I gits de smoking tobacco.[19] Same
as money ain't hit? Yas suah, I believes in my signs."

"No'm I ain't lived in this community all my life," she replied
to my question. "I wuz bawn in 1868 in Cotton Valley, not fur
over the way in dis county of Macon. Yas'm." She kept on as she
leaned forward slightly in her chair, folding her arms in her lap,
gazing straight in the fire. "My ma an' pa had leben chillen,
seben boys and four girls. Ums de oldes' girl." Her sister sat
there witnessing every statement. That was about all she could
do for Miss Becky always did the talking when she had company.

---

[18]See Browne, *Popular Beliefs from Alabama*, p. 191, nos. 3232–33.
[19]See *North Carolina Folklore*, vol. 6, p. 545, nos. 4087–90, on itching as the herald of
good news.

"Did all of your sisters and brothers get a chance to go to school?" I asked. "Yas ma'm, ev'ry one uv us went ter school 'ceptin' Laura an' she died 'fore she wuz oler 'nuff ter go. Yas ma'm I loved my gwine ter school an' I had good teachers too. I went ter school til I was in de fifth grade. I coulder went on but all dem wuz in my class dey married an' I jes' stopped 'cause dey all stopped but I coulder went on two more years. We allus had ter stop an' go ter field 'bout March an' dat's reason we didn't git no fudden de fi'th grade. I sho' lacked school."

"I bet your dad fed you all, too," I said. "Fed us," she repeated. "I say dat man fed his younguns! My dad ud buy bar'ls uv sugar, flour, sacks of rice an' things lak dat. He kilt plenty meat. Chile, de hardes' time I evah seed wuz since I been married." She looked at me and smiled as she assured me that she had never really suffered for food. She reminded me however that she has had to turn in close places to keep things going. She got up, went over to a little pocket hanging on the wall and pulled out her pipe. She laughed heartily as she held it up and said, "Dis is my satisfaction."

She came back, sat down and continued her conversation. "Yas suah, we wore good clothes. Homespun, osnaburg,[20] das whut all de chillun wore den. Dey wuz good close. We allus went ter Sunday school an' my ma an' pa dey had fambly prayer ev'ry mawnin' an' on Sunday, ev'ry one had ter git on dere knees." Her sister witnessed this fact, rose and said, " 'Scuse me, lady, I sho' is glad I met yo', hope ter meet yo' ag'in. Sorry I got ter go but I must go now." Her sister Becky asked to excuse her and she went to the steps with her sister and there they chatted a few minutes.

She returned shortly, seated herself near the fire and began to tell me more about herself. "I bin married, les' see," she began counting her fingers. "Les see, I married in 1886; yeah I married Lester Ford in 1886. We had leben chillun. I wuz jes' as good a woman as my ma wuz. She had seben boys 'n fo' girls. I

---

[20]Osnaburg was a rough, strong fabric of coarse flax yarn. Homespuns and osnaburgs were commonly purchased for plantations in antebellum days; see Charles Sackett Sydnor, *Slavery in Mississippi* (Gloucester, Mass.: Peter Smith, 1965, reprinted from 1933), pp. 24–25.

had seben girls and fo' boys. Eight of my chillun livin'. I got three dead."

The smiles left her face as she began thinking of her children who have passed on. She began, as she sat up straight, folded her arms across her bosom, "My oldest son got killed. He wuz gamblin', he was a gambler jes' lak his dad. He got shot ter death in Cincinnati durin' de war. He come ter his daddy's funeral in 1918. I sez, 'Son don't go back an' leave me, yo' dad done gone lef' me; you stay heah wid me.' He sez, 'I can't stay.' I sez, 'Well if yo' go yo' ain't comin' back,' jes look lak I had ter say dat to him." In a pleading manner she reached her arms out as she continued, "I begged him so hard not ter go back. My ma she beg him too. She sez, 'Son I feel lack I ain't gwineter see yo' no mo'.' Sho nuff in three weeks my chile was shot down, an' wuz buried three weeks fo' I knowed anything 'bout hit."

"Penny, she died in 1927. Po' chile, she jes' staid sick, complainin' wid her side an' stomach all de time. She stayed sick right round three years, den she died. She had jes' reached twenty-one when she died. My baby Hattie, she died wid de whoopin' cough when she wuz six months ole. Well, dem's gone on ter glory an' I got ter git dere. Dey done worrin' in dis old hard worl'. Dey lef me heah to worry, I'll meet dem someday. Yas das three I got done lef' me." "That is sad to think about," I said, "but you still have quite a few children to cheer you." "Yas ma'm, but dey all married but two boys an' jes' one uv dem is here, Lester, dat's my baby boy; he name for his dad. Den I got two gran'sons heah wid me. Dem three boys dey help me wid my farm ev'ry yeah."

Gazing into the fire, Miss Becky suddenly seemed amused on a different subject, for she burst into a roar of laughter and before I could ask her what she found amusing she began, "I wuz thinkin' 'bout my secon' husban', Johnnie Miller. Das his name. My fust husban' wuz a gambler. My secon' pick wuz a no 'count preacher. I quit dat thing in one yeah. Every time he sees me he ask me to let's go back, but if I keeps my mind I never will." I joined her in her laughter this time. She put another piece of wood on the fire and lit her pipe and leaned back in her chair as if she never was happier in her life. She continued about her second husband, "Ums doin' well an' ums gwineter let well enough do. Yo' see Miller jes' didn't know how ter pervide fer no fambly, dat's all 'tis ter hit. I allus believe in havin' plenty ter eat. I wuz raised dat erway. No, yo' see Miller, he had three chillen 'n I had eight, dat wuz lebben; thirteen wid me an' him. Miller would go ter town an' buy a twelve pound sack of flour jes' as big as anything and yo' know dat wuzent no mo' dan enough fer one good meal fer aller us. I sez ter him one day, 'Yo' let your daughter cook fer you an' I cook fer my chilluns.' Dat didn't do any good fer I had ter always be givin' dem sumpin' fer ter cook 'cause he wouldn't have nothin'."

"Honey," she said, "my chillen sez one day ter me. 'Maw us gwine ter leave heah cause we ain't gwineter take care of dat lazy no 'count man yo' done up an' married.' I didn't want my chillen ter do dat. I lef' dat man an' me an' my chillen we move heah. I treats him nice whenevah I sees him. He jes' wouldn't do; dat's all 'tis ter hit an' we jes' didn't wanter take kere of him an' his three chillen. Me an' my chillen we do de bes' we kin for each udder."

The whistle blew for twelve o'clock and Miss Becky jumped to her feet in surprise that it was so late. She exclaimed, "Laws is it twelve an' I done set heah an' ain't seen about de lady no dinner?" "Please," I said, "do not think of dinner for me. I always have my dinner at four and never care for anything to eat so early." She made me feel quite welcome to anything she had and assured me that it was a pleasure to her to feed company at her house. She said, "That's the reason I work so hard so I allus have plenty fer myself and others too."

Then she began to tell me about her community club. "Ev'ry yeah, for about thirteen years I have been havin' a little community club. We has twelve members an' each dese members pay a little along till August. By dis time dey each must have four dollars. At Christmas time dey each must be done paid in five dollars. Den we takes dis money an' buy rashuns in August and at Christmas. We gits heap mo' by buyin' in bulks lack dat. We git lard, flour, an' sugar. We go ter de chain store, he treats us nice. See dat's a good way ter do. Work together an' we all has plenty all de yeah, near 'bout hit!" "My, that's fine," I said. "Yas'm I ast de Lawd ter help me an' make a way 'n He'll sho answer prayer. Me an my granddaughter wuz both members so dis Christmas we had ten dollars. I got thirty-two pounds lard, forty pounds sugar, and six twenty-four pound sacks of flour an' den we had some lef' fer ter git flaver, soap an' little things lack dat. Come on," she said, standing up, "Come on, go in de smoke house an' let me show you what I got."

She continued to talk as we walked slowly out of the room into the hall, on out the door. "We got our seketary, president an' treasure. We allus sing an' pray in our club an' jes' have a good time. When we gits ready ter buy we gits us a wagon, goes ter town (Tuskegee) an' buys our things."

When we were into the yard I mentioned several nice-looking chickens that I saw. "Yas'm, I got 'bout eighteen hens. A'terwhile dey all gwineter be layin'." By this time we had reached the smokehouse. She unlocked the door and stepped in. "See," she said, "I got my meat packed down heah in salt in dese here boxes. I kilt two hogs 'n I got a can of lard and three gallons over. See in heah." She was raising a lid from a large wooden box. "See dis is whut I got from our little club." There was her sugar and flour all packed securely from rats. Then she displayed several sacks of peanuts, ten or more sacks of peas, including purple hull rice peas and speckle peas. On a shelf were a large pan of cracklin's, and several jars of canned fruit. "My, but you have plenty food in here," I said. "Yas'm, I has ter turn 'cause I gwineter feed my chillen an' den I lacks ter have plenty ter 'vide wid others. Yo' know das whut de Lawd wants us ter do."

"I tries ter git dat welfare to give my boy some work ter do but dey won't do hit. I jes' made three bales of cotton las' year. Yo' see one bale goes fer rent. One bale fer fertilizer an' money ter run de farm. Den das one bale to git clothes, sumpin' ter eat an' I got all three of dese boys heah. No dey won't give my boy a lick of work to do. But Becky gwineter make hit. God gwineter help Becky 'cause she trusses Him. Dem welfare folks dey give me nothin' but eye water fer to cry. Looks lack dey down on me but thank God you can't keep a good man down. I sent all my chillen ter school till dey jes' wanted to quit." We were now on our way back to the house. "Pretty soon," she said, "I'll be milkin' all three of my cows an' dat helps out whole lot. One thing, I ain't got no syrup dis yeah, but das all right too, 'cause I take sugar an' make my syrup. I jes' dare yo' take de Lawd wid yo', He sho' make a way outer no way."

"Sit down," she said as walked back into the room. "I ain't tole yo' 'bout my sellin' candy. Um sellin' candy fer a comp'ny. Yo' see." She showed me a card with several places to punch and a box of bars of candy. "Punch one," she asked me. I punched one and a card came out with five cents on it. I gave her the nickel and told her to keep the candy and sell it. "Ain't dat luck?" she smiled. "Thank yo' ma'm." She went to an old trunk, opened it, got out several pretty pieces of cloth and a pretty spread. "Dis is whut I got sellin' candy, dese four pieces. Dere is four yards in each of dese pieces. See," pointing to two dresses already made and hanging on the door, "I done made two, dey ready ter wear. I has ter do all lak dat ter keep agoin'. My chillen dey tries ter make me sit down but I can't sit down. I jes' got ter keep agoin'."

Her daughter, who lives just across the road came in just here and said, "Ma, they are havin' a party down the road. I think I'll go." Before she had finished, her mother was sighing, "Umph, umph, I jes' don't lack dem parties. Mos' of de youngsters cut up so dese days. Dey gits ter drinking an' fighting. Honey, ma wish yo' didn't want ter go, 'cause I be worried till yo' come back."

"Well, I guess I won't go." She assured her mother that she didn't want to "cause her no worry," and she went out. Miss Becky gave a sigh of relief. "It's so mucher trouble gwine on; I hates ter see um go to dese frolics. When I wuz a girl de boys didn't cut up lack dey do now. We would play nice games. I kin 'member how I useter love ter play Stealin' Partners. We would all git in a ring, each one have his own partner and one odd one would be in de ring, den we'd sing:

'Rosie, Lady Rosie
O..o..o Rosie
Rosie Lady Rosie.
I got a house ter put yo' in,
Rosie Lady Rosie.
I got a house ter put yo' in,
Rosie, Lady Rosie.'

All us would be clappin' our hands and pattin' our feet.[21] O, we had a good time," she laughed. "Den we useter have cake walks; dey give a cake ter de one whut walks de straightest. I useter git all dem cakes. O man, I could strut straight."

She got up and walked across the floor to show me how she useter strut. "I can't strut lack dat now, I got rheumatism in dese ol' joints now," she laughed. "But you do get about fine," I said to her. "Yas'm I been had good health, scusin' I useter have the toothache 'n I done had all of dem took out now. Dey useter give me so much trouble dat I won't let um put no more in my head; dey might hurt." She laughed at herself for this.

"I nevah had a doctor in my life. Wid all my babies I jes' had a midwife but she wuz good ez a doctor. She gid me a quart of whiskey wid ev'ry one of my chillen. Jes' made a toddy fer me an' let me drink it till I had had a quart. Yas'm dat's whut she'd do. Den she would make me stay in de house fer a whole month. Dat's reasons we ole folks so much mo' 'count dan our chillen, 'cause we tuk kere of ourselves."

"When my chillen wuz comin' up I didn't have no doctor neither. I jes' give dem tea an' home remedies. When all my chillen dey had de whoopin' cough, I would git someone ter kill me a crow. I take dat crow, boil him down wid salt. I take dat likker and give it to dem whut got de whoopin' cough an' hit sho' help dem.[22] Den when dey had de measles, and chicken pox I made dem go in de henhouse backwards an' come out forward, den I gi'e dem shuck and ginger tea an' I nevah had a minute's trouble wid nary one."[23]

"I 'member one time I jes' had chills an' chills and jes' couldn't git well. Dey tole me to steal jes' as much sugar cane as I could hold. I did this an' do you know I didn't have another

---

[21]Probably a play-party game of the courtship and marriage variety, many of which begin with a person in a ring.

[22]Browne, in *Popular Beliefs from Alabama*, p. 30, no. 433, records similar recipes using jay birds instead of crows.

[23]Corn shuck tea and ginger tea were two common folk remedies for measles, and some sympathetic magic from one's relationship to chickens was believed good for chicken pox; see Solomon, *Cracklin Bread*, pp. 140–41; and Browne, *Popular Beliefs from Alabama*, p. 79, nos. 1331, 1344.

chill! Yas suah, take de Lawd wid yo' an' use yo' head an' yo' boun' ter git erlong."

Miss Becky wore an odd but pretty little blue cap with white stripes. She wore a blue print dress with small white flowers in it and a blue and white check apron with a bib and a thick red sweater. Her hightop shoes had thick soles and she wore thick ribbed stockings. She weighs one hundred and sixty-five pounds and is about four and a half feet high. Despite the fact that she has no teeth, her face is full and round and there beams an everlasting friendly smile. "So glad yo' come ter see old Becky, I loves company. Wait a minute." She went out and soon returned with a paper bag. "Heah, yo' plant dese little rice peas in your garden. Dey taste jes' lack English peas. Den when yo' be eatin' dem yo' think of me. You wouldn't eat no dinner wid me, yo' jes' got ter have sumpin' so I give yo' dese peas. Don't you throw dem away, neither, yo' plant dem so yo' kin see how good dey is when dey green. Yo' come back ter see me ag'in."

Janey Gets Her Desires

by Rhussus L. Perry

This very attractive and convenient farm house is north of Tuskegee. The cream-painted house sets about a hundred feet from the Franklin and Dadeville highway. It is a pretty little bungalow that is sure to get a second look from passers-by. On the porch are pot flowers and porch chairs with white slip-over covers. On each side of the gate entering the lane leading up to this lovely house is a rock column about four feet high in which are growing pretty cedars. Several bushes of Crepe Myrtle are growing just inside by these columns. Green shrubbery grows along the rock-lined lane up to the yard where verbenas are blooming along the walk to the concrete steps.

The lawn is a thing of beauty. There lies on the left of this large lawn a lively rock garden where grow zinnias, verbenas and daisies. A large, shady pecan tree stands to the left of the lawn about fifteen feet from the left corner of the porch under which are two green lawn chairs. Pretty green shrubbery, some flowering, grows all around the house. A picturesque little flower garden of roses and other flowers lies on the right back side of the lawn where flitter bees, butterflies and humming-birds. A fence of shrubbery divides the front yard from the back yard. Setting on the right in the back is a large barn and stable; nearby is a chicken house and other little houses for various uses. There are lots and lots of Plymouth Rock and white Leghorn chickens in and around the stable. Peach, fig and pear trees are hanging with luscious fruit. A flower garden is in the back also. A well with concreted curbings is on the back with a rope and bucket hanging from a post over the well. A dipper and a cup are hanging there for passers-by. Of course this well is to be replaced very soon by the government pump system. The government also has the Dixie line electricity out on this farm.

When I told Janey my mission, she hesitated at first. After I explained why and for whom I wanted the information, she agreed to give it to me. So many people visit this rather unusual woman who has achieved an enviable reputation. She was peeling peaches and they were nice, ripe, soft ones. She likes to share, so we both enjoyed the luscious fruit. As we ate she began to tell me about herself.

"I was born right here in this community in 1876. I can remember very well how religious and good my mother was. She was a faithful Christian and always had family prayer. She taught us to kneel when we would pray. I can remember that my dad would sit up as we kneeled because he wasn't a Christian. My mother's daily Christian living and praying con- verted my dad. He joined the church and became a deacon. This made my mother happy. She lived to see all of us join the church."

"My parents were farmers and always worked hard and tried to teach all of us to work. My dad was brought here from Georgia a slave. Right here on this same spot my dad and mother bought 320 acres which belonged to the white people to whom my parents had been slaves. The white people said that they wanted their Negroes to have the land."

"I started to school when I was seven years old. My first teacher's name was Mr. Rich Pots. Oh, I was so happy to start to school. I worried mother long before it was time for me to start to school. We could not start to school until we were seven years old. I do not remember having one fight in school. There were two distinct classes in our school: one of these classes was called fat boy's class, and the pretty girl's class to which I belonged."

"I can remember how I always wanted something pretty for the house even when I was a little girl. I made my first quilt when I was about eight years old. When they would ask me what I wanted the Santa to bring me, I would always ask for vases for the mantel when I got a house of my own. I had seen large seven-room homes, about three of them in the commu- nity; of course they belonged to white people. I was a little girl but I had hopes of some day owning a seven-room house, nicely furnished, like those three seven-room houses in our commu- nity. Even though I had never seen a Negro in such a house, I believed that it was possible for anyone to work and save and get a beautiful home. And if this was possible I had a mind that I would be one to own such a home. Aside from a beautifully furnished home I longed to own a fountain pen, a watch and chain and a pair of nose glasses."[24] Here she laughed and said, "I have to wear glasses now and I don't find it so pleasant as I dreamed when I was a girl."

"I learned from my mother at an early age to love Sunday school and church. I remember a sermon the pastor preached when I was a child, but [already] a Christian. His text was, 'Delight Thyself in the Lord, and He Shall Give Thee the Desires of Thy Heart.' I believed this statement, together with my mother's faithful Christian life, helped me to struggle and strive to get those things which were the desires of my heart. Yes, I believed that if I would try to serve the Lord that he would help me to realize my desires. I always went to Sunday school and church and tried to do what I could in my church and community to help make it better. I tried and still do try to help in Christ's program to evangelize the world. I may can't do much, but I do all that I can as far as I know."

"I was not able to go on as far as I wanted to in school. So anxious was I to go to school that when I had a chance to go to Tuskegee, I was happy even though I did not have but fifteen cents. It was in 1895 I went to Tuskegee. At this time you did not have to pay an entrance fee. I worked in the day and went to school at night. I worked the first year in the teacher's home. I worked the next year for Mrs. Penny and the next year I worked in the sewing room. I had only one apron, but I washed that apron in the evening; I would get up early, iron that apron on the lamp chimney and make a clean appearance the next day. I got so bare for clothes that Mrs. Richardson, Capt. Richardson's wife that's at the Institute (she was a Miss Laura Mabry then), went to the 'barrel room' and got me some clothes.[25] At Tuskegee in those days the northern white people would send barrels of clothes down for poor children. The room where they kept these clothes was called 'barrel room.' They had plenty children who needed them. In those days we had plenty fine smart

---

[24]Pince-nez.

[25]Laura E. Mabry is listed on faculty and staff under "Laundering" in a 1901 publication; see Max Bennett Thrasher, *Tuskegee: Its Story and Its Work* (New York: Negro Universities Press, 1969 reprint), p. 211.

children who would come to school bare and penniless. They were poor but ambitious and Booker T. saw to it that these poor ambitious children were given a chance. I was one of these children who wanted a chance. I was given a chance and I worked as hard as I studied. My health failed me and I had to stop school. As I recall about my fifteen cents that I had when I entered school, the funny thing I had that fifteen cents when school closed. I was afraid if I spent my fifteen cents, something would turn up that I needed it worse for, so I held tight to that money."

"I decided to get married. I was only fifteen when I married the first time. I married Henry McBride. My life was shocked by a mob who lynched him. A man was found dead and they suspicioned that my husband did it. They had his trial but the jury split on it. So the side that wanted him hung took him and lynched him."

"I didn't let this coward me down. I decided to work and try to make a mark in life so that someone would know that I lived and had not lived in vain. Booker T. Washington would go round lecturing to farmers: he would always tell us to bring something to town with us to sell so we could have a little cash to get the things we needed without going in debt for everything. I took this in and profited by it. Then Mr. Washington would teach the farmers to raise plenty food stuff. This I did and it meant much to me. When he would send county agents around I always cooperated with them and I always found that they could help us in our farm problems."

"I made a sad mistake when I married my second husband. He was the type who did not want anything. His name was Johnny Leonard. We had land where we were trying to farm. This land was just washing away. I did not know anything about terracing, but I did know that if a ditch was dug across the field it would prevent the washing away of all the rich soil. My husband seemed perfectly satisfied about the land washing away. I studied the directions of the wash and I decided we would dig ditches to prevent it. I told my husband, Johnny, about what I thought should be done. He cursed me out, but I was determined about what I thought was right so I marked the ditch by digging holes along and then argued with Johnny until we argued into a fight and then he helped me to dig the ditches. This would happen every spring. An argument, fight and then the ditches. I would rake the ditches and help with all the hard work around the farm for I wanted something. I boarded the teachers, took in sewing and did every thing I could possibly do to try to fix up my little humble home. We had only one room and a dirt floor kitchen. But I had seen over to Tuskegee the nice toilets and I wanted one. I wanted a dining room too, so I tore down an old shed that we did not need and built a toilet myself. I took some of the boards and made a partition in my kitchen and made a dining room. The neighbors saw my toilet and my other fixings around so they followed. I was the first in my community to own a toilet. Before this time we all had thought the woods afforded a good enough place for a natural toilet."

"I kept on trying to make little additions to the home and trying to fix it so it would look attractive and this would make my husband mad. We just could not agree. He treated me so bad that I just went to court and asked for a divorce. Well, the court gave him everything, even the forty acres of land we worked together and bought. I did have forty acres of land my father left for me. But I did not have a mule or nothing to start my farm on the following year. But I still remembered, 'Delight thyself in the Lord and He shall give thee the desires of thy heart.' I still had faith in God."

"I had gone through so much bad treatment from my husband that I had nervous indigestion and the doctor had to put me on malted milk for a long time. When the deacons asked my husband why we parted, he said, 'She's too damned high-minded. She wants too much.' "

"I had a son in Cincinnati, Ohio. He decided to come down and help me on the farm. This was in 1918. After the crops were laid by, my son Lawrence McBride went to training camp at Tuskegee Institute. We made eight bales of cotton for which I got forty cents a pound. The government gave me fifteen dollars for my son and this helped me to pay the debt of $1,011.75 and to buy back the forty acres which the court gave my husband. I struggled hard this year to do these things. I did a lots of peddling and working at night. At this time I was so anxious to pay my debts and start fixing up my home that I had one dress for Sunday and going to town and one pair of slippers which I bought for fifty cents. I went to church and was not shamed for I believed so strong that if I delighted in the Lord and His works that I would have something someday."

"While my son was in training at Tuskegee he met and married Dottie Woods, oilwell queen. She helped me lots at that time. I had someone working on halves and I always carried good insurance on my little home. When the house burned, my insurance was paid."

"Mrs. Laura Daily and Mr. Robert Thurston was demonstrators at this time and is yet.[26] They taught me how to do proper terracing and to plant winter cover crops which has improved my land so very much. I continued to peddle to help myself so as to keep out of debt. I wanted to put that insurance into a new home. Mrs. Daily made my plans and helped me with the plans for this new home which I am in now. The house cost two thousand dollars. The insurance was seventeen hundred. I put that into the house and furnished it and moved into it in 1930. Right after this the prices on cotton dropped to five and six cents per pound. This left me with a big debt. I had another hard struggle, but I kept faith. In 1933 the government had the farmers to plow up their cotton and was allowing ten cents a pound and estimating a half bale to the acre. I had twenty acres planted. So I pulled through that dark spot. I have gladly followed the plans of the government ever since. It has helped me to have clear today my one hundred and eighty acres of land. The government is making it possible for us to enjoy electricity and pump system of running water. God bless the Roosevelts. Theodore Roosevelt gave farmers rural delivery and then comes F. D. Roosevelt and gives the farmer the joy of bright lights and running water. And F.D.R. has helped us in so many ways that we no longer feel forgotten. If I did vote I surely would vote for Roosevelt to be president another term."

"Well, I just keep on thanking God for letting me see the most of the desires and enjoy the things I used to long for. I recom-

---

[26]The farm demonstration teams set in motion by George Washington Carver of Tuskegee Institute.

mend anyone to delight in the ways of the Lord and He will surely give you the desires of your heart."

I should think Mrs. Janey Leonard certainly has the desires of her heart. As well as pretty outside and attractive, her home is very attractive inside. It is on the farm but as modern and attractively furnished as any city home. In the living room is a beautiful mahogany living room suite, a victrola, a library table on which sets an attractive table lamp. On the mantel are two very pretty vases. A pretty vase sets on the victrola. A large what-not rack in a corner with what-nots on the shelves, a smoking stand and a magazine rack, pretty scrim curtains with drapes and everything harmonizes beautifully in her rooms. All the floors are varnished and have becoming floor coverings. The guest bedroom has an oak vanity bedroom suite, white curtains with pastel floral drapes and becoming wall pictures and vases. The other two bedrooms are lovely, furnished with maple furnishings. The dining room has a rich oak dining room suite of nine pieces. A very attractive and gorgeous oblong mirror hangs over the buffet. The bathroom is furnished in white. The kitchen is very attractive. The wood and coal stove is soft green and yellow. Convenient shelves and a cabinet add to the convenience and neatness of this kitchen. A pair of snow white curtains with three rows of varicolored braid hang at the two windows. The pantry is inviting. Every shelf in this spacious pantry is filled with canned fruits and vegetables, jellies and jams. Excellent taste is shown throughout this lovely farm home in color, harmony and furnishings.

Mrs. Janey Leonard is now one of the highly respected citizens of Macon County. She is active in religious and civic organizations and president of one of them. She says she is happy. She says she always felt that people should live to be known, to be useful and to be looked on as one worthy of being an example for someone else.

At Father Timmons' Home

by Rhussus L. Perry

On a bright November day the fields were bare, the trees all adorned in their autumn colors. Despite the barren fields, there were lovely flowers in Father and Mother Timmons' clean and well-kept yard. There were marigolds, bachelor buttons and winter pinks. The cotton had been planted close up to the small yard, and around the house were several chickens of different kinds, a turkey gobbler and two turkey hens.

Noticing the cotton so very near the house, I asked, "To whom does this cotton patch belong?" Mother Timmons replied proudly, "It's ours; me and Timmons', yes dis is ours." Father Timmons interrupted, "I kin pick 'bout twenty-five pounds a day, too; can't pick mor'n dat 'cause my back gits so tired." He placed a hand on the small of his back as he continued, "I ain't what I use to be, an' yo' know my feet keep cold winter and summer, I dunno why."

By this time we had reached the rickety steps. Mother Timmons said, "Go right in our shack. 'Tain't much, but yo' welcome; so glad yo' come." After I had gone up the steps which had two or three holes worn in them, she came up bending down, using her hands to help herself. She wore a print dress pretty and clean and her hair was neatly done. She gets about splendidly to be eighty-three years old.

As she and I sat on the clean porch which was worn with age, talking and watching the turkeys strut among the flowers which adorned the yard, Father Timmons, who had gone into the house, came out presently with a good, juicy baked sweet potato. Smiling and bowing, he offered me the potato, saying, "We ain't got any dinner fit to offer yo', but here's a good ol' yeller yam, if yo' likes 'em."

Mother Timmons began talking about Tuskegee Institute, which gives them a satisfaction almost equal to that they get from their religion. Mother Timmons began by saying, "I've been goin' ter dat skule fer over fifty years. I jes' love it an' all dem teachers up dar." Then she folded her hands in her lap and shook her head. "Lawd I loved Booker T. I hated ter see 'm go.[27] I 'member once he wuz talkin' in de chapel and it wuz crowded plum full. Lawd I hates ter tawk erbout it. He wuz tellin' us how we otter live and love one 'nuther and have entrus in each udder." She gestured with palms downward to help explain the great emotion that she felt, and swaying her frail body she continued, "I wanted ter cry so bad, but I wuz shame ter cry dar in de chapel, so I took my hanchuf and crammed in my mouf. I put my head in my lap. I done fust one thing en ernuther. I wuz jes' 'bout ter holler." When she began again tears were shining in her eyes. "I wanted to hug Booker T. Washington in his coffin. I patted his face. I rubbed it. I jes' didn't want ter give 'm up."

I attempted to get her mind off Mr. Washington, asking, "Mother Timmons, do you remember when you were a little girl?" Her face beamed, "Yes, chile, I wuz a little girl in slavery time but I didn't have no hard time lak most niggers. My folks belonged ter old man James Greese, and Moster Greese didn't 'low nobody ter beat his niggers an' he didn't 'low white folks pullin' his little nigger chilluns' years lak de res' did. Why, he never hit a one of us a lick. And the good thing 'bout it all, he 'lowed de mothers all ter keep de chillun t'gether. He wouldn't sell chillun from de mas and pas. Mos' Greese got sick, en he sent fer all his niggers an' tole dem 'meet me in heben.' "

Father Timmons interrupted here by saying, " 'Twertin dat way wid me. My mother died when I wuz two weeks old, and da wuz er woman what nursed me til' I could eat an' git about. Den I wuz 'lowed ter stay in de white folks' house and help roun' de place, hunt turkey nesses. Old Ben Mott was his name. Dey wuz right kin' ter me. Dey give me one quilt ter sleep on and one ter kiver wid. But Old Moster had a son-in-law name Tony, and oh, my stars, he hated niggers. You know, dey jus' give little boys a shirt, no pants, and many times dey would twist my shirt over my head and beat me fer nothin'. When boss Tony cum fer ter

---

[27]Booker T. Washington set up Tuskegee in 1881, well within the memory of the people interviewed by Rhussus Perry. He died in 1915; see Marks, *Who Was Who in Alabama*, pp. 186–87.

live wid Mos' Ben I had ter git out. He 'lowed he didn't want no nigger ter live in de same house wid him. So den I had ter git down ter de quarter to live wher de other niggers lived. I had ter go fum house ter house an' beg um ter let lil' Henry come in. And honey, do yo' know, some of 'em 'ould holler at me 'fo' I c'u'd git ter de steps, 'doncha come in here; no room in here fer yo'.' Den it would be almos' dark 'n' I had nowheres to stay."

I interrupted here by saying, "You can well appreciate a home of your own, can't you?" A smile played over his face as he said, "Yas child, das reason ol' Timmons worked so hard when he young. Working to git all my chillun a home. I got eight, an' all eight of dem got forty acres of land." As he continued he leaned back in his chair like one confident of security. "President Roosevelt, he's a fine man, he believes in giving a man a chance. I b'lieves dat de Congress should be de fines' an' greatest church in de world; yas sir honest, upright, looking down on de poor wid a eye of pity jes' lak Roosevelt try ter get dem ter do. Yas sir, de President he wants us ter even be able ter read, us old folks. Way back yonder in slavery de paderole would git a nigger fer tryin' ter learn ter read."

"Paderole?" I asked, "what was that?" He burst into laughter as he began to explain, "Chile, de paderoles wuz ter keep bad niggers from gittin' worse, and ter keep dem from running away. Dey wuz unmerciful white folks. Sometimes dey tie you on a log and whip 'til de blood jes' run down." He laughed again and continued. "We use ter sing a song 'bout dem." He raised a hand as he began:

Please ol' moster don't whip me!
Whip dat nigger behin' de tree.

O, run nigger run, paderole ketch-u
O, run nigger run, jes' 'fore day.

I run, I run, I run my bes',
I run right close ter dat hornet's nes'.

Paderole run, dey run da bes'
Dey run right in dat hornet's nes'.[28]

As I started to leave, Mother Timmons said to Father Timmons, "Give her some our sugar cane. She got good teeth. Chew it, chile, and thank Gawd the paderole won't getcha."

---

[28]"Paderole" is a corruption of "patroller"; this song remained a popular folksong for a century after emancipation. See an almost identical version in Byron Arnold's *Folksongs of Alabama* (University, Ala.: University of Alabama Press, 1950), p. 121, and another version probably originally from Alabama in Newman Ivey White, *American Negro Songs* (Cambridge: Harvard University Press, 1928), p. 168, no. 23.

Jakob Hawthorne, Sculptor

by Rhussus L. Perry

In the ceramics division of the trades building, Tuskegee Institute, I found Jakob Hawthorne, a little brown-skinned man, about five feet tall and weighing about 130 pounds. He has keen, searching, clear eyes and a gentle, firm look. As I advanced toward him his eyes met mine and he smiled. His smile was full of kindness and understanding. All around me were students. On the floor were small piles of clay of various colors. Mr. Hawthorne greeted me with a warm handshake and gave me permission to watch the students working.

I wanted to know something about the little piles of clay, just where all came from. I was told that the clay, which is in seven hues, is found right on and near the campus. A group of girls were sorting the clay so as to get a purple color. Some of the lumps of clay were streaked with four or more colors, and the students, using a knife, separated the streaked pieces into color groups. Two large tubs were sitting close together. One was full of water; the other contained clay with just a little water above it. In getting clay ready for use it is first put into this tub almost full of water and is left there until wet through. It is then run through a very fine mesh which separates the clay from the sand. Hawthorne used a parable to explain: "Just as the good and the bad live together in this world, so does clay and sand," he said. "Just as the good Lord promised to separate the wheat from the tares when he comes, so do we separate the sand from the clay by use of a sieve."

When he had finished I asked just why the clay was put over in another tub of water. He explained that there was no water in this tub but that the clay is quite soft and it is put in here to settle. "The water, you see," he said, "is from the wet clay; just strained." He then instructed a student to take a ball of clay to a plaster vat. This was the next process in removing the water. A student then took the clay and pounded it for several minutes on tightly stretched cloth that was fastened to a work table. This was continued for several minutes. Mr. Hawthorne explained that this gets the air bubbles out. If holes or bubbles are left in the clay, heat penetrates the air holes when the clay is placed in the kiln and will cause the pottery to break. After the pounding a student took a piece of the clay and carried it over to a fine string of wire which was stretched tight, attached to a table. He tossed the piece of clay through the wire so as to cut it in two pieces. In this way the wedging of the clay is tested. If it has been wedged enough the cut will be smooth; if not the cut will show air holes.

We walked over to another group of students and I watched them as they cut small coils from clay, rolled them, stacked and shaped them as desired. With a wet knife they would smooth it together and shape it as they built. Mr. Hawthorne said, "This reminds me of our duty to our children. They should be shaped into usefulness as they grow."

Since we were very near the kiln, I asked Mr. Hawthorne if he would let me take a peep into it. "Oh," he said, "the door must not be moved ever so little until the oven is thoroughly cooled. If it is opened before it is cool the pottery will crack and break." Through a little hole covered with glass I looked into the oven and saw several small conical objects along with the pottery. They were leaning like candles when warm. These, Mr. Hawthorne explained, serve as a thermometer. They stand according to the heat. "We read the heat by the cones. When the cones go over or collapse, the oven is as hot as we need it to be," he said.

When I noted a beautiful white swan sitting on a shelf, I inquired, "Is this used as a model?" He smiled and said, "One of our students made that." He led me to his office where there were several shelves upon which were pieces of finished work. "All this is work done by students," he told me. There were dogs, buttons, plates, cups, saucers, vases, lamps, toys, book ends, busts. A student had almost completed a bust of Dr. George W. Carver, Tuskegee's famous Negro scientist. "You see," he said, "students who take up this work are fitted to work in factories or begin a little business of their own." "That's great, Mr. Hawthorne; you must have been inspired to do this work," I said.

He offered me a chair. I made myself comfortable for I could see that an interesting story was coming. He narrowed his keen searching eyes as a smile played over his face, and began: "When I was quite a small boy my father, Rev. R. E. Hawthorne, took me to see an art exhibition in Cincinnati, Ohio. In the surging crowd I was lost from him and when he found me he scolded me severely for not keeping up with my sisters who were in our party. I told my father that I was trying to find a bust of Frederick Douglass. Dad said, 'Son, you will not find a bust of Douglass here.' I was amazed," and he gave a shrug of his shoulders and looked in wonderment, living that hour all over again. "I said to my father, 'Teacher says the truly great people are perpetuated in marble and bronze. And Douglass was truly great.' My dad replied, 'Yes, son, I know, but we shall have to produce our own artists of our own race to portray our great men.' "

Drawing his shoulders up and with a determined look Mr. Hawthorne continued, "Well, I made up my mind that day I was going to make busts and statues of our great Negroes and put them where people can see them. That day my dad set me to thinking. I began to feel a responsibility to my people. Yes, I would perpetuate our great men and women in marble and bronze. Despite the hardships that I have met, the opposition and lack of confidence shown by my own race, I have devoted my time and money to taking masks and modeling busts of my people. You will find them scattered in schools and colleges throughout the United States and some in South America, the West Indies, and Canada."

"But back to Douglass," he was saying as a look of deep concern passed over his face. "I modeled Douglass under trying and peculiar circumstances. In Washington, D.C., beset with rent and food problems, I had worked in vain for three days trying to produce even a semblance of a likeness when suddenly God led me to the Washington Zoo. I say God led me because when I am working at a problem of any kind whether that problem is in clay or finance I pray for guidance; then go as far as I can with the means I have at hand, and invariably something turns up a solution. So I know God led me out to the zoo that day I was trying to model Douglass. The minute I walked in the zoo, a lion stood up as if to say, 'Take note!' I noticed and cried, 'There he is! My model, at last I have you.' " We both laughed heartily as he continued. "From that day, I formed a theory that all human beings resemble some animal, bird or reptile."

I said, "Your dad gave you the first inspiration to model and the lion gave you help to model your first truly great man." "Yes," he said, "that dad of mine was great. His name was Elijah. Even though he was a slave, he managed to learn to read and write when a boy. He was a slave of United States Senator Garrett Davis of Bourbon County, Kentucky. Senator Davis had a son who was about the same age as my father and frequently they would fight. One day dad gave Garrett Jr. a whipping which caused the boy's nose to bleed. Young Garrett's mother didn't like it and told my dad that she would see that Garrett, Sr. whipped my father for that. The Civil War was being fought and although a mere boy, my dad wanted to join the army. To avoid that whipping from Senator Garrett, he decided to run away and join the army. Oh, but he tells of some blood-curdling experiences. My dad joined the Union side of the army. One of the men on the opposing side was fighting and tried to take dad for a servant. Dad barely escaped being killed. In the fight he got a sword belonging to one of General Morgan's men. I have that sword now. I cherish it as a precious heirloom, and intend to keep it as long as I live."

"Believe it or not," he said as his face beamed, for he seemed happy as he talked of his father, "fate brought my dad and Garrett, Jr. together after they had grown up. It happened that Mr. Garrett Davis, Jr. was chief clerk in the pension office in Washington, D.C. My father was now a popular minister. I was working for Dr. Hrdlicka[29] in Washington, D.C. when my dad visited me, and informed me that he had learned that Mr. Garrett Davis, Jr. was chief clerk in the pension office and suggested that we go to see him. I replied, 'What? After bloodying his nose, running away and all that? Besides, you know he is grown up now, and aristocratic and all. Aren't you afraid you will get a cool reception?' 'I can't help it,' said dad. 'I want to see that boy.' So we went over to the office. Dad told the attendant to tell Mr. Garrett Davis that there was a man to see him, and in a few

---

[29]Ames Hrdlicka (1869–1943) developed the Division of Physical Anthropology in the U.S. National Museum beginning in 1903; see *Dictionary of American Biography, Supplement Three 1941–1945* (New York: Charles Scribner's Sons, 1973), pp. 371–72.

minutes a rich-looking, stout, handsome fellow came our way. My heart grew faint, for I hated to see my fine, proud old dad's feelings crushed. I just knew Mr. Garrett would receive a Negro caller coolly. He approached us, looked at each one of us with a stern but kind stare. Then my dad spoke. 'You don't remember me, do you?' For a second he gazed in wonderment at dad. Then Garrett, Jr. grabbed him in a close embrace. There were tears in their eyes, and they were living boyhood days over again. I walked away a few steps to avoid more of the scene, for I, too, was becoming sentimental."

"After they had talked a while, dad called me and told him I was a sculptor and that I was working there for Dr. A. Hrdlicka, the curator of the division of physical anthropology in the National museum. Mr. Davis said, 'You must be good if you work for Dr. Hrdlicka. What are you doing?' I told him that Dr. Hrdlicka had hired me to assist Mr. Frank Mischa in modelling the government exhibit for the Pan-American Exposition. As I related the story of my work for Dr. Hrdlicka to him, he seemed as interested as my own father. He said, 'Well, well, Elijah, just look what you have produced! You beat me.' He insisted on dad dining with him but previous engagements prevented. We both were happy. Dad had lost and found again a friend."

I interrupted him to say, "It must be wonderful to enjoy association with fine people like that." "Well, yes it is," said Mr. Hawthorne. "It is pleasant to remember." Then he continued with a recital of his experiences in modelling. "I assisted Dr. J. W. Pryor, head of department of physiology, State College (white) of Lexington, Kentucky, for two years in illustrating anatomy for a textbook, and Dr. Burris A. Jenkins, president of the old Transylvania University, Lexington, Kentucky, in making a miniature model of the main building of the institution, to be sent to the Louisiana Purchase Exposition at St. Louis. Then Guiseppi Moretti, an Italian sculptor, had me to assist him with one of his important commissions. An industrial company hired me to model a replica, two inches in height, of the Columbus Memorial which stands in front of the Union station, Washington, D.C., to be sold as a paper weight on Columbus Day."

"I have enjoyed working with teachers also in several of our colleges and schools," he added. "For two years I taught ceramics at the State school, Pine Bluff, Arkansas. Professor B. F. Hubert had me to give a course in correlated art in the summer school, 1932, of Georgia State Industrial College, Savannah, Georgia. Professor H. Council Trenholm, president of Alabama State Teachers' College had me to give his teachers a similar course. Dr. Joseph J. Rhoads used me as guest lecturer on fine arts at Bishop's college, Marshall, Texas, in 1935 and to teach art in the summer school of 1935 and 1936."

"It seems a paradox, that notwithstanding my avowed intention to devote my life to modelling busts and figures of Negro life, my best commissions with the exception of two have come from the white race. Two things my race must develop: confidence in the ability of their own race, and appreciation of art. A Negro artist who must depend upon his own group for support is to be pitied. I cherish the fact that John L. Webb gave me the job of modelling Judge L. J. Winston, founder of the Woodmen, in bronze. It is now in the cemetery in Natchez, Mississippi. For this he gave me $1500. I have modelled busts of Booker T. Washington, Paul Lawrence Dunbar, Frederick Douglass, Rev. C. T. Walker, Bishop Richard Allen, Bishop John E. Hurst, Mr. John L. Webb, Rev. E. C. Morris and many others. Last year Father Bruno Drescher, a Catholic priest of Chicago, commissioned me to model and cast one hundred statuettes, one foot in height, of Blessed Martin DePores. Father Drescher wrote me these kind words: 'I do not believe there is a sculptor in the United States who can excel you in producing a likeness.' "

"In 1903 I was called to Louisville, Kentucky, by Attorney William Marshall Bullitt to make a plaster cast of a trunk of a tree and the surrounding ground where R. C. Whayne, a merchant, was alleged to have committed suicide. Two white sculptors had been previously offered the job, but both considered the venture impractical since plaster poured upon the ground will not relieve. On my arrival, I went to Mr. Bullitt's office, and found him alone. While I was consulting with him, in rushed a white man exclaiming, 'Eureka!' and signalled Mr. Bullitt to follow him into another room. After being out of the room a few minutes the two men returned and Mr. Bullitt explained to me that the gentleman present had been offered the job first, and had now found a way to do the work. He further explained that this gentleman who was a sculptor would spread a sheet upon the ground and that the weight of the plaster poured upon it would cause it to conform to the various configurations. He further volunteered to repay my railroad fare and also to pay for the loss of a day's work. I replied, 'That will be all right if you want a reproduction of the sheet rather than of the ground.' "

"The sculptor said, 'That's the only way that it can be done.' Mr. Bullitt turned to me and said, 'He says that's the only way that it can be done.' I simply replied, 'I heard him.' Mr. Bullitt asked, 'Can you make the direct copy without the sheet?' I replied that I could. The sculptor exclaimed, 'He can't do it! Mr. Bullitt said, 'Hawthorne, he says you can't do it.' Again I said, 'I heard him,' and again Mr. Bullitt said, 'Now, are you sure that you can do this?' Whereupon I replied, 'I can.' Turning to the sculptor, Mr. Bullitt said, 'We will have to employ this other man since he says he can do the work.' Here I was fully convinced that the color of your skin does not always matter with a white man. It is the ability to do a desired job well that counts. 'Get your hat, Hawthorne,' he said, 'let's go.' "

"We sat on the street car silently for eight slow miles. We finally arrived at Jacob's Park where I was shown the spot to be reproduced. The work was finished and set up in the court room as an exhibit in the evidence. So realistic was the ground and tree here represented that the opposing counsel, Attorney O'Neal, accused the defense with mutilation of private property, his view being that I had literally undercut the ground and tree and brought the natural scene into court. When I was called to the stand Attorney Bullitt asked, 'Hawthorne, what is that?' pointing at the cast. 'It is a plaster cast,' I replied. 'Can you prove it?' asked Attorney Bullitt. 'Yes sir,' I said, taking a knife from my pocket, sticking it in the tree and revealing a white spot of plaster. This aroused quite a commotion in the court room as there were many others beside Attorney O'Neal who thought the cast was an actual figure."

"Two things in my early life prepared me for this successful undertaking. One was the accident of poverty so that I could not afford to buy modelling clay, and had to use mud. In making my casts from the mud I learned by experimenting how to make the plaster relieve. The other was a thing that happened when I broke a limb from my father's favorite peachtree. Overcome with the temptation to secure a peach I leaped high into the air to lower the limb so that I might get the coveted fruit. To my consternation the whole limb came down, peeling the bark for several inches. Knowing that my father would soon return from his church duties I hastily instructed my younger sister to gather all the peaches from the limb while I ran into the house, secured my box of paints and painted the scar a deep Van Dyke brown. It looked as if it were almost decayed. The scar was retouched with turpentine several times until it did not shine, and the detached limb was hastily deposited in a rock quarry several yards from the house. When dad came he missed the big limb from the tree but for his life could not account for it as he did not see any scar. To this day, although this incident helped me in coloring, I always feel guilty of having deceived my father." I joined him in laughing the matter off.

"I will tell you this and then I will let you go." He was too polite to say he would have to go; it was now ten minutes past twelve, and the class had been dismissed by his assistant while he lingered on to give me the information which I so eagerly sought. "I can never forget the words of Booker T. Washington when I took his life mask. He was dictating the answer to a letter received from a man who had asked him to state the thing for which he was most thankful. Mr. Washington began by saying, 'First, let me say, I am thankful that I have something to do. A man who has something to do is to be envied. A man who has nothing to do is to be pitied. I would not care to live in a world where there are no difficulties to be met and no problems to be solved.' These words have stayed with me," Mr. Hawthorne exclaimed.

"I would love to see that mask, Mr. Hawthorne," I said. Readily consenting he reached down, picked up a hand bag, opened it and carefully lifted the mask which was wrapped in black cloth. The mask looked so much like the head of the real man that I was amazed. Smiling he said, "Does it look like him?" "My, but it does!" I assured him. "See the pimples, the lines and the expression of his face. There they all are as in life."

Mr. Hawthorne said he was graduated from the Chandler Normal College, formerly located at Lexington, Kentucky. Then he studied two years in the art department of the New England Conservatory of Music at Boston, later spending two years in the Cincinnati Art Academy. He also studied pottery making, glazing and firing in the summer school of the Pittsburgh Normal School in Pittsburgh, Kansas, and has taken various extension courses.

One of the life histories from the Alabama Writers' Project was about one of the Alabama writers herself. Woodrow Hand wrote an extensive life history of Gertha Couric, author of the article that follows. Mrs. Couric was a native of Eufaula, apparently of a family of some social standing—Hand described her as "an attractive woman just past forty," "steeped in the traditions of the Old South." Her husband's death in 1918 left her with a six-year-old daughter to support, a depleted savings account, no income, and no job experience. She launched a successful restaurant business and at the onset of the Depression moved on to a series of major hotels in the South, including the Tutwiler in Birmingham, as hotel hostess. Couric eventually moved back to Eufaula, again running a dining room, and shortly before this interview with Hand fell and broke her ankle. Three months in a cast forced her to give up her job and at that point she got an appointment to the Writers' Project.[30] One of the most prolific writers on the project, she contributed ten life histories from the Eufaula area. Most are descriptions of mill workers, too short to be very detailed, as in the one printed earlier in this section. An interesting longer account of two older women successfully running a 400-acre farm already has been published as "A Day on the Farm" in the Terrill and Hirsch edition of Such As Us. *The following account is Couric's longest life history, curious in that it is the history of a man through the eyes of his wife.*

Bob Johns, Fisherman and River Rat

by Gertha Couric

Bob Johns lives on the banks of the Chattahoochee River in a little four-room cottage, high up and with concrete steps leading to it. Bob has five children, all living and all married but the

---

[30]See Woodrow Hand, "Gertha Couric—Hotel Hostess, WPA Worker," in Alabama life histories, FWP—Couch Papers.

youngest boy. He married Lizzie Brown about twenty-five years
ago. She is an expert laundress. Lizzie has never had any
children of her own. She tells her story in this way: "Bob just
heired his children. All five of them are bastards, but Bob gave
them his name; ain't none got the same ma. But Bob has been
mighty good to all of them."

"Bob has been a fisherman all of his life. He started when he
was just a little boy. Me and Bob been married nigh unto
twenty-five years. His youngest child was just two years old
when I married him. His ma was dead and he and Bob was
living down here all by themselves. He had a woman that
cooked and looked after little Bob for him, and his other chillun
was living with their mas. Bob always took care of them. I mean
he supported them, clothed them and fed them. The two oldest
boys are fishermen with him. He pays them just like he does his
other help. His two girls live up North."

"Little Bob lives with us; he railroads. I loves him just like he
is my own and he sho is a smart and good boy. He ain't married;
hope he won't; nigger gals is so trifling these days. Ain't got no
morals a-tall."

"Bob says the best he can recollect is he was about ten years
old when he first started to fishing. He is sixty now. So that
means he's been fishing fifty years. The way he started was this.
Dave Johns, Bob's pa, owned this place on the river. I'll tell you
about Dave later on. He owned this house we live in now, only
we have added two rooms and a porch and a lots of other
things."

"Mr. George Vaughn had a little one-room house further
down on the river. You 'member him? He's been dead now 'bout
twenty years. Well he is the man that learnt Bob to fish and
swim. At first Bob said he used to follow him about just like a
little puppy; would get up before day and go with him in his
bateau a-fishing. In them days they used to seine in the
Chewalla Creek; it's ag'in' the law now.[31] Mr. Vaughn learnt

---

[31]Unrestricted seining was outlawed only in 1907 in the legislation accompanying the
establishment of a state department of fish and game; see *Code of Alabama*, July 27,
1907, vol. 3, *Criminal*, prepared by James J. Mayfield (Nashville, Tenn.: Marshall &
Bruce Co., 1907), p. 544, sec. 6901.

him how to set out traps and lines; he learnt him everything there is about fishing. He makes good money at it. Mr. Vaughn learnt all the older white men in Eufaula to swim and Bob learnt all the niggers. Whenever anybody ever fell in the river or jumped in to kill themselves, Bob and Mr. Vaughn would always do the diving to find the bodies. Since Mr. Vaughn has been dead, Bob's been doing it and many a body has he found. Folks don't drown themselves like they used to, though, I am glad to say."

"In Bob's young days—he don't do it now—he used to swim across the Chattahoochee right here at the wharf four and five times without stopping, and they says it's third to the swiftest river in the world; and it's terrible wide. They call him the 'river rat.' When he was a young man he lived on the river, slept in a tent, camped there. I thought it was awful but he would do it. Now, he is not, well, his heart is bad, he works too hard. Gets up at four in the morning. I get up and cook his breakfast. He goes all day without food and when he comes home at night he eats too much. Yes'm, he is a fisherman right. In the days when the steam boats was a-running, them was the days for Bob. The *Kelly* and the *Bradley* and the *City of Eufaula;* he never missed a boat. He could hear her miles long 'fore he could see the smoke."

"When Bob gets through in the day, you know the winter days are so short, he puts his lines out at four o'clock in the afternoon, then comes home. I always have a good hot meal for him with plenty of coffee. He won't eat fish except now and then. He smells 'em so much he turns ag'in 'em. He likes his collard greens and beef steak."

"Now he goes back at eight and gets his fish off his lines and puts 'em in the fish boxes all along the sides of the river. That keeps 'em alive. The boxes have a wire top that lets the water in. He has four and five men that work for him. He owns twelve bateaus. He has his fish boxes miles up and down the river and creeks on both sides. He changes 'em every now and then. He fishes mostly in the Chattahoochee River, but he works the Chewalla, the White Oak and Barbour Creeks. His average catch a day is about two hundred pounds; sometimes a hundred and fifty and again two hundred and fifty. He don't fish on

Saturday and Sunday. He's got religion. He wouldn't fish on Sunday for nothing!"

"Bob couldn't get along without his little 'nip' when he is working; its so damp and foggy and wet on the banks. He would die with pneumonia sho' if he didn't have it. But I ain't never seen him drunk in his life. He knows how to take it. It's a pity these other nigger men and white gentlemens too don't know how. Bob is honest too. That's his religion. He would cut off his right hand before he would sell a fish that wasn't all right. His fish are all breathing and wiggling on his lines. He works every day and night from January 'til June, then stops off in June. In the summer months he has his fish frys.[32] Don't sell fish in the summer because it's too hot to keep them. When he has his fish frys, the fish are still alive; that's why they are so good."

"Bob is famous for his fish. He puts out his nets (he don't seine) from January the first 'til the fifteenth of March. Then after that he just hooks and lines. In September he starts back to work. He don't work in the Christmas month though."

"He has certain days to sell his fish in different places. He sells four lines 25¢, 50¢, 75¢, and $1.00 depending on how many and the kind of fish. He has better luck 'catching' at night than he does in the day. The best time is in the full moon. He catches channel catfish, bream, rock fish, mud cat, eels and any fish that runs in the stream he sho' gets 'em. He sho' is lucky and they calls him a expert. If he comes across a tainted fish he gives 'em to the niggers. They hangs around him like Grant around Richmond. The stronger a fish smells the better a nigger likes 'em."

"He has made good money too. He has a car; 'tain't much of a car, just a fish car. He sells his fish in Eufaula Tuesdays and Wednesdays. Thursdays and Fridays he goes out of town. He don't go hisself though; he sends one of his men. They peddle Georgia Thursday; Cuthbert, Dawson, Albany and little places. Then Friday they peddle Alabama; Clayton, Comer, Midway and Union Springs. He has regular customers and always sells

---

[32]In much of the South, annual summer fish fries seem to have preceded Fourth of July barbecues; see Blount County Historical Society, *The Heritage of Blount County* (n.p., 1972), for one woman's reminiscences.

out. Saturdays he sells 'cut fish' to niggers. 'Cut fish' is the big red fish he cuts in small pieces. The red fish he catches weighs from eight to twelve pounds and more.[33] All the red fish he gets in the week time, he puts in his fish boxes and keeps live 'till Saturday morning. Then 'bout four o'clock he gets up and with one or two of his men he gathers 'em up and cuts 'em in small pieces; puts 'em in push carts, takes 'em up town and before nine o'clock he is sold plum out to niggers and poor white folks. Then Bob comes back home and has a day of rest. He sho' needs it, cause he is sho' overworked. There is a lot of folks right here in Eufaula been living here all their lives, ain't got no idea what a big business the fish business is right here."

"He has had some narrow escapes too. Fell in the river lots. Course he is a fine swimmer, but this last time his clothes and boots was so heavy it was hard to swim and the current was swift. He lost his gun and his bateau. The bateau was overloaded; that's what made it sink. He is a good bateau maker too. He makes his own boats. He also makes boats for sale. They are row boats."

"Fish bite better when the moon is full. He has a camp on the mouth of White Oak Creek, on the banks of the Chattahoochee River. He uses spring lizards and stump grubs to bait his hooks and trot lines. A trot line goes from one side of the river to the other with heavy weights on it. The spring lizards are caught in little branches or springs, under leaves and moss and make fine bait. A 'set hook' is just one hook, close on the banks, scattered up and down sometimes a hundred or more tied on willow trees or put on sticks stuck in the bank.[34] Some of these set hooks catch catfish overnight weighing twelve pounds and over. He fishes too with a basket made cone-shape, out of white oak or hickory strips. This is baited with old cheese or peanut meal or sour meal put in the baskets at the bottom of the river or creek bed. A wire is tied to a tree on the bank to hold it. It is made just like a rat trap. If a large fish gets in it, it can never get out. He puts all these lines out at night. His fishing is done mostly at

---

[33]Redfish is one coastal name for the channel bass or red drum (*Sciaenops ocellata*), but the fish referred to here is probably river redhorse (*Moxostoma carinatum*).

[34]Also locally called "bank hooks" or "limb lines."

night. He has little nigger boys that gets most of his bait; his
spring lizards and his stump grubs. They find the stump grubs
mostly in old wood, old stumps and old trees. Stump grubs are
worms," she explained.

"I'll tell you a secret, missey, I know you won't tell, but that's
all right, I ain't gonner call no names. Many a night Bob comes
home just a-laughing. A lot of these white gentlemens that goes
a-fishing, if they don't have no luck, they buys a string of live
fish from Bob. They goes home with a string of fish just
a-kicking. They strut up town and tells everybody and their
wives and brags about what a fine fisherman they is. That is
what you calls 'fish caught with a silver hook.' Bob has the silver
jingling in his pocket and he is glad."

"I told you that he don't sell fish in the summer, but he has his
fish frys from June till September. He makes right good money
at it. It depends on how many comes. He gets fifty cents a
person. They always lets him know about how many is coming
so he will know how much to fix for. They brings the pickles,
the bread and the beer and 'things.' I means liquor. He fur-
nishes the fish, the onion bread and the coffee. It ain't no easy
job. If it is a big fish fry, say fifty men or more, he fishes two
nights all night long straight running. My God, how them men
can eat fish! Some eat ten and fifteen apiece. You know a drink
or two before eating sho' gives you an appetite. I help him
always at the frys; help him cook."

"He has a long wooden table that he made. We have two large
coffee pots that hold two gallons apiece. We puts two pounds of
coffee apiece in sacks in each pot. That makes enough coffee.
We have over a hundred tin cups and use paper plates. We
make two fires. Get our wood first thing, then we cleans our
fish. That's not hard; we are used to it. Then we make our onion
bread, 'hush puppies.' To make 'em you cut up a pair of onions
real fine, mix that with meal, add salt, make in small balls and
fry in the same pot the fish are fried in. Put 'em together. When
they rise to the top they are done, a golden brown, piping hot,
and are they good? We uses as much as three and four gallons of
boiling lard. Our frys are sho' wuth fifty cents a plate."

I asked Lizzie how she liked living near the river. She said,
"It's lonely sometimes, when the wind blows at night. Sounds
are lonely, the hooting of an owl from away down the river, the

whip-o-will, the bullfrogs, crying for rain; and the crickets. I don't like to hear no screech owl; that's a sign of death.[35] When the river overflows, Bob checks out. He takes out his traps, boxes and lines. We are too high up on the bluff for it to come to our house. It's a big river and it gets over in Georgia terrible."

"Bob's good and steady now. Before I married him he was one bad man after women in his young days. He ain't no more. We are both getting along. Bob was proud of his pa, Dave Johns and his ma, Mandy. Dave been dead 'bout fifteen years. He was born in Virginia and was Lieutenant John's bodyguard. Went through the War with him until Gettysburg. He died on the battlefield there in the arms of Mr. William Ray of Eufaula and as he was dying gave Dave to Mr. Ray. After the War Mr. Ray brought Dave back to Eufaula with him and built him a house on the bluff. He was carriage driver and butler for Mr. Chauncey Rhodes. He married Mandy Thomas and they had seven children, Bob being one of the youngest. Bob always likes to talk of his father."

To have one's home on the high banks is pleasant; Bob's home is on such a bank. One can look across the lovely Chattahoochee; see the sun rise and set; see in the moonlight and starlight the deep, swift river and the expanse of fertile savannahs below it. The Alabama side—all down the steep one hundred and fifty foot bank of Bob's home—nature has landscaped lavishly with an abundance of green growth, oak and hickory trees, long and short-leaf pines, white and rare mirica, seven-bark, heart-shaped leaves of red bud, magnolias starred with blossoms, blooming elderberries, mulberries festooned with gray moss; lacy maiden-hair ferns hanging in bunches from the marl banks. In the spring the yellow jasmine, dogwood, honeysuckle and red bud give color to the green. All of this glorious beauty spreads to the water's edge. Sandy beaches reach along the opposite shore. A silvery ribbon of road starts at the filigree-like steel bridge, and runs its way on to the inviting tree-covered rises where the river curves. Nestled in all this loveliness is the cottage of Bob Johns, fisherman and 'river rat.'

---

[35]Browne, in *Popular Beliefs from Alabama*, pp. 191–92, recorded eight similar Alabama views of screech owls as harbingers of death.

Part Four

From Urban Mobile and the Rural Coastal Plain

Jack Kytle was described in more detail in the introduction to the Coosa River stories in Part Two. As assistant director for the Alabama Writers' Project during its life history writing phase, he was the only writer with funds for travel. His story from Washington County deals with the Alabama Cajan community, a group of uncertain relation to the Acadian stock of Louisiana.[1]

Jake Gaw, Cajan Turpentiner

by Jack Kytle

There is a desolate stretch of gullied, sandy land on the western banks of the Tombigbee River, in Alabama's southwestern corner. The land is poor, covered by cutover pine timber and scrub oak. Raw gashes, with tin turpentine cups nailed beneath them, are on all the pines; but the resin drains sluggishly. The trees are too small to produce a steady flow. Threading through the region are dim logging roads, neglected for years, and filled with stump ends and brush. They are flanked by forests inhabited by razorback hogs, wild turkey, deer, and other game. And far back from the roads, in isolated places and sometimes as many as ten miles apart, are squat, weathered huts that house a people of vague racial origin.

This is the land known to Alabamians as the "Cajan Country." Here for more than a hundred years dark, solemn men, women and children have existed on what they earned from turpentining and lumbering. Now, with these resources almost gone, many of them admit that they are facing an uncertain future.

The Cajan houses never have more than three rooms, and most of them are either one or two-room structures. The windows have no glass panes, no screens. Plain pine boards nailed to hinges keep out the winter winds, and in summer flies swarm through them unmolested. Many of the Cajans have withdrawn so completely into isolation that they are unable or unwilling to

---

[1]Carl Carmer, in *Stars Fell On Alabama*, pp. 258–59, gives three local and mutually exclusive accounts of Cajan origins.

obtain outside aid. Their means of earning a livelihood have almost disappeared, and most of them live in bitter poverty. Others struggle to better their condition and are unwilling to admit that the future is without hope. Jake Gaw is one of these.

He is a wiry Cajan, nervous of movement. He is in his early thirties and has lived in Washington County all his life. As long as he can remember he has worked in turpentine and lumber. His father was a turpentine and lumber worker before him. The father, however, sometimes managed to pay all his debts and still have some money left. Jake says he has not been able to do this. The father even managed to buy forty acres of land; but the trees were larger and more plentiful then, and prices were better.

Jake Gaw and his family of three live in an unpainted pine-board cabin of three rooms in a community called Happy Hill. Like several others of his people, he married a white woman, and they have two children—a girl twelve years old and a baby boy. Gaw is proud of his people, claiming good Spanish and Indian blood.

He stood surveying his land with solemn eyes, his dark head bare and erect. Ditches pierced the sandy earth between the slim pines. The land looked as though it had never been turned by a plow, but Jake Gaw said, "Maybe I can a-grow something here; I theenk it might make corn, yes, and some cotton." He turned as he stood in the weed-flanked trail and looked back upon his cabin, some fifty yards away. "See," he said, "I have jus' built her. She's a purty house, I theenk; better anyway than the one we moved out of about three miles over yonder. She still needs steps and a ceiling. Maybe I can a-get to that later on." The cabin stood, stark in yellow newness, among the small pines, some of whose branches brushed the roof. All of the windows were without panes. The weeds and brush had not yet been cleared from the yard, although Gaw explained that he would get to this task later. A large circular block of pine, apparently sawed from the stump of a tree, was placed before the front door to serve as a temporary step.

Gaw walked with his visitor up the newly beaten trail, and together they entered the cabin. In what he called the front room was an iron-post bed, better than those usually found in

Cajan houses, and a somewhat battered dresser. A rag rug, gay in its red and blue coloring, was on the floor in the center of the room. His wife sat on the edge of the bed, her baby cuddling at her breasts. She said loyally, "One good thing about this country: it may be lonely, but we never have to worry about being robbed, as you people do in Birmingham. We never have had anything stolen from us out here, and even when I am alone, I never bother to lock a door."

She shifted the baby to her knee and bounced him until he laughed gleefully. "Of course, our place isn't pretty now," she admitted, "but we will improve it as we go along. I teach over at the Cajan school, you know, and I have very little time now to tidy things up. I just have to leave a girl here with the baby, working at odd times about the house. You see, I have not even had the time to hang my pictures."

Gaw led the way from the front room into the kitchen, where a squat wood stove stood in one corner. In the center of the room was a long pine table upon which was heaped a small cluster of commodities. These included salt pork, lard, salt, a paper sack filled with flour, and another with corn meal. He explained that they eat only the simplest things, "because, you see, I am the cook; and I can't a-cook much. My wife, she too tired for anything when she gets done with the kids up there in school."

The visitor was not taken into the other room, but a glance through the open door revealed only odds and ends of furniture. These included a chair bottomed with calfskin and a washstand. Several pictures yet to be hung were on the floor, leaning against the rough walls. Returning to the bedroom, Gaw drew up chairs about the large open fireplace in which burned a blaze made of pine knots. He talked then about the turpentine business. "It's a-no good," he explained. "It hasn't been for a long time. A man, he can't a-live on fourteen cents a day, and that is all the turpentine brings a gallon. Resin, it brings only 'bout four cents a pound. One time there was a-money plenty to be made in these woods. Some people got lots of it. But now the trees, they are jus' too little. It will take years 'fore they grow up to be any good again."

"I used to get some work in the sawmills 'bout here, but mos' of them have a-closed down now. It's got to where there's no work for anybody. I sometimes walk all the day around to my turpentine cups, but it's awful to fin' such a little bit of resin. It makes me theenk that we're a-jus' wasting our time fooling around with it. I theenk maybe some big industry should a-come down in here, even if I don't know what it would be. So many of our people could be helped that way. Something's got to come, or else they must go away somewhere. But they're all like me, I guess. I was a-born on this place; I helped my father here, and it would be a bad thing to leave. I don't think any of us will a-have to leave. Something's bound to come along."

"We've been lucky in a way, me and my family. When my wife's teaching, we get along as well as mos' anybody. That gives us better'n twenty dollars a month. I jus' don't know what I'd a-done without her." Elizabeth Gaw glanced at her husband, drawing the baby closer. She smiled a little, saying, "We never suffered for anything, and we've been together more than twelve years." She is a sturdy woman, short and a little plump. Her eyes are brown and frank, her hair dark and done up in a knot at the back of her head. Fourteen years ago she came to Washington County from her home in Bessemer, Alabama, to teach in the Cajan schools. And teaching here she fell in love with Jake Gaw, "because he was the most considerate and most lovable man I had ever known." They were married, and she said proudly, "We agree on about everything; we never have any quarrels." She glanced again at her husband, brushing strands of hair away from her face with her free hand, and he nodded solemn agreement.

Jake and Elizabeth Gaw have never minded the antagonistic attitude of some people living in Washington County who oppose the marriage of whites and Cajans. In this county, Cajans are classed as "colored people," and a great deal of concern has been aroused by the problem of intermarriage, which is by no means rare. The Gaws agree: "Our marriage is our own business. So long as we are happy together, why should it concern anyone else?"

Their daughter, Faye, attends the Cajan school, where she is in the fifth grade. The school has only seven grades, and after she finishes, the Gaws hope to send her to high school; perhaps to college. They realize that she can never attend high school in

Washington County, where anyone with a trace of Cajan blood is forbidden to enter the white schools; but they have made plans to complete her education, even if she is forced to attend school outside of Alabama. She is a shy girl, large for her age. Her features are like those of her mother, but her eyes and hair are a shade darker. She hopes someday to study music although there is not a piano in her community. She has no means even of obtaining the latest sheet music, because Cajans seldom venture into town, and they never have the money to buy anything except necessities. But she hums the few religious hymns and spirituals she has learned.

Jake Gaw, like nearly every other Cajan, has only a limited education. He can read, and he says that he can do fairly well at the task of writing a letter; but he admits that most of his learning has come from his wife. She is a graduate of Jacksonville State Teachers' College, and she taught him to write after they were married. He says that he wishes he knew more, and for that reason he is anxious for his children to have an education.

"What we need here," he said in his drawling tone, "is a high school for my people. If we could a-get the high school, then we might someday have a college. The Negroes have their college up at Tuskegee. Why can't we have one? Why, those kids over in my wife's school are bright as they can be. They learn everything fast. Jus' think what it would a-mean to them if they knew they could keep learning past the seventh grade. How would you feel if you knew the State wouldn't a-give you a chance to get any further?"

He shook his head slowly, looking into the fire, but his wife said, "I have children over there who would grow into fine men and women if they were given a better chance. There is nothing lazy about them, no matter what the people over in town (Chatom) say. They want to learn. I tell you, when children come to school without any breakfast, and many times without enough clothing to keep them warm, they have something about them that you won't find in every child."

"You were over at the school to see those children," she said to the visitor. "You saw children who were without shoes, and it was cold this morning. You also saw that some of the children's eyes are very bad; that they need glasses badly." She paused a moment, looking into the fire. Then she said, "I wish I had enough money to take all of them to Mobile and buy them some glasses. It must be terrible with your eyes hurting you all of the time. Isn't it asking a little too much to expect cold and hungry children to learn a great deal! Of course, we are always planning something better for them, but it seems that we never have enough money. We are talking about setting up a lunch counter, to be run on something like a cooperative plan. I don't know whether it will work, but it's worth trying. Anything would be better than watching them stand about the grounds at lunch time without any lunch to eat."

Jake Gaw, like his wife, resents the claims of some that his people are shiftless and unwilling to help themselves. "You will find lazy people everywhere," he said, "and you will find some smart people, too. I don't a-believe anybody could call me lazy. Since I was a boy, I have been up before daylight, and I never stop a-working until it is after dark." He flung a glance at his wife. She smiled and nodded.

Neither Jake nor his wife takes any active interest in either local or national politics. They do not vote, and as Jake explains, "I guess the people who do the electing know what they are a-doing; anyway, I hope they do. I think that Mr. Roosevelt has done his very best to help the poor class of people, but one man can't a-do everything. We need hundreds like him, and we need some of them right a-down here in Washington County. Why, I tell you, if people knew how some of us have to live, they'd be dumbfounded. There are lots of Cajans who'd a-get out and do something if they had somebody to set them on their feet just once. But you know it's hard to do anything when you are kept busy trying to jus' get up something to eat. If these woods weren't full of wild game, lots of Cajans would be hungrier than they are. But it won't take no time down here to get a 'possum, rabbit, or squirrel. And now and then, we get a wild turkey."

Gaw says that he has often been without money, but that he has never asked anyone for help. "I have always a-managed to get along some way or other," he said, "and I guess I can a-keep getting along that way. I found out a long time ago that most people won't a-help you unless they are a-going to get something out of it. But I guess that's jus' people's way. I don't a-blame them none for it. I'm not the kind that runs about asking favors. I tell you, when things was so bad back in 1932, I'd a-get up in the mornings, and I swear I didn't know where I was a-going to get something to eat for the day. But I got it, jus' the same. I guess life's like that; you got to scratch for everything."

Jake believes in religion, which is not true of many Cajans, but he says, "I've never a-seen much good in setting up in church and listening to a man talk. And anyway, I'd rather stay at home on Sundays. It's so far to the churches that we don't get a chance to go much, but my wife always says that she would like to go every Sunday. I guess that she would, because she used to go before she came off a-down here. The way I see it, if a man a-lives right all the time and does the best he can, he'll a-get to Heaven right along with the church-going people."

It was getting late now, and the visitor rose from his chair to leave. In the kitchen there was a sound of meat frying, and the pungent odor had come into the front room. The daughter, Faye, was cooking supper. Without rising from his chair, Jake said, "You can't a-leave without eating. Stay with us and get something under your ribs before you go." Mrs. Gaw seconded the invitation, apologizing, "You won't find much to eat, but you are welcome to anything that we have." When the visitor explained that he had to get back on the highway before good darkness, Jake followed him to the door where the circular block of pine served as a step. He said, "When you come back maybe I'll a-have my house done. I want to ceil her and clean up the yards good. I theenk then she'll be as good as anybody could want." His tall figure was framed in the darkening doorway. He did not respond to a farewell wave of the hand, but he smiled a little.

*Annie Lee Bowman was born in 1881, according to the old
family Bible, and was the youngest of six sisters. In her early
years she was a schoolteacher. When she wrote the following
account she was fifty-eight years old, unmarried, and living
with her brother-in-law and two sisters in Atmore.*[2]

The Hanks

by Annie Lee Bowman

Rosa Hanks is the mother of nine children, four of whom are
dead. Enora, the oldest, is married and lives in Dothan, where
she now teaches. Her other four daughters are also teaching.
Cathy, Shirlee and Amy teach nearby and stay at home while
Andrea teaches in Columbia, Alabama. The youngest child,
John Robin, is still in high school. Since the girls are profession-
ally employed, Rosa's family lives somewhat better than the
average colored family. Each of the girls makes thirty dollars a
month and Rosa makes some on the side with her washing.
They are now trying to redeem their home which they lost
during the depression. To do this they will have to pay five
dollars a month to the government for the next seven years.[3]
This is much better than paying rent.

Down the highway through the Atmore Negro quarters, this
house stands—somewhat better looking than the other make-
shift structures which the Negroes call their homes. A gate
gives access to a neatly trimmed and freshly swept front yard.
An old half-blind Negro was in the back yard cutting wood when
we arrived. To the question, "Is Rosa at home?" came the reply,
"Yes Ma'am, she were in there an hour ago," as he shuffled into
the house to find her. Rosa came to the door with an invitation
into the parlor. This room has a living room suite, piano, and a

---

[2]Information from Mrs. Joe Brock, Atmore, in telephone conversation with editor,
August 28, 1981. Mrs. Brock was the wife of Annie Lee Bowman's nephew. She married
into the family in 1937 and remembers that Annie Lee and other women visited and
worked on a writing project in the late thirties.

[3]The Home Owners' Loan Corporation was one of the first major programs passed by
the Roosevelt administration; this monthly payment was probably to HOLC.

rug on the floor. Rosa hospitably invited me to come in her room as she had a fire in there. The fireplace had an old iron pot on the coals. "Yes, I'm trying to save fuel by cookin' my dinnah on the fire," she explained.

The room has two beds, covered with neat cotton counterpanes, a sewing machine and three chairs, one a rocker. She has been sewing on quilts and she proudly displayed three that she has recently pieced. The girls' room has a bed, table, wardrobe, dresser and two rocking chairs. In the guest room is a neat bedroom suite, a wardrobe, washstand, a rug and two chairs. John Robin's room also serves as the pantry. Rosa says that she keeps her canned fruit there; and she displayed the kitchen and dining room, which are quite clean in appearance. She said, "The girls warned me this morning that if they left without cleaning up the house, I would neglect it and company would surely come and now, sure enough, you're here."

Just then the door opened and her half-blind husband walked in. He appeared to be about seventy-five years old. He told me that he could see a little since he was operated on. He then proudly declared that he could work his own garden, and he then pointed out the window to prove it. "I couldn't give satisfaction by hiring myself out to anyone else," he added, "but I can pick cotton a little. The bolls are so big and white that I can see many of them and feel the rest. So you see I can do a good day's work yet," he explained.

"Today, our new governor goes in office.[4] I kept telling the old lady that I wish we had a radio so we could hear his inaugural address. Well, he has a load on his shoulders and I guess he is a lot like school teachers. We walk into the room the first morning with high hopes, but before it's over, we are just doing the best we can."

He went on about the Federal government, "I don't believe there's going to be any tenant farmers any more, since the government has fixed it so the tenant farmer can get half the subsidy. The landlords will just hire help and you can work it or let it alone which means that most of them will work at any price

[4]Frank M. Dixon was inaugurated January 17, 1939; see Jesse M. Richardson and Herbert R. Padgett, eds., *Alabama Almanac and Book of Facts 1955–1956* (Birmingham, Ala.: Vulcan Press, 1955), p. 52.

to keep from starving. The government has just made two classes of the American people. The lower class has turned to beggars; the higher class has turned to grafters. That comes from putting so much money in their control." He then asked if I had read about the tenant farmers in Arkansas.[5] Then he left the room to go out in the garden to work. I wondered where he got his information, until I noticed the Montgomery Advertiser and the Mobile Register lying on the sewing machine.

Rosa was born in Monroe County, one of seven children. Her father, John Carty, was a slave before the war. He didn't remember much about slavery, however, for his mother and father were freed when he was a child. They kept the name of Carty, their master. When Rosa was four years old, her father and his family moved to Wilcox County near Pineapple and lived there as tenant farmers until she was grown. Before going there he had been a tenant farmer for David Watts. In 1911 the family moved to Escambia County where farming conditions were better, and the father worked here for John Maxwell and Mr. Wagner until he died.

Rosa again took up the conversation. "I stayed with my ma longer than any of her seven children. All the others married and left home and I decided to become a teacher. I begged my ma and pa to let me go to school. They finally consented to let me go to the Colored Industrial Seminary at Snow Hill. I worked there in the laundry for my board." She sat for a while, gazing out the window. "Them was happy days. I just loved it all. I finished the eleventh grade and took state examination. I then taught school for three years. Then I married at the age of

---

[5]The events that interested the man being interviewed revolved around the Southern Tenant Farmers Union that had been organized in Arkansas several years earlier. Partly because of STFU pressure, the Department of Agriculture had ruled in 1938 that tenants and sharecroppers should get their government checks in their own names, so owners could not automatically absorb all the subsidies for reducing acreage under cotton. This plan backfired when owners simply decided to evict sharecropper families. The STFU helped organize a highway protest of those evicted in southeast Missouri. Farm Security Administration photographers were among the journalists there, and the whole scene got massive national publicity; see Donald H. Grubbs, *Cry From the Cotton: The Southern Tenant Farmers' Union and the New Deal* (Chapel Hill: University of North Carolina Press, 1971), p. 181, and H. L. Mitchell, *Mean Things Happening in This Land: The Life and Times of H. L. Mitchell, Co-Founder of the Southern Tenant Farmers Union* (Montclair, N.J.: Allanheld, Osmun & Co., 1979), pp. 171–79.

House. Mobile, 1938. Lee, FSA.

twenty-five. I had done give up hopes of ever marrying by then, and sometimes I wish I never had."

She confessed that she had a very desperate love affair when she was very young. "Lord how I loved that man," she recalled. "He was no account so ma, she just broke it up. I grieved so hard after he married that the neighbors said it was a sin to covet another woman's husband. I went to church one day and the preacher said it was a shame and disgrace to grieve over spilt milk. I've seen him several times since and it seems now that I am just meeting a dear old friend."

"I was teaching at Wallace when Roy Hanks' wife died. She was giving birth to a baby girl. It wasn't long before he came a courtin'. I decided that I was getting to be an old maid. If I ever married I had better take him. I never loved my old man but I respected him. After I bore him nine children, I couldn't give him up. He got sick and blind and I'm certain that it's my duty to keep up with him."

"After we were married, I went with him to Camden to live. He was teaching there. Roy taught school for twenty-five years.

I was ailing that winter and was homesick for pa and ma. When school closed, we moved back to Escambia County. Roy kept teaching and pea-patching until three of my children were born. He only made twenty-seven dollars per month and I can tell you them was hard times. He finally quit teaching and went to work at a sawmill for Mr. Harry Patterson. Pay was better there and he worked for fourteen years at this mill. In 1926 it closed down. By that time I had raised most of my family. Four of them had died. The screech owl screeched in the chinaberry tree by the door.[6] Them was bad signs and I knowed right away that something bad would happen."

At this point Rosa paused with a sorrowful sigh as those sad memories came back to her. She got up and walked about the floor before she continued her story. After her children's death, her husband's eyes began to fail. He would not tell any of the family about it, but they could tell by his feeling and fumbling around. This incapacitated him for holding a job, and he has not worked regularly since. Those were hard times for Rosa and her family. Old Roy lost his sight entirely. According to the doctors, a cataract had covered his eyes and sight was impossible without an operation. There was no money in this poor family for one. Rosa continued, "To keep from starving I gathered my four girls and John Robin and went to the field to hoe. I put the baby in a corner of the fence in a big cotton basket, and there we hoed, picked cotton and strawberries from morning until dark. We kept together some way, sometimes I wonder how."

Rosa was interrupted by John Robin coming home from school. He is a big overgrown boy who will finish high school this year if he passes his grades. Rosa ordered him out of the room to go help his father get the wood cut but as I looked out of the window, I could see him going to the playground with a ball under his arm. Rosa saw him at the same time and declared, "That is the most trifling boy I have ever seen. I'll get him yet for this. I don't know what's goin' to become of him." Like many of her race and sex it is plain that she seems not to put any dependence in any boy or man. It was further shown when she made a remark about Roy. "My ol' man is not brutal—jus' shiftless, but I guess it is because of his health."

[6]See Part Three, footnote 35.

Rosa spoke of the possibilities of the future. "Now, if I can keep my girls at home for seven years longer, we can pay off the mortgage; but one of them has a suitor—a teacher at Freemanville who has been paying her court. If the other two has ever had a beau, I don't know it. I reckon though it would be better for them to marry before one of them should disgrace herself. But if I even so much as mention such things to them, it makes them mad. They always claim that they are old enough to take care of themselves. But I don't know and nobody else knows what a girl might do. After all my raising them right; I always made them go to the Methodist Church with me and tried to bring them up in the straight and narrow way; but I didn't spare the rod either. But if some wolf in sheep's clothing should ruin one of my daughters by big promises and honeyed words, I wouldn't leave it up to the Lord. No ma'am, not me."

Rosa said of her husband, "We were speaking about Roy's eyes. He was a terrible care, a man ailing and me with a living to make, but one cold day I was sitting in my room—brooding, praying and wondering what we were going to do. We had no wood and nothing else much. When I heard a knock I went and opened the door. You could have knocked me down with a feather. Mr. Harry Patterson, a man Roy had worked for fourteen years, stood in the door. The spirit rose but I said to myself, 'Down spirit, wait 'til Marse Patterson goes home. Then you can do all the shouting you want.' He had heard of our plight and had come to see about taking the old man to a hospital for an operation. I have never been so happy since I was in Snow Hill in the seminary." Roy Hanks was carried to the hospital and the cataract was removed, so that he can now see some out of that eye; but a cataract has covered the other one.

The girls came in from school and greeted us courteously. They were dressed alike in plaid skirts and red topper coats. Their mother's training showed in their pleasant manners and self-possession. Shirlee had a headache; so she lay down on the bed. Cathy went to make a fire in the stove and fix supper. She remarked that they never had but two meals a day. That was breakfast, and supper when they got home from school. Shirlee, regardless of her headache, was in a talkative mood. She began to tell about incidents that had happened that day at school, and soon was telling all about their school life.

"All the time that we were working in the field, Cathy and I were planning to go to school. We didn't see how we could for we had no money, but we didn't give up hope. After we finished high school, we wrote to the Alabama State Teachers' College in Montgomery, the school for colored. The principal got a place for us to work in Cloverdale with some of the rich white people and go to school. We borrowed some money from Mr. Jones, a banker, and promised to pay him in the summer by working on his farm. This we did. He was glad to help us. It didn't take much, just train fare and a few clothes. We worked hard at the white folks' house and went to school during the day. We stayed all that first winter."

"The next year we couldn't be spared at home. Mama couldn't take the load by herself. Andrea and John Robin were still in high school at home. The next year Cathy went back for four months, and the summer following she went for three months. That winter we both stayed in school. Andrea was large enough to work and help at home and Papa was assigned to teach an adult school. Cathy was able to teach the next winter but papa lost his job after he began teaching. We have both been teaching for three years now and Andrea, with the help of Federal aid, spent three years in Huntsville school. She is now teaching in Columbia, Alabama. We miss her very much but we are making a living. When school closes, we work in the field."

François Ludgere Diard of Mobile, journalist and local histo-
rian, was with the Alabama Writers' Project from its very
beginning. As supervisor of the Mobile district for four years, he
probably is due much of the credit for the volume and quality of
Mobile area writing in project files. Diard wrote just one life
history, the following study of a twenty-four-year-old hobo he
encountered on the streets in Mobile. Diard in his choice of
subject may have been influenced by W. T. Couch, who sug-
gested that Alabama writers read Thomas Minehan's then-
recent book, Boy and Girl Tramps of America.[7] *Diard had some*
reputation as a writer before the FWP began, and the Alabama
Writers' Project may have encouraged him in this direction.[8]

Sharon Suffolk, Knight of the Road

by François Ludgere Diard

On Friday night, January 20th, 1939, at exactly six o'clock
when the Angelus was ringing loudly from the towers of the
Cathedral of the Immaculate Conception at Dauphin and Clai-
borne Streets, after eating supper I took a stroll out Dauphin
Street to Hamilton Street to where the New York Bakery is
located. This bakery has the reputation of making excellent rye
bread and delicious candied macaroons, which I generally purchase every Friday afternoon if financially able. When I had
reached the opposite of the back of the Cathedral, there was
standing at the northeast corner of Franklin and Dauphin
Streets a young man of five and a half feet in height. He had on
a thin slip-on blue-gray sweater, brown trousers, and a brown
sport shirt which he wore under the sweater. A pair of un-
polished black shoes encased his feet, and he carried under his
arm a heavy black overcoat. I was walking with my face cast
downward heavily thinking, and when I looked up to step onto

---

[7]Thomas Minehan, *Boy and Girl Tramps of America,* illus. with photographs by the
author (New York: Farrar & Rinehart, 1934).

[8]Diard wrote at least one book afterwards, *The Tree: Being the Strange Case of Charles
R. S. Boyington* (Mobile: Gill Printing & Stationery Co., 1849), about an 1834 murder
and hanging.

the curb of the sidewalk, I saw the young man had a pair of the frankest and sincerest blue-gray eyes I had ever seen in a man's head. He was looking at me for a moment with a stare of suspicion, and I knew then he thought I was a detective of some kind, for he soon hurried away to the opposite side of the street and vanished from sight in the shadow of the automobiles.

I continued a block further to the bakery and purchased the loaf of rye bread and the macaroons I was going after. All that night I had that young drift-in's face before me and the expression he wore on seeing me, for he was a fairly genteel, nice looking young man with regular features and a head of rich, sandy hair. The next day came and I was still thinking of the young man and the strange way of crossing the street and getting out of my way. At one o'clock when I was returning from lunch and on my way to the post office, I chanced to pass through Bienville Square. My shoe string at this point became untied, and I stopped at a bench in the center or circle nearest the pathway I had entered by, and on placing my foot upon the bench to tie my shoe, I saw the same young man. He was talking to an old-time transient who, from his face and appearance, had had many experiences of life on the road. I said to the young man: "Young fellow, why did you vanish across the street by the Cathedral last night when you saw me? I didn't mean you any harm."

"Well, I'll tell you," he answered. "I was afraid you were a dick and would run me in. Last night the bakery shop and one quarter was my last salvation—buy something to eat, or get a two-bit flop for the night. Kindly excuse my language of the road, please, as I am a knight of the road." He smiled as he repeated his last sentence.

I sat on the side of the bench with him, as I learned from his talk he was a prospect for a fairly good story, and showed every sign he had been a high school student. "You have had a lot of experiences in life, I suppose," I said, "and I am going to get you to tell me in your own words all about yourself and this knocking about the country."

"Yes, I have had a lot of experiences all right," he said. "I saw a moving picture the other day called *Arkansas Traveler,* and

Bob Burns played the character lead to perfection.[9] This picture came right near to my own experiences, that is, the hobo camping ground and the kindness of some of the characters in the picture, for I've stopped at just such hobo camping places in the jungle, and smelt the odor of canned goods cooking over a pine-knot fire. So you really want my life's history? As I expect to stop this road life and locate here in Mobile, yes, good, old Mobile, after one more trip back west. The weather of Mobile is ideal, so I might as well locate here, and in the future I reckon you will see lots of me."

"Now for the life history," I urged.

"You see, I was born at Ellenburg, Washington State, on September 11, 1914. I am the son of Elizabeth Gilpatrick and Bert Suffolk. My mother used to sing an Irish song called 'The Rose of Sharon,' and she named me Sharon after the song. So you see I am a baby named for a song. My father was a government engineer, and the last work he worked on was the Grand Coulee Dam in the State of Washington, located on the Columbia Basin. He then tried to get a job on some engineering project in a southern state, but the length of the job didn't justify him moving down south. Then he went to work for the Washington State Lumber Company, and in cutting timber was killed by a falling Sequoia tree at Cle-Ellum, Washington. This happened in 1928, when I was only fourteen years of age, and both my father and mother are buried in the Ellenburg Cemetery. They were the parents of three children, two boys and one girl. I am the baby, and am twenty-four years of age."

"I was first sent to Ellenburg Public School at the age of seven years, and continued at the public schools until I reached the age of nineteen. I always had good merits at school, as I always tried to study hard, and I loved writing, geography, history and reading. In childhood I used to roam the woods with a Yakima Indian boy by the name of Jim. He always greeted me with 'Chickawaloa!', which means 'Heap Big Pale Face.' This is the

---

[9]Bob Burns was described as a "folksy comedian and humorist who after radio success appeared in several light films," among them the 1938 "Your Arkansas Traveller"; see Leslie Halliwell, *The Filmgoer's Companion*, 4th ed. (New York: Hill & Wang, 1970), p. 121.

common way of greeting a white man by the Yakima Indian tribe in Washington State. This red-skinned boy friend never liked his Indian name, so he took the plain name of Jim. There was one old Indian named Old Bill, who came from the Yakima Indian reservation, and he would cross the canyon to where I was herding sheep, and I would talk with him for hours and learned much about the Indians and their ways. He often shared my lunch and was tickled to get what was called a mutton stew I made. He, however, despised cheese very much, as it was not good for his system."

"My first work where I earned any money at all was during summer vacations as a sawyer, cutting Sequoia timber, a California redwood. You see, when I was fourteen I went in for cutting timber seriously. This was in the northern part of Washington State about 125 miles northwest of Seattle, at Bellingham. I worked at this timber cutting at Bellingham about seven months. I then went into working on a cattle ranch tending stock. I worked for a man named Mr. Richard O'Riley. When I first met Mr. O'Riley I had already started out to roam on the road over the country. I met him on a fast freight train between Salt Lake City and Ogden, Utah. I thought then that he was just a plain out-and-out tramp, or knight of the road. I was attracted to him by his gentle manner and kindliness, although he was dressed in almost rags like a great many other tramps. We were bound for parts unknown. He told me, however, if I went to Pendleton, Oregon, I could get a job during Rodeo season at $125.00 a month and board or food, exhibiting fine Jersey cattle. I had figured to get up into the Idaho country to pick potatoes. I left Mr. O'Riley at Pocatello, Idaho, and proceeded by myself on a freight train."

"I next went to Boise, Idaho, where I picked Irish potatoes about six or eight miles north of Boise. I stayed there near Boise for about eleven weeks during June, July and August of 1935 of the picking season. I left the town of Boise on September 1 headed for Pendleton, Oregon, to get the Rodeo job Mr. O'Riley had told me about. When I reached Pendleton, I called at the Rodeo cattle corral, filled with all spirit of obtaining the job, and when I asked for a ranch hand I told him I was looking for a man named Richard O'Riley and asked where he could be found. I was told to wait by the ranch hand and he would call him. He said there was only one Richard O'Riley in that section that owned cattle. I had told this ranch hand I had met a man by the name of O'Riley on a freight train, who had told me about the Rodeo job. I was doubtful and leery that it was the right Mr. Richard O'Riley I had met on the road; so when I came face to face with the Jersey stock owner, I saw to my great consternation that the Mr. O'Riley I thought a tramp was a leading cattleman in that section. He was dressed like a lord, and had on a fine riding outfit, riding hat and other pieces that went with it. He greeted me with a smile of welcome and a handshake. He immediately put me to work for him in charge of displaying his fine Jersey cattle, and at the salary of $150.00 a month, what do you know about that! I asked him the next day why he had taken to the road. He replied that he wanted to see what life was."

"I lived at Mr. O'Riley's home, a fine residence of about fourteen rooms or more, and furnished superbly with the best of furniture and household effects. I ate three meals a day at his table, and was treated while there like one of the family, although I slept in the bunkhouse like the rest of his ranch hands. Mr. O'Riley was a single man, and two of his brothers and a sister lived with him. His sister was his housekeeper. His older brother was an invalid from infantile paralysis since he was eleven years old. I soon found that this invalid brother was a great admirer of Franklin D. Roosevelt. The O'Rileys were devout Catholics. I found this Irish family the kindest I had ever met. They said a Catholic prayer at table for grace, and I was also made to learn it."

"I remained with Mr. O'Riley for six weeks after the Rodeo closed, and worked with his ranchmen at a lesser salary than the Rodeo job. I took to the road again on November 15, 1935, although I was asked to remain with the O'Rileys as long as I wanted. The day I left Mr. O'Riley brought me into town himself, and saw me off on the passenger train. He said, 'Son, anytime you will come back your job as ranch hand will be open to you.' "

"I left the passenger train at Casper, Wyoming, where all the sheep herders gather to get their winter supplies. I stayed at

Casper about two weeks, then I caught a Union Pacific freight train and crossed over the Rockies headed for Chicago on a cattle train, but was delayed in Omaha by railroad detectives for two days for investigation. When I was released I continued on to Chicago on another freight train. I took the highway Lincoln U.S. 30, and caught a ride for Indianapolis. Here I stayed at the Salvation Army that night after arriving. This last was in the beginning of the winter of 1935. I mean heavy winter had set in. I then headed for Toledo, Ohio, and stayed there about a week. I couldn't find work, so I proceeded on to Cleveland. I stayed in Cleveland at the Government Transient Bureau about three weeks. I washed dishes in Mitchell's Cafe at the corner of East Ninth Street and Superior Avenue. I left Cleveland and went to Pittsburgh, and here stayed at the Improvement of the Poor at Duquesne Way. I stayed in Pittsburgh for two weeks, leaving for the road again, and reached Bloomberg, Pennsylvania, where the State Teachers College is located. While standing here on a street corner, I met a fellow by the name of Albert McDevitt, who got me a job helping to paint houses. I got three dollars a day. This was shortly before Christmas, 1935. I stayed in Bloomberg until February 17, 1936. While I was there I fell head over heels in love with a beautiful young lady, a Miss Thelma _____, who was a State College teacher, and we had planned to marry, but financial troubles arose, for I lost my job at painting. When I met her I was boarding with her mother. I left but returned, and continued to stay at my intended fiancee's home until March 22, when I started for the road again and headed south."

"From Bloomberg I went to Harrisburg, Pennsylvania, which place I left, after staying for the night at Betheda Mission, and continued taking the highway for Baltimore. In Baltimore I worked for three days at the Baltimore Highland Country Club at cleaning up the place. I left Baltimore and headed for Washington, D.C. I stayed overnight in the capital at the Volunteers of America, and left next morning headed for Richmond, Virginia, where I stayed for the night at the Salvation Army. I left Richmond, and started for Danville, and got stranded between the two towns and slept out in the woods. This was the last week of the month of March and it was rainy and cold. I got into Danville the following day, then caught a transportation truck out of Danville for Louisville, Kentucky. Out of Louisville I took the highway for Cincinnati, and there stayed at the Transient Bureau for two days, when I caught a freight for Columbus. At Columbus I stayed at the Transient Bureau, and I then started back on the highway to Indianapolis and stayed there at the Wheeler Mission. Leaving Indianapolis I went to Chicago, but soon was out of there for Davenport, Iowa, where I stayed in the railroad yards in a box car. The next morning I was lucky, for I caught the Union Pacific freight for Grand Island, Nebraska. At this place I made good connection to Cheyenne, Wyoming, and there caught a train next morning for Salt Lake City, and stayed there overnight at the police station. Next morning I caught a freight for Pendleton, Oregon, and had the good fortune to see again and stay at the home of my good friend, Mr. Richard O'Riley. From Pendleton I went to Walla-Walla, Washington State, and stayed overnight at the City Farm, leaving the next morning and arriving that evening in my hometown of Ellenburg, Washington. Gee, it seemed great to be again in my old home! I went out immediately to my sister's place about seven miles north of Ellenburg, and remained with her for three months. Of course my sister, as she always is, was glad to see me. I visited all the old familiar places where I had played or gone in childhood, or worked, the Yakima Indians and some old friends."

"I left my sister's and started down the West Coast to Portland, where I stayed for a week, and then proceeded on to Pendleton and went back to work for my old friend, Mr. Richard O'Riley. This time I worked for him for four months, which was during the latter part of 1936. I tended cattle here as before. I quit one morning suddenly as the wanderlust had again invaded me, and I took out on the highway for a little town called Mancos, Colorado. I tried to get a job here with a man named Percy Starr, who had struck gold at a creek thirty miles from Mancos. Unfortunately he had all the men he wanted just then; but I was told to come back anyway by him later on and he would see what he could do. I didn't go back, but struck out for Julesburg, Colorado, another one of the almost deserted towns where gold was still being panned. I stayed here a little over a week and got little odd jobs to live on. This was the spring of

1937. I left Julesburg and started east, and came into a little town called Missouri Valley, Iowa, which is about eighty miles north of Omaha, and landed a job there with a fellow I knew by the name of Arthur Emsley working with a construction company, the Rust Engineering Corporation, whose home office was Davenport, Iowa. I worked with this company for about five and a half months to September, 1937. As soon as the job was completed I left for Chicago. I stayed in Chicago in a lodging house at 195th Street and Commercial Avenue. I got little odd jobs and paid $1.50 a week for my room. I remained in Chicago until November, 1937, when I finally got disgusted, and started further east and got into Huntington, Indiana. I met up with a fellow there who told me I might get on with Hagenback and Wallace's Circus. I started for their headquarters at Peru, Indiana, and I decided when I got there that I wouldn't apply for a job, because I didn't like circus life. I then decided to go on into Ohio, and went to the town of Dayton, and tried to get work at the rubber plants, but without success. Left Dayton and went to Akron and tried the Goodyear Rubber Factory, also without success. I left Akron for Youngstown, where I tried to get a job with Youngstown Street & Tube Company, but was told to come back later on. I decided to go from here to a town called Warren in Ohio, and applied at the steel mills in that section for work, but failed, so went back to Youngstown, and while there stayed in the Argonne Hotel, conducted by the Salvation Army, at $4.50 a week for board and room. I had secured a job in a tailor shop with a tailor named Ernest Hetrick. I stayed here from November, 1937, to March, 1938. I ate Christmas dinner as well as New Year's with Mr. Hetrick and his family. After starting to work for Ernest Hetrick, I ate dinner at the Salvation Army barracks on Thanksgiving. The latter place had no turkey but good roast beef, which answered the same for a poor man. When I returned home from that Thanksgiving dinner at the Salvation Army barracks, Mr. Hetrick asked me what did we have for dinner, and I told him roast beef, so he said, 'Well, on Christmas and New Year I invite you for a turkey dinner with my family.' "

"One night while I was lying in bed I was thinking of trying to locate my older brother, James, who had left home a year previous to my mother's death in Ellenburg, and was said to have gone to Pittsburgh, and was driving a yellow cab, so I decided to leave Youngstown and go to Pittsburgh to look for my brother. I had left Mr. Hetrick's employ in March, 1938, but I failed to find my brother in Pittsburgh. I left Pittsburgh and went back again to Bloomberg, and this time again landed a job with the Bloomberg Paint Company. I worked here painting until August, 1938. I left Bloomberg and went again to Harrisburg. I stayed while here in the same Betheda Mission, and did odd jobs throughout the city until the latter part of October, 1938. I decided it was too cold in that section of the country, so turned my course towards God's country, the sunny South, where the weather generally fits your clothes. I went to Baltimore, but didn't stay, and went on straight through to Richmond, Virginia. Here I stayed at the Salvation Army haven for a night, and I left next morning on U.S. Highway 60 to Lynchburg. That night I made it from Lynchburg to Danville, where I stayed at the Salvation Army. The next morning I caught a ride from Danville to Greensboro, North Carolina, and landed a job cleaning the elevator shaft in Hotel Greensboro, a three weeks' job. When this was completed I left Greensboro on U.S. 29 to Salisbury, and then took Route 150 through to Shelby, and then U.S. Route 74 from Shelby to Forest City, North Carolina. This was during the first week in December, 1938. From Forest City I took Highway 74 to Asheville, where I got a ride direct to Atlanta, and stayed overnight at the Salvation Army. I got a ride next morning to Savannah, went on through Savannah to Orlando, the orange center, where I stayed overnight, going next day to Miami, however, stopping for a night and day at Fort Pierce on my way, and eating Christmas dinner with an elderly couple who invited me into their home as I called at the back door to ask for something to eat. After reaching Miami I worked for two days doing odd jobs. It was now the first week in January, 1939, and I got a ride from Miami to Tampa. After eating dinner in Tampa I got a ride that afternoon to Tallahassee, where I stayed overnight, proceeding on Highway 90 to Marianna, Florida. The police station in this town was my lodging place, and I rested fairly well here after a hard jaunt. The next morning I went to Milton, Florida, where I stayed overnight at the Tar Works. Here is the most comical side of my long jauntings over the good old U.S.A. When I reached Pensacola the next day from Milton, I decided I wouldn't stay long. At Pensacola I talked with a few floaters, who told me to watch out for the immigration officers on the road out of Pensacola to Mobile. Mobile was the next town on my way over Route 90, and I had heard from quite a number of men on the road that Mobile was a clannish and friendly town and a fellow could get by there very easy, if he attended to his own business and didn't publicly mooch on the streets."

"While I was standing on the outskirts of Pensacola trying to hail a ride west toward the City of the Azaleas, two immigration officers came along in a car headed toward Mobile. My concern at this moment was to get to Mobile, so after I suspected who they were and remembering what the floaters had told me while in Pensacola, I decided to keep my mouth shut if questioned by them. It was the ride to Mobile I wanted, for my feet were tired out. These immigration officers asked me where I was going, and I answered, "headed for home." They asked me where my home was, and I told them at Ellenburg, Washington State; but they doubted me and accused me of being a Canadian, because of my sallow blond type, and, perhaps, because Ellenburg was in a state near the Canadian line. I then told them I wasn't doing any talking (while telling them this, I was smiling to myself), and to go ahead and hold me for investigation, which they did. I was told to get into their car, and they proceeded toward Mobile through Baldwin County and over the bridge across Mobile Bay. I was taken by them after reaching Mobile to the rear of the new U.S. Court House and Custom House, where they parked their car. I was taken then into the building of the Immigration Office. Here these officers again accused me of being a Canadian, and I only smiled and took it as a compliment, for Canadians are generally goodlooking people."

"One of these officers said, 'How do we know you are from Washington State?' I answered in turn, 'How do you know I am from Canada?' They said, 'It is just as broad as it is long.' All this time I was chuckling up my sleeve and prided myself for being clever, while they were playing dumb. In my heart I knew I had done nothing wrong, and I had full confidence I would be free again in a few moments and walking on the streets of the town most of the floaters have praised—Mobile. Of course, as I had not had a charge placed against me, they had no right to search me. In the minds of both of them they still entertained I was Canadian, and this they insisted, but when I pulled out my Social Security Act account number, they were so astounded they could only stare at each other and then at me."

"One of them said, 'Why didn't you show us your Social Security card back there on the outskirts of Pensacola?' 'Well, if I had,' I said, 'I wouldn't have got a ride to Mobile, and then you didn't ask me to.' They both agreed I had put a clever piece of work over on them, and one of them said, 'This is the first time anybody ever put something over on us in a long time.' "

"But they both acted good sports, for I was given the price of a fifty cent meal and a quarter to get a bed with, and they agreed it was well worth the seventy-five cents it had cost them, and then wished me the best of luck on my way back to the west coast. That night, which, as you know, was Friday, January 20, I went to the Salvation Army on Conti Street near Joachim Street to get a bed, but was turned down, being told they had no fund for housing transients. I then went up Dauphin Street as far as Franklin Street, and was standing opposite the Cathedral waiting to make a touch for another quarter, when a man came along who I at first thought was a dick, not knowing he would the next day, as you know, meet me by chance in Bienville Square and prove my friend. I dodged out of sight among the automobiles parked alongside the Cathedral, and went on down to Royal Street and got a twenty-five cent room at a rooming house run by a man named Heustis King. Today I started to leave for New Orleans on my way back to the west coast, but I've decided to remain over the weekend and maybe a little longer and wait for some mail. It looks like rain for the weekend, but I'll be happy to be on my way toward the west coast."

As I started to bid him goodbye and Godspeed, he began to recite the following lines of a song, and a smile filled his frank and sincere blue-gray eyes:

"In the big Rock Candy Mountains,
  Where you sleep out every night,

Handouts grow on bushes,
   And you are never in a tight.
In the big Rock Candy Mountains,
   Where you never change your socks,
And the little streams of alcohol
   Come trickling down the rocks;
In the big Rock Candy Mountains,
   Where the jails are made of tin,
You're no sooner locked into the jails
   Till you walk right out again.
In the big Rock Candy Mountains,
Where the bulldogs all have rubber teeth,
   And the hens lay hard boiled eggs.
I want to go where there ain't no snow,
   And the wind don't blow
In the big Rock Candy Mountains!"[10]

---

[10]A hobo song that had become popular with the general public; see Margaret Bradford Boni, ed., *The Fireside Book of Favorite American Songs* (New York: Simon & Schuster, 1952), pp. 113–15. A reader might wonder if Diard took this down verbatim or simply added it as a final flourish to the manuscript.

Ila B. Prine, one of the most prolific Alabama writers of ex-slave narratives in 1937–38, wrote six life histories from November 1938 through January 1939. All six are substantial accounts from Mobile County places like Crichton, Navco, and Bayou la Batre. The following study of a Japanese immigrant is a departure from the stereotypical rags-to-riches pattern of immigration.

Teiichi Mayumi, Nurseryman

by Ila B. Prine

On the Moffatt Road in Mobile County, several miles from Mobile, is the Pineview Nursery, partly owned and operated by Teiichi Mayumi, a Japanese. The Pineview Nursery is located on low ground on a gravel road leading from the paved highway. The entrance is by a driveway on the east side, through a gate covered by an orange and black pagoda. The driveway winds among plant beds and hothouses up to Mr. Mayumi's home, which is separated from the nursery by a hedge of many different types of shrubs. Most spectacular of these is the pyracantha formosaca, which strikingly suggests Japanese origin. Taller than a man of average height, it is a solid mass of bright red berries, almost as large as marbles, on boughs which droop like those of the Japanese weeping cherry. The office of the Pineview Nursery is a plain, square, white building in front of the Mayumi house.

Mr. Mayumi himself is a short, stout man whose skin is more brown than yellow. His hair is short, straight and black and his bright black slanting eyes sparkle when he talks. He has been in America since 1906 and he never expects to go back to Japan; he has no desire to. The years have changed his country so that it no longer seems familiar—and they have also changed Mr. Mayumi so that his countrymen no longer recognize him. More than three decades of outdoor work under the hot southern sun have burned his skin from yellow to brown. "When I went back to Japan fifteen years ago," he said, "people thought I was a Filipino. One day I was standing on a street corner scanning a newspaper. Some children passed by and said, 'Look at that Filipino reading a Japanese paper.' "

"I have no desire to go back to Japan to live. It's a strange country to me, for I left when a very young boy and everything has changed so. I have been back only once since leaving—so long time from home I have strange country. If my father and mother had lived it would be different. Even all my school friends are gone or dead. If I go back, nobody knows me— strange people to me." Only a trace of the Japanese speech is noticeable as Mr. Mayumi tells his own story.

"Now, I only have two brothers and one sister in Japan and they are strange to me. Their religion is different. So you see I no longer belong in Japan. I am American. I have never taught my children to speak the Japanese language. I am contented in this country. The government protects my people here, but if I were in South America or Mexico, and someone wanted my property, they could take it."

Mr. Mayumi's specialty is propagating plants. "I sell them to other nurserymen," he explains. "That is called 'lining out.' Lining out is much more profitable than just raising stock, because you sell quicker. So many of the nurserymen quit propagating, because everybody can't propagate successfully. If you get the plant a little too warm, or too dry, too wet, too cold—no good. Just a little carelessness will kill many thousands of plants overnight."

"Many years of experience taught me to grow many millions of azaleas, small trees, camellia japonicas and evergreens. My business is one of a kind that cannot use machines. Most of the work is done by hand. I now have nineteen men employed; they are all Americans. Later on in the winter months I will employ from twenty to twenty-five men. With my years of experience with propagating plants, I get ninety-five out of every hundred to grow. At that rate it pays. But so many growers cannot get that proportion and that is one of the reasons I started in the lining out business. I am connected with all nurserymen and florists in the United States. I have membership with the Associated American Nurserymen."

Mr. Mayumi was born in Osaka in central Japan in 1887, one of a family of six. "I was so full of ambition," he says, "and wanted a change, after graduating in agriculture from Osaka University. Having heard that America was a land of plenty, I came to America. I thought I could pick up gold along the highways. But you may be sure I found that you get hold of money only by hard work."

"I left Japan when I was twenty-one years old and came to Texas to work in the rice fields. That was in 1906 and I stayed there until 1910. That was hard work in the rice fields, no tractor, no machinery of any kind, just four or six mules to a plow. Plow all winter long; then, in February and March, disc and harrow. In April, sow and drill. Then, when rice come up about six inches high, start irrigation. Every section of the field had to be surveyed carefully, sometimes square, sometimes circular, so that no one section will be over three inches high. Let water stand until July or August on the rice, stop irrigation, then it is ready for threshing."

But Mr. Mayumi was not satisfied in the rice fields. "I see I get nowhere there," he says. "I see people make good selling orange and pecan trees. So I leave Texas in 1910 and come to Grand Bay, Alabama. I thought when I come to America you could make five dollars picking strawberries and grapes. But I soon learn better. I believe in human luck. There are smart people, poor luck. They work hard, but still have poor luck. Then there are some people not smart, but have good luck."

"When I first came to Alabama, it was when the orange tree boom was on. So I start an orchard and sell trees in Bayou la Batre and all around. Then I bought thirty acres here on Moffatt Road, good sandy land to plant orange and pecan trees. This land is good to dig up big roots of trees. But, soon after I buy here in 1923, big freeze come and kill all the orange trees. Then I had to start something else. This land here is not so good for shrubbery, but I have bought eighty acres more on the Howells Ferry Road—much better land."

"After I come here to this country, I go back to San Francisco in 1916 and marry my wife, who came from Japan. I never see her before I marry her but she make me a good wife. We had four children and nine years ago she die, leaving a three-weeks old baby. Nobody wants to take the responsibility of my children, so I do the best I can. All my children in school. My third child is a girl in the seventh grade at Chrichton school. My baby is in the fourth grade. One of my boys is in Auburn, Alabama Polytechnic Institute, studying landscaping and horticulture. This is his second year. The other boy is studying business administration and commerce at Spring Hill College. I do not try to persuade their character—everybody different character—but I hope they will make good businessmen. I tell them they can see what I need here is business education, or the ability to sell after I raise my nursery stock. In fact the whole country needs more commercial knowledge. The farmer today cannot sell his products at a fair price after he raises them. I tell my boys, if I was smart enough and had commercial knowledge, how much better I could do. I don't want to impress them for bad. I tell them give good things, reasonable price. I don't make much money, but I have established good reputation."

America's most important problem, Mr. Mayumi thinks, is reforestation. "We have much more extreme weather now than we once did," he says. "People cut down so many forests. People no longer care for the trees given them. I believe in higher control. Thoughtless people destroy recklessly and the One who controls all things tries to replenish where man destroys."

"I believe that, in our own lives, we must look to a higher control. We must be contented today and work hard tomorrow. We must cooperate and have forgiveness to each other. The trouble today, everybody wants their own way, nobody give in. We should have community spirit, be good neighbors. Peaceful-ness and happiness should govern all our lives. I do not go to church myself, but I send my children to church and Sunday school. We have a church building in Orchard, Alabama, and my children went as long as a minister came to teach them. Sometimes the Baptist come, then the Methodist, and last the Presbyterian had charge of it. But, for the past year, nobody come, so my children have not gone anywhere. But, just the same, I believe in a higher control. I think people in this country are getting too far from this control and it will take a conflagra-tion like Noah's flood to bring them back."

The final three life histories of this volume were written by Lawrence F. Evans. He wrote six in all, one from Bayou la Batre and the rest from Baldwin County, where he lived. Evans's background was unusual. A student at Howard College and Mississippi College, he eventually got his degree in herpetology from the University of Southern California with a minor in journalism. Expeditions took him across Latin America, Africa, the Philippines, and Australia, and during them he wrote for the Associated Press, National Geographic, *the* Chicago Daily News *and the* Los Angeles Times. *Before signing on with the Writers' Project he was editing the Gulf Breeze CCC paper in Foley.[11] Perhaps some of Evans's naturalist background can be seen in his questions in "Master Abel, of the Grover Cleveland" on shrimping. "The Potter" is a shorter account, the street directions at the end pointing out the close relation all Alabama Writers' Project writing had with the state guide. W. T. Couch liked the "Plain Country Doctor" account, calling the doctor a "good man, good attitudes—stout fella."*

Master Abel, of the Grover Cleveland of Bayou la Batre

by Lawrence F. Evans

I stopped the car on impulse and walked behind the shrimp factory where the *Grover Cleveland* floated lazily in the bayou. Aft, basking in the sun and whittling a piece of pine board sat the master.

"May I come aboard?" I asked.

Master Abel spat a mouthful of tobacco juice expertly across the deck, but did not look up. "Aye," he said. The thirty-eight-foot deck of the *Grover Cleveland*—the boat was built during the administration of that president—was as clean as an eggshell, and shaped almost like one. Coiled lines rested neatly fore and

---

[11]See vita enclosed in letter of March 7, 1939, Miles to Couch, FWP—Couch Papers.

aft and shrimp nets and trolls[12] were neatly stacked. An upper and lower bunk showed spic and span through the cabin doorway. I passed the engine room and noted that the machinery shone as if burnished only a moment ago. No crew was aboard but then Master Abel (everyone called him Master Abel) was a crew in himself and the *Grover Cleveland* looked as if ready to putt-putt out into Mobile Bay or the bayou or the Gulf of Mexico—or anywhere, simply by a command. Yes, the *Grover Cleveland* was ready for her next trip to sea for a load of shrimp.

Now Bayou la Batre, long noted for her fishing industries and especially for shrimp, boasts of three shrimp factories, and although the factories maintain fleets of boats with two and three men as crew of each, some of the shrimp men prefer, if they can, to own their craft.

"Working a factory boat is like being a share cropper," said Master Abel. "I been in this here business thirty-five year and it don't pay to work for a factory less'n you own your own boat. Crewmen gets everything furnished and the factory gits a share of the shrimp brung in besides taking out the money the crew has spent for food and oil. Jist suppose that the crew has been out for a week and don't catch no shrimp. What have they made? Well next time they go out they'll probably catch a good haul but they'll owe two weeks grocery bill as well as a oil bill and maybe they've lost a troll or a net wu'th say fifty dollars. They ain't made nothin'. Me I'll take my own boat every time. I furnish everything and sell the shrimp to the factory and what's mine's mine."

"Have I got time to answer some questions about the business? Well I guess time is what I ain't got nothin' else but. Since I owned this boat nigh on to eighteen year all my time is spent with her out on the water when it's time to go fishin' and sittin' here where I can see the factory on one side and my house on t'other. My old woman can call me to dinner from here and the factory can tell me hit's time for me to go on out and bring in a load of shrimp."

"Yep, they allus tell me when it's time to go out. We got a Union and every man gits his proper turn. One fellow goes with me and we share on the shrimp when we clear expenses.

---

[12]A trawl, a bag-shaped net towed behind a boat.

Expenses run pretty high with gasoline in the motor so we use paraffin 'stid o' gas. Yes, she works all right. But when shrimps bring a good price we use gas anyway. No good now. Don't seem to be nothin' in nothin'. Remember last year during the sea-son—it's the best season now—I made more'n two hundred dollars a week for three weeks, clear profit."

"Yep, that's a lot of money in anybody's town—but don't last long. I didn't make more'n half that the rest of the year cause the bottom dropped out of the price. Can't bring in more than thirty barrels in one load sometimes and then again they might be times when I stay out all week and don't git fifteen barrels. The *Grover Cleveland* can take aboard thirty-five barrel!"[13]

"How do we find shrimp? That's easy. Sometimes the water's a little muddy and then ag'in you can smell 'em. We drop a test troll down and see if they're there. If they are we just shut off the motor and drift and put out our nets and trolls and two men handles them pretty easy. We put 'em there below deck and ice 'em until we git up to thirty barrels. We have to weigh them and keep 'em iced below deck until we git in. Hit's easy. 'Less you're out in the gulf where you have to go a hundred feet to find 'em on the bottom. Now, shrimp is runnin' (they run in schools) up the bay and we git 'em in thirty feet of water all up Mobile Bay as far as Fairhope—that's thirty miles. 'Course they only run in there this time of year, 'cause the water's salty. Springtime when the rivers empty in the bay shrimp goes out in the Gulf. That's harder and shrimp ain't so good then but we could still make a livin' at it if the government would let us. Now we have to stop four months, on account of a law of some kind."[14]

"What do we do then? Well them that's got boats can fish for redfish and trout and flounder and mackerel. I do. And git by on it—but not so well."

"Them that ain't got no boat mostly has to go on the WPA and things like that. Some jist go on relief 'cause with all the fishermen on Dauphin Island and in the bayou they's a lot o'

---

[13]A barrel, a standard measure for oysters and at one time shrimp, was defined by Alabama state law as early as 1896 as two containers each 14 inches high, 17 inches in diameter at the bottom and 21¼ inches in diameter at the top; see *Code of Alabama* 1975, vol. 7, *Conservation* (Charlottesville, Va.: Michie Co., 1977), p. 223, sec. 9412–27.

[14]Probably a seasonal regulation established by the Alabama Conservation Depart-ment.

men here. I growed up here and been at this game since I was eighteen. 'Member when I married my wife—she was a Bosage and her people was French who settled here in 1786—they warn't more'n a hundred men working shrimp. They worked it all year and made a good livin'. Why seventeen year ago I bought this boat for $2500.00 and built that house you see over there besides. They're both mine. Boat's still wu'th two thousand dollars in anybody's money. House ain't wu'th nothin'. Have to keep that boat up to make a livin' sich as it is. But this here boat is better'n most o' the new ones the factory owns. Wouldn't trade with any of 'em. Hell no."

"Is shrimpin' a hard life? Yep, it's hard, but I guess everything else is too. Harder on my old lady than on me. Don't mind stayin' out for a week or ten days when she's rough in the Gulf and Bay, but the old woman might not like it so much. Been at it too long now to know anythin' else. We git out in a storm sometimes and might run out o' grub. Always make my helper do the cookin' so don't worry me much. Git fish and shrimp to eat when there ain't nothin' else. Ain't touched a shrimp in nigh on to five years now, though. Sorta git tired of them. Family still eats 'em. Me and the ole woman got eight kids and it takes a lot o' grub for kids. Yep all living. Had lots o' sickness but they's all pulled through. Guess it's the ole woman that's done it. The grown boys are still with me. Shrimpers too. They go out on different boats. Thataway, we don't have all our eggs in the same basket and we always got a chance to have somethin' comin' in. Nope, they ain't married, 'cept one girl—she's been married three years—married a shrimper and he works on a factory boat."

"Nope, I don't mind you seein' my house and ole woman. Neither of 'em is much to look at but they'll do yit, even after all the years they've been through. Say, you ain't no revenue man are you? You know this here boat use' to run liquor from Cuby to Mobile an' ever since then I been bothered with revenue men. You ain't! Well then go on up to the house and visit the ole woman. She's cookin' dinner. Shore it's alright. Glad to talk to you—ain't nothin' else to do."

And Master Abel of the *Grover Cleveland*, captain and owner of the ship, stayed where he was, sitting in the sun, whittling and chewing his Brown Mule tobacco. A gentle breeze swayed the craft on the lazy bayou as I walked down the gang plank. From there a path led through the rank weeds to a ramshackle, paintless house that might have been of Civil War vintage. The path led into the back yard where garbage, fishing paraphernalia and tin cans greeted my approach with many odors. From behind a pile of washtubs a three-year-old boy jumped to life and ran into the house yelling, "Ma! here's a man." I followed the rotting picket fence around to the front, eluded the shaggy chickens and two scrawny puppies, stepped over the broken doorstep and onto a porch with one straight-back chair sitting sedately against the wall.

My knock brought the "ole woman," and Master Abel was right. She was an old woman. There wasn't a tooth in her head. Her dress looked as if the thin calico was the only garment she wore. She appeared anemic, was stooped, and snuff dribbled down one corner of her mouth. The three-year-old child stayed behind her thin legs and peeped out with questioning eyes. Through the door I could see the living room.

"Captain Abel sent me up—may I come in?"

"Shore," said Mrs. Abel as she opened the screen door whose lower half was entirely devoid of screen.

There seemed to be plenty of furniture, such as it was: old, broken-down, weatherbeaten and on a bare floor. A bed with a quilt spread neatly over it sat against the wall in the corner. There were numbers of straight chairs with rawhide bottoms scattered about. But the house was dirty and disorderly. Two doors opened to other rooms. One was a bedroom with two beds unmade. The other door led to the dining room where an unpainted table was being set by a girl of approximately fourteen years of age. The table was barren of any cloth.

Mrs. Abel excused herself and went and spat her snuff out. But she didn't talk much. She said that with her hands so full of feeding nine people there wasn't much time for her to know what was goin' on. And further, with shrimp bringing only seven dollars a barrel and her menfolks to look after when they couldn't average more'n three barrels a week, it wasn't like it used to be.

"Sometimes," said Mrs. Abel, "me and the two girls at home now pick shrimp in the factory. We don't make much. Could make about nine dollars a week if we could work regular, apiece. But we git about two or three days when they are the busiest."

"How do you spend your spare time, Mrs. Abel?" I asked. "Law me," she said, "I ain't got no spare time. Hardly time to go to church what with four kids in school this year. They go to the parochial school. We're nearly all Catholic down here, you know—and lookin' after three grown men I'm too busy to worry about havin' spare time. 'Course I go to all the church affairs and sometimes they have a party. Sometimes we can let the kids go to a picture show but most times they don't have the chance. Keep them busy too. Then they's Union meetin'. I attend when I can, 'cause the shrimp pickers oughter go to that too. I been kinder puny the last two or three year and we ain't gone nowhere nor done nothin' but try to make a livin'. I can remember when my grandpere—he was a Bosage (and she said this proudly)—was living. He was the grandson of the first settler of Bayou la Batre. There was jist a few people who shrimped then and everybody could make a good livin' at it. But now since there's about two thousand people in this town, most all of them make a livin' shrimpin', oysterin' or fishin'. Leastways they try to. Guess we do about as well as any of them—except in the summer when most of the fishermen go on relief and we can't because we own this house and the *Grover Cleveland*. But I ain't kickin'. We got five good boys and three nice girls. Don't never give us no trouble. All of 'em work in shrimp when they git big enough. Antoinette—she's in the kitchen—can't work at it now on account of the new law 'bout age or somethin'.[15] But we're pretty well fixed. Most fishermen ain't got a place to call their own. Our roof leaks and the house needs fixin' but still it's ours. Guess we're pretty well off."

Half a block north of Master Abel's house and beginning next door to the shrimp factory a rickety, unpainted fence encloses seven "shot-gun" houses,[16] their front doors open to the paved

---

[15]The Fair Labor Standards Act of 1938, commonly known as the Wages and Hours Law, is still the basis of U.S. law regarding the employment of children. It also set forty cents an hour as the standard wage; see "Child Labor" in the *Dictionary of American History*, rev. ed. (New York: Charles Scribner's Sons, 1976), vol. 2, pp. 23–24, and "Minimum Wage Legislation," ibid., vol. 4, pp. 352–53.

[16]The front door of a shotgun house is in the gable end, and the one, two, or three rooms are all in a line; see a Mobile County illustration in Eugene M. Wilson's *Alabama Folk Houses* (Montgomery, Ala.: Alabama Historical Commission, 1975), p. 53.

street but their back doors open on a branch of the shrimp factory. Just behind the shrimp factory is the bayou, mother of the industry, resting complacently on her sandy, dredged bottom.

But houses is not the name for these hovels. They are all of a pattern, long, ugly, unpainted, dilapidated, with a half porch caving in and pasteboard patches here and there for window panes. One does not need to enter to feel the hopelessness and desolation of the occupants. Ill kept, with scrawny, stooped women sitting on the doorsteps, tousel-haired and dirty-faced children; nondescript garments hanging on a wash-line between the buildings, all make a picture of despair.

These are the homes of shrimpers who work for the shrimp factories on "shares." Here live the wives and daughters of the men who go to sea and fight for an existence; here live the women who strip their fingers to the bone, beheading and picking the shrimp, so that they may earn a few dollars to eke out the meager earnings of husbands and fathers.

Two blocks north and two blocks west another factory group presents a similar appearance. But there are more houses and a large colony. Still another factory is one-half mile west of town on Shell Road where appearances are in no wise different. Scattered throughout the city of Bayou la Batre, shrimpers live in houses that they have once owned but now merely rent. Some three hundred families make a living working in shrimp in the dreamy, drifting town of Bayou la Batre. Drifting in a sense of knowing no other thing to do but catch, pick, pack shrimp and wait for the next season to do it over.

It was noon time and I bid Mrs. Abel and her shy little boy good day.

The Potter

by Lawrence F. Evans

"Well, now I'll tell you. I don't think being a potter is so much different than being anything else. Of course there aren't many good potters, especially in this section but when they's a good need for good potters we can git 'em. I remember when I came here from Choctaw County thirty years ago there was several men who thought they were good. It wasn't long before the Weavers, who own the pottery here at Daphne was using just me and the other fellows were gone. I've trained twenty men during the thirty years and I imagine some of them would be glad to be here now if there were enough business."

"Isn't business good? Well it's like this, sometimes it's good enough for me to keep two helpers here at the wheel. You see I do everything by hand, but most time I just use one helper. He's a good one. Of course in a place as big as this there must be other laborers too. We employ about six or eight people here normally. There's seven here now."

"Do I make a good living? Well I guess I do, seems that my old lady never kicks much; though I always say a woman is like a mule, they'll wait thirty years to get to kick you in the back. But we got six children who are all in grammar and high school. Two will finish next year. Got a forty-acre farm on a mile out o'town. Got potters clay on it too and when this is over here guess I'll start me a plant of my own."

"What do we make here mostly? We make charcoal burners most o' the time. There ain't no other place in the United States can turn out as many good charcoal burners as we can here in such a short time. No other place in the South that makes them at all. Then we make strawberry pots, oil pots, vases, flower pots, urns, crockery, and knick-knacks. Guess we can make most anything. The man from the government said we had the best clay here of any in the State. The clay's been here for centuries and will be here for more centuries. Guess we won't give out at all. This plant goes back to before the Civil War. Union soldiers burned it during the War. Heard tell of the people who owned it when it opened, named McNary from Scotland. Seems they made supplies for the United States Army. Built Fort Boyer with brick made here in 1809. Don't make brick here no more though. Expensive. Easier to make good stuff by hand."

"What's that, mister? What's the funniest thing I ever made? Well I guess the funniest thing I ever made is what I'm a-makin' now. A frog. Yessir, a great big bullfrog. Seems that they's a call for 'em to go in pools. Make 'em in a mold and bake 'em and then they paint 'em green and sit 'em in a pool and they'd fool even a little frog's grandma. Look real in the water. Can't say as I like to make such crazy things but then they's money in it. Gotta pay a helper here. He mixes the clay and hands it to me at the wheel. We can turn out as many frogs in a day as we'd sell in a week."

"Then there's these crazy water pitchers, look like they was about ready to turn over but they don't, kinda think they are funny. Lots of new-fangled notions. Remember in an election once I made a model of a man who was runnin' for office. Opposition wanted him. They never did use it 'cause they dropped it and broke it into smithereens before they could do what they intended to do. Always wondered what they were going to do with that clay man."

"Do we have salesmen out? Yes and no. That is there is salesmen, but they work for themselves. Charcoal salesmen and coke and hardware men, etc. We don't hire no salesmen. It ain't necessary."

"O sure. We give the school kids in the county all the clay they want. They use it to make maps and things. Can't see how they make maps of it 'cause when I went to school they made maps in books on paper. But that's what they do. Like to see the kids have it to play with, too. They mold and make animals and toys with it. Come here from all over the county and Mobile County too. Always give 'em some clay."

"Say listen, mister. I'm gonna ask you something. Do you know anything about the Wage and Hour Bill that Congress just passed?[17] Wish I knowed if I gotta pay my helper twenty-five cents an hour. Can't do it. Ain't fair. If I pay my helper twenty-five cents an hour we'll both be in a pickle 'cause I'll have to work him less and less and so will I. Seems kinda funny to me that a man can't say what he will pay a feller who's working for

---

[17]See footnote 15 in this part.

him. If the money is satisfactory to the feller that's working for him it ought to be satisfactory to the government. Looks like you gotta turn your radio on the government every morning and listen and see can you go to work in your own shop today. Reminds me of a story of a farmer I heard. Did-j'ever hear it? Well it seems a farmer wasn't gittin' along so well and a lady came by from the government and said if the farmer would plow under ten acres of his cotton the government would send him a check for it. He did and the government sent him a check. Then a man came by and said if he would kill ten of his pigs the government would send him a check for them. He did and they did. Then a lady came by and said, 'Mr. Jones, how many children you got?' But he wouldn't tell her. She said, 'Why won't you tell me how many children you got? I'm from the government.' He said, 'Well a man came by and said kill ten pigs and I'd git paid and I did. A woman came by and said plow under ten acres of cotton and I did; and now you ask me how many kids I got and I won't tell you!' "

Then Ed the potter waited for me to laugh, slammed a fifty-pound piece of clay on his wheel, dampened his clay-covered hands in a pan of water, spat a mouthful of tobacco juice on the voidless clay and started the motor. The clay on the wheel began to turn slowly while he inserted his hand in the center. The interview was at an end. I watched him while he skillfully placed a cleft in the center where his hand had been. The bit of clay began to spread out and up. He used his hands on the outside and in two minutes there was a complete, red-clay charcoal burner about eighteen inches in diameter and flat on the bottom. He ran a cord under the burner, inserted a pair of tongs and lifted it off the wheel for his helper to remove to a shelf where it waited for the oven with the others.

Ed works in the front end of a dirt floor shed whose size approximates 100 by 50 feet. The floor and wall shelves were lined that day with charcoal burners of two sizes. Huge strawberry jars sat in rows on the ground. Small jugs and pitchers were scattered here and there on shelves and floor while his most peculiar product was the frog he mentioned to me. All these pieces were of a similar rouge shade and were waiting for the hour when they should be baked in one of the two huge furnaces in the open yard. Two warehouses nearly as large as the main plant were stored with flower pots and more charcoal burners and strawberry jars. The plant may be reached by going one block south of Daphne Post Office, where a ten-foot black and white sign points two blocks west. Daphne is on the paved road known as the Bay Shore road from the Bridgehead and five miles due south.

A Plain Country Doctor

by Lawrence F. Evans

"Another baby coming," called Doc to his assistant as he replaced the telephone receiver. "Everything's ready, doctor," she said, handing him a bulky little black bag. Doc reached for his hat and turned to me. "Look, you come along," he said; "We can talk on the way." "Let me stop and get a magazine to read while you're working." "You won't need it; you're going to help me."

When we were in the car Doc continued, "You know, I believe I remember this patient. I think I came out here nine years ago. It was one of the toughest obstetrical cases I ever had; a case of version. That's where the child's head fails to make the proper passage, and the feet and head are exactly backwards. The woman had pains and convulsions for eleven hours. I thought I was going to lose them both. I finally failed to get the head right and had to deliver the infant feet first with forceps. Everything was wrong; but they both did fine. I think this is the same woman, living in the same turpentine camp."

He reached a straight stretch on the sandy road and pressed harder on the accelerator. "Look, Dr. Joyce," I said, clinging to the door handle, "let's start at the beginning and talk about what has happened during your life." "Sure, but there's nothing terrific, I reckon," he replied. "I am the son of a Methodist preacher. The male members of our family have see-sawed back and forth between the ministry and medicine as far back as the record goes, even when my family lived in Scotland. We've lived in the South for six generations."

"I reckon I always wanted to be a doctor. When I was a boy I was always giving sick animals medicine and cutting into them if they didn't get well. I took two years of pre-med work at Southern University. But when I got out of there, I didn't know how I could go ahead with my medical studies. You know how poor preachers are. So to get money for the rest of my course, I went to work in the circulation department of the Evening Herald. Then my grandfather died, and I went home for the funeral. There, the subject of my training was discussed. Well, they all said it was just too bad; all except my bachelor uncle Tom who was a doctor and owned a drug store at Fitzgerald. He made me a proposition to come and live with him, work in his store in the summer, and go to school in winter."

"I finished at the University in 1916 and went back to Fitzgerald to help Uncle Tom. I felt that I could begin paying him back, and at the same time be getting a little training as an intern. The Government solved the problem of accredited hospital internship, because the World War came along and all young doctors were admitted as first lieutenants in the Army. Some of them were given full credit for internship, and I was one of the fortunates ones. I spent two years in various camps, including some base camps and spike camps. I've forgotten some of the camps now, but I had plenty of experience with men's diseases."

He slowed the motor as we approached a group of shanties. "Must be the place here," he said. "We'll stop and see." We heard a shriek inside one of the shanties, and he immediately cut off the motor. "This is it, all right," he said. "Come on in." "Well, look, Doc Joyce," I protested; "I believe I'll just wait out here. I can hear enough without going in." "Come on—come on," he said with a flash of impatience.

A fat Negro woman met us at the door. Four Negro children, apparently between the ages of three and seven, were scattered around the filthy room. A three-legged stool was beside the bed, where the midwife had been sitting. She had sent her man two miles to telephone, and we had arrived before his return. "Doctor, somethin's wrong," said the midwife. "Ah can't do no good. You remembers this woman; she's Alice Lee." "Yes," the doctor said, "I remember attending her. How many has she had since?" "Well, ah's delivered five, doctah, and you done brought de fust one."

Doctor Joyce went over to the groaning woman. "This seems to be another case of version." After an examination he turned to me and said, "Very similar to the other one I was telling you about. This should be less difficult. The fact that several children have been born since then makes it easier for her now. Get me some clean cloths—clean, now," he ordered the midwife, "and put some water on that stove to boil; plenty of it."

The doctor removed his coat, turned the lining out, and laid his instruments on it. When the water was boiling he told me to put all the instruments in the pan. He took a hypodermic needle with a long point and jabbed it in the woman's arm. I tried to see the vein under her thick black skin but could not. All I could do was help him hold her arm. The patient writhed and groaned until the anesthetic took effect. She looked silently at the doctor through glazed eyes. He began another examination just as she had more convulsions. The doctor finished and the midwife brought hot water in a rusty tin pan in which he washed his hands, drying them on a faded, but clean sugar sack. He walked across the room and sat down on a woodbox beside the cook stove.

"You might as well sit down and relax," he told me. "How long?" I asked, but he only shook his head. "Then we might as well go on with your story," I said. "You were still in the army, remember, when we got here."

Farm house cleaning. Coffee County, 1939. Wolcott, FSA.

"Well, let us see," Doctor Joyce mused. "When the war was over, my commanding officer offered me a good place in his hospital in Minnesota, but I'd had enough of snow and ice. I just couldn't accept. Another superior officer offered me a place as a contract surgeon in a small New Jersey town. I finally agreed to accept this one, and before I was discharged, went up to look around. It was all right; but about that time I received a message that Uncle Tom was sick, and wanted my help as soon as I could come. Naturally, I gave up the place in New Jersey and returned to Fitzgerald."

"Uncle had influenza, and it was six months before he was on his feet again. By that time the State Board of Health had given me a clean practice bill, recognizing my Army internship, and I was taking care of Uncle's practice. By the time Uncle was ready to take over again, a job came seeking me. Dr. Waters, of the State Board of Health, asked if I would be interested in being assistant State Health Officer for two years. I accepted immediately."

The doctor jumped to his feet and was at the bedside in an instant, although nothing had attracted my attention. "Hurry," he said, "hurry over and hold her feet!" The footboard of the bed was so high that I could not stand on the floor and reach her feet. So I got up in the middle of the bed and propped my back against the footboard directly behind the doctor. I took hold of her feet, and just as I got set for what I thought would be strenuous exercise, the doctor climbed off. It was not time yet. Feeling very foolish, I climbed off the bumpy mattress and went over to sit on the woodbox. On second thought I washed my hands, drying them on a pocket handkerchief.

We sat for a long time before the doctor spoke again. The house grew dark and the children began whimpering. The midwife sent them to a neighbor's house. Then she lighted an oil lamp with a smoky flue, and added pine knots to the fire in the stove. A chilly wind came through the cracks in the walls, and around the pasteboard window panes.

"It's not as bad as the first case I took care of," the doctor said. "She's had more experience. Still it's not the easiest thing in the world. The chances are always slim in a case of version." He spoke as if he were talking to himself. "What about complications, Doctor Joyce?" "The possibilities are greater in a case of this kind than in any other," he said. "She's stopped having convulsions. With the exception of the position of the infant, there is no reason why there should be any other than normal action from here on."

"So you spent two years with the State Board of Health, and then what?" I asked. "I got married and moved to Carter, and I've been here ever since. That's all there is to the story." "Not by a long shot, man. Your medical life was really beginning then, and so was your home life. What about it, Doc?"

"I met Karen when I was with the State Board," he said. "She was Miss Karen Metcalf of Stimson. I thought she was the sweetest thing in the world, and still do. When she agreed to marry me I felt that I wanted to settle down. She had a brother who had timber and land interests down in Mulder County. When he asked me to come along with him on a fishing trip I discovered Carter which was then a little town with growing pains and possibilities."

"When we got married, I remember that they dragged an old pair of shoes behind a Ford for two blocks—with me in them." Doc laughed. He seldom laughed aloud; just a series of chuckles, with his funny wrinkles quivering. I had to laugh, too, because his little bay window hopped up and down like a fishing cork when he laughed. He reminded me of my childhood idea of Santa Claus.

His laugh died as suddenly as it had come. He was at the bedside before I knew what was happening. It was time. He motioned me to take my position back at the foot of the bed. The midwife stood by with the pan of steaming water and some cloths. Somewhere she had found a clean sheet, yellowed with age. She spread it over the patchwork quilt that covered the patient. The doctor's hands worked swiftly under the sheet.

Beads of perspiration on her brow, the woman lay still except for an occasional muscular contraction that shook her body. At such times, my hands slipped on her large ankles. A low moan came from the patient as the doctor brought a gray and red bundle of flesh from under the sheet. I did not look again. A faint mewing struck my ears; then a resounding smack brought a very life-like wail. The midwife took the infant and carrying it to the woodbox, begain bathing it in the rusty tin pan of steaming water. The doctor finished his work and stepped off the bed. I got down, wanting to go out the door, but thought better of it. I would have washed my hands, but everything was being used.

Doctor Joyce took some instruments from the hot water and returned to the bedside. He worked for several minutes, and then while washing his hands, gave instructions to the midwife. She was grinning at the newborn baby, paying little attention to the doctor. Once more he went to the bed and felt the mother's pulse, looked in her eyes and mouth, gave her a pill to swallow, and then began putting his instruments in his bag.

"You stay with her tonight and call me in the morning," he said to the midwife. "Cigarette?," he asked me, as he flipped two from his case. I looked at the new baby while the doctor was lighting his smoke. It was asleep in the quilt on the woodbox. "It's a fine boy," the midwife said, "Name him Herbert," I suggested. "That's the doctor's name." She grinned at me but said nothing. The mother slept. When the doctor turned on his way out and told the woman to take good care of the mother and child, that was the last I heard of the obstetrical case. I was definitely glad it was over.

"Well, sir," he said, when we were in the car again, "when I came here sixteen years ago, there wasn't such a thing as a road; just a trail and a rough one at that. I've ridden horses, buggies, and Model T's all over these piney woods. Sandy trails used to give me the dickens. Nearly every time I started home I'd get stuck. Once I was going to see a pneumonia patient down in the Tucker neighborhood and got stuck in the mud. It was three hours before I could get away to see the patient. I lost that patient. But it was usually when I was returning that I got stuck in the mud or sand—mostly sand. Good roads have changed lots of things. Bringing babies to the world was a big task sixteen years ago but now most people come to my office and go to the hospital. Medical science and rapid transportation and communication have eliminated lots of hazards."

"I started to count the babies I had helped into the world the other day, but something came up to stop the count. It's a large number, though. I put their birth in a little black book, and always send a birthday card to each of them. It keeps my office assistant busy when she has nothing to do. The other day a pretty young lady, fifteen or sixteen, came into my office, threw her arms around me, and kissed me, saying, 'I'll bet you don't know who I am.' Well, I didn't, but I found out that she was one of my babies. The family had been living in California since she was three years old. I had sent her a birthday card every year. You know, I didn't mind that sort of remembrance a bit." The doctor chuckled again.

As we were getting into town I looked at my watch and saw that we had been gone four hours. "We'll run by the office and see if there's anyone waiting," the doctor said, "and then we'll go over to the house and eat. You've earned your supper." I said nothing, but I didn't feel as if I would be able to eat.

When we arrived at the office, a little man with blood all over his head sat there holding his face in his hands. He did not look up when we entered. Across from the man sat a large woman who looked more like a farmer than the man did. She had large angular hands and a bony face. "I hit him over the head with a shovel," she explained to no one in particular, and then added as an afterthought, "He was drunk." "Come in," said the doctor, "we'll have a look at it." His voice was cheerful as he motioned me in with the couple.

In the back room, Dr. Joyce seated the man in what looked like a barber's chair. He switched on a light over the chair, washed his hands, and began examining the wound. I saw a nasty looking laceration on the little man's head, and a bump that appeared as large as a baseball. While the water was heating over the doctor's spirit lamp, he laid out a scalpel, a razor, a pair of medical scissors, bandages, adhesive, and reached over to a glass-enclosed shelf for two bottles of fluid with long scientific names.

The little man was still silent. He did not act drunk. The woman said, "I told him if he ever came home drunk again I'd knock him in the head with an axe, but I couldn't find the axe, so I grabbed a shovel." The blood had run down on the little man's brown shirt. The wounds must have been inflicted several hours earlier, and no first aid had been given.

"I told him," the woman started again. The doctor glanced up from cutting the little man's hair, and she stopped talking and stood in the corner. Doc washed the wound with a hot towel, soaped and lathered the head, shaved the entire top and both sides. With a scalpel, he began working on the huge bump. The patient raised up stiffly, squirmed, and sank lower in the chair. The doctor motioned for the woman and me to hold his arms. He opened the wound to remove the dust and dirt, swabbed it with iodine, and drained it. The little man gritted his teeth and perspiration broke out on his forehead. When the doctor began taking stitches the patient grunted each time the needle pierced his flesh.

"I told him," the woman began once more. "Suppose you wait in the other room," said the doctor. "Everything is all right now, and we'll be through in a few minutes." He finished sewing the wound, bandaged the scalp, and helped the man out of the chair. "Come back tomorrow at four o'clock," he said. "You didn't ask the name, Doc. Do you know them?" "No, I don't know them, but they'll be back tomorrow."

After washing his hands he wrote something in a little black book and said, "Let's go home and see if we can find something to eat." When we reached the house, twelve-year-old Mary opened the door, flung her arms about her father, and kissed him on the forehead. Still wearing pigtails, she was growing up tall and straight. She took our hats. "Where's Tommy?," Doc asked. "He's asleep; it's far past his bedtime," replied Mrs. Joyce, coming from the dining room to greet us. "I didn't know we were going to have company, but there's enough for you both. I'll make coffee and you can have it with dessert."

Doc sighed as we sat down at the table. "This doctor's life gets pretty humdrum," he said. "Deliveries, tonsillectomies, fractures, lacerations—one bogs down. An appendectomy is a highwater mark for a country doctor. Sixteen years I've put in on this field with no kale to show for it, and not much science left. But when I came here, women were faring little better than animals at childbirth. I feel better about that."

"We have a little money made by careful management of inherited property, but I have made little money from my regular practice. You see, about ninety percent of my patients are farmers and their families. Sometimes they are unable to pay their bills for years, and some never get them paid. If they should pay as quickly as a doctor is expected to answer a call, then we'd be sitting pretty. But crops go against farmers about fifty percent of the time."

"But I was just thinking the other day that the Lord has blessed us. I've always found inspiration in the church. Something my dad taught me to do was tithe. I've always done that. Seems that the Lord blesses people in more ways than one when they tithe. Karen tithes to her church, and I to mine. She's a Baptist and I am a Methodist; we just never worried about belonging to the same church and it worked out all right. We don't go to church as much as we should, but we take part in all the activities that we are able to support."

"You know, I began from the first giving a tenth of the first payment for my services to the church, and I've been doing it ever since. I'm just a plain country doctor; as the country people say, I'm 'the man with the little black bag.' I'm no good at any special disease, no good at any special operation, just a plain country doctor. But I've delivered a lot of babies. My work is just fair, and there are better doctors. But I have had patients with me for sixteen years."

"I've been fortunate enough to hold a job for four years as contract surgeon for the local Civilian Conservation Camp. When the lads enroll they are healthy, and it's my duty to keep them that way. I go down every morning at six o'clock for sick call and stay about an hour. Treatment consists mostly of first aid, caring for colds, athlete's foot, and shots for such diseases as pneumonia and diphtheria. A company first aid man calls me in case there is something he cannot handle."

"Listen, Doc," I urged, "you haven't told me about your unusual cases yet." "They're all unusual. But I'll tell you about a strange accident case that occurred about eighteen years ago before I came to Carter. A lad was beating his way somewhere on a freight train. He slipped and fell under the train, and had both legs cut off near the trunk. We hurried him to a hospital, where we found that he had a fifty-fifty chance. While he was in a delirium that night the nurse stepped from the room to call for help. He tried to get up. The strain was too much on his heart, and it just stopped beating. We had a difficult time locating his relatives, but finally found that his mother lived in Connecticut.

We wired her to ask what to do with the body. She wired back that she didn't care what we did with it; she didn't want it. The railroad finally took the body and buried it on the right of way. She was one of the few unnatural mothers I ever heard of."

"This was another case I remember well. About ten years ago a Negro woman brought a twelve-year-old boy in and asked me to look at his head. He had a scalp disease, and the head was so swollen that it looked like a black balloon. I lanced his scalp and found it full of pus. He had to keep coming to me for months, and every time he came his mother brought a dime or a quarter, saying that she had no more. His head was cut until there was not an inch where a scalpel had not entered the skin. But he finally got well."

"After that, the mother came in every month or so and brought a dime. She kept this up for years. I don't know how many times she came in, or how much she brought, for I never kept books on it. It was too insignificant. Then last Saturday she came in with fifty cents, and asked as she gave it to me, 'Doctah, how much mo' does I owe you?' "

" 'Mildred, you've been a faithful person about paying your debts,' I said without looking in my books. 'I think that the fifty cents will pay us in full, and so I'll give a receipt. By the way, how is the boy? I haven't seen him in several years.' "

" 'Doctah, I don't know how dat boy is; he's been in de jail house in Atlanta for nigh onto two years now.' "

" 'Well, I'm sorry about that. Here, though, let me write you a receipt.' When I got through writing the receipt, it read, 'Pay to the order of Mildred Woods, ten dollars.' 'Now, Mildred,' I said, 'you take this to the man at the window in the bank, and don't come back here unless you're sick.' You know," and there was a grin on the doctor's face as he told this, "Mildred came back in the afternoon when I wasn't in and left the ten dollars with my secretary, telling her that I had made a mistake. Isn't that one for the book?"

Appendix:
The Unpublished Life Histories
from Alabama

Three Alabama life histories were published in 1978 in *Such As Us:* Gertha Couric's "A Day on the Farm," Nettie S. McDonald's "Green Fields Far Away," and Jack Kytle's "A Woman's Like a Dumb Animal." All three were taken from W. T. Couch's FWP papers, as were twenty-seven of the twenty-eight life histories in this volume. Fifty-six remaining accounts in the Couch papers are as yet unpublished. These are listed below alphabetically by author, along with some description of length in typed pages, locale, occupation, and description of subject.

Barnard, George S., writer from Dale County
   1. "A Negro Cook's Day," 5½ pages, Ozark. Subject is female, thirty-one years old.

Cain, Maude, writer from Tallapoosa County
   2. "Bertie Turner," 4 pages, Alexander City. Rural boarding house keeper.

Clark, Luther, with the editorial department, Jefferson County
   3. "Looking Around With a Hay Farmer," 6 pages, McCainville, in Sumter County. Farmer, seventy-two, and wife and son.

Couric, Gertha, writer from Barbour County
   4. "Midwives are Called 'Grannies,' " 6 pages, Eufaula. Seventy-seven-year-old full-blooded Indian woman.
   5. "Three Workers of Cowikee Cotton Mill," 6 pages, Eufaula. A mill fireman and part-time farmer and two older women weavers.
   6. "The Hughes Family," 4 pages, Eufaula. A couple who worked fifty years in the mills, husband a "loom fixer," wife a weaver.
   7. "Mill Workers," 1½ pages, Eufaula. Retired mill worker, female.
   8. "Ed West—Installment Collector," 3 pages, Eufaula. White furniture store employee collecting mainly from black clients.
   9. "My Time is Mighty Nigh Out," 6 pages, Eufaula. Elderly black washwoman, possibly ex-slave.
   10. "Fifty-Two Years in the Cotton Mill," 6 pages, Eufaula. Seventy-two-year-old retired mill worker; he began as a sweeper.

11. "Midwife and Farmer," 7½ pages, Eufaula or vicinity. Sixty-year-old midwife.

Dobson, Noma, writer from Talladega County
12. "Veteran Newspaper Man," 5 pages, Sylacauga. Active seventy-eight-year-old newspaper editor.

Evans, Lawrence F., writer from Baldwin County
13. "Story of a Minister's Family and Life," 9 pages.
14. "An Oysterman," 6 pages, Bon Secour. Young boat owner and wife.
15. "Sam, the Turpentine Chopper," 4½ pages, near Stapleton. Black couple in their early twenties.

Hall, Covington, writer from DeKalb County
16. "Mountain Thinker and Experimenter," 3 pages, near Mentone. An innovative farmer and small miner.
17. "Mountain Merchant-Farmer," 3 ½ pages, near Mentone. Country storekeeper and farmer.

Hand, Woodrow, with the editorial department, Jefferson County
18. "Gertha Couric—Hotel Hostess, WPA Worker," 13 pages, Eufaula. Active writer and restaurant manager in her early forties.

Harper, Edward F., writer from Jefferson County
19. "Hobbies, Pets and Children," 12 pages, Ensley. Young couple, husband a blacksmith with TCI.

Hartley, Helen S., writer from Mobile County
20. "Shrimping on the Schooner Barney Geneva," 6 pages, Bayou la Batre. Owner of shrimping boat.

Heflin, Wilson L., writer from Jefferson County
21. "I Wouldn't Be a Farmer," 19 pages, set on a bus going from Birmingham to Winfield. College boy on way home after summer work in Birmingham.
22. "People Call Me a Loan Shark," 7 pages, downtown Birmingham.

Klein, Preston, writer from Lee County
23. "The Truitt Family—Tenant Farmers," 4 pages, near Opelika. Young parents, six children.

Kytle, Jack, with the editorial department, Jefferson County

24. "River Drifter," 6 pages, near Talladega Springs. Older fisherman and his wife.

25. "Jim Lauderdale: River Wreck," 4 pages, near Talladega Springs. Former fisherman, miner, and moonshiner; wife and children moved away.

26. "Dead Man of the Coosa River," 5 pages, near Talladega Springs. Another old and solitary fisherman.

27. "Uncle Bud Ryland, the Coosa Fisherman," 8 pages, near Talledega Springs. Yet another solitary fisherman.

28. "River Widow: Portrait of Poverty," 7 pages, near Fayetteville. Unemployed widow and children.

29. "Pattern of Ignorance," 4 pages, near Talladega Springs. Former farmer, now fisherman, about forty years old.

30. "By the Glory of God," 4 pages, near Talladega Springs. Fifty-eight-year-old black farmer of three hundred acres.

McDonald, Nettie S., writer from Jefferson County

31. "Coal Miner," 10 pages, Birmingham. Mine foreman and part-time farmer.

Marshall, Bennett, writer from Jefferson County

32. "Some Grow Old," 5 pages, Birmingham. Boarding house proprietress, over sixty years old.

O'Brien, Susie R., writer from Perry County

33. "Ellawhite Mill Village," 4 pages, Uniontown. Wife of man who worked in this California Cotton Mill town thirty-five years.

34. "The Alexanders," 3½ pages, near Hamburg. Tenant farm couple (wife age forty-two) and children.

Petterson, Josephine, writer from Mobile County

35. "Life Story of a Swedish-American," 12 pages, Mobile. A sixty-seven-year-old Swedish immigrant who moved to join relatives when she was thirty; a series of occupations.

Prine, Ila B., writer from Mobile County

36. "Life in a Shrimping and Oyster Shucking Camp," 7½ pages, Bayou la Batre. Husband, seventy-seven, and Cajan French wife, sixty-seven, in a packing company camp.

37. "Mandy Johnson, Midwife," 5½ pages, Cottage Hill. Older black woman.

38. "Story of Auguste Mollie," 5½ pages, Navco. Feeble eighty-year-old French immigrant and his black housekeeper.

39. "It Ruins Oysters to Wash Them," 9½ pages, Bayou la Batre. A seventy-year-old fisherman, his wife and children.

40. "Lena Cash, Octogenarian," 11 pages, Crichton. An eighty-eight-year-old woman, former seamstress, Louisiana native.

Reese, Marie, writer from Lowndes County

41. "Holly House," 8 pages, Lowndesboro. Middle-aged tenant farmer, also a mechanic, his wife and children.

Rogers, Adelaide, writer from Montgomery County

42. "Mrs. Blanchard, Professional Mother," 15 pages, Housekeeper and day care worker, most of the account on an earlier marriage.

43. "Gab'ul, Chime Dat Harp!," 12½ pages, Montgomery. Seventy-five-year-old black farmer turned fortuneteller and conjure man.

Tartt, Ruby Pickens, writer from Sumter County

44. "Seeking Salvation," 6 pages, Livingston. A black widow in her early fifties whose husband died in a convict mine.

Waldrep, R. V., with the editorial department, Jefferson County

45. "I Wanted to Keep a Good Horse," 10 pages, Red Bay. A seventy-year-old small-town doctor.

46. "Lord Loafer," 11 pages, Red Bay. Grave digger and town character.

47. "Bony Winchester," 8 pages, near Red Bay. Sixty-nine-year-old farmer.

48. "It's Hell to be Popular," 10 pages, Birmingham. A high school girl.

49. "Pink Petree," 10 pages, near Red Bay. Country store owner.

50. "John F. Davis," 9 pages, near Red Bay. Postman and innovative farmer.

51. "J. P. Epps and Son," 9 pages, Red Bay. Drygoods storekeeper and wife.

52. "Luke Warn: He Ain't Talkin'," 11 pages, Red Bay. Black farmer, around seventy years old.

53. "My Boys an' Me Died in the War," 15 pages, near Birmingham. A seventy-year-old farmer and former country storekeeper.

54. "Jack Hodge," 6 pages, Red Bay. Reclusive farmer.

Williams, Jennie Sue, writer from Jackson County

55. "Frank Coffee," 3 pages, Bridgeport. Seventy-two-year-old black farmer, preacher, and former day laborer.

56. "Isaac Slaughter," 6½ pages, Bridgeport. Ex-slave and former butcher, approximately ninety-four years old.

Bibliography

Collections:

Alabama Writers' Project, Works Progress Administration Materials. Manuscripts Division, Alabama State Department of Archives and History, Montgomery, Ala.

Federal Writers' Project, Papers of the Regional Director William Terry Couch. Southern Historical Collection, University of North Carolina, Chapel Hill, N.C.

Federal Writers' Project, Records of the Works Progress Administration, Records Group 69. National Archives, Washington, D.C.

Books and Articles:

Acts of the General Assembly of Alabama, session of 1876–7. Montgomery: Barrett & Brown, State Printers, 1877.

Acts of the General Assembly of Alabama, session of 1894–5. Montgomery: Roemer Printing Co., 1895.

Adams, Edward C. L. *Congaree Sketches; scenes from Negro life in the swamps of the Congaree and tales by Tad and Scip of heaven and hell with other miscellany.* Chapel Hill: University of North Carolina Press, 1927.

Agee, James and Walker Evans. *Let Us Now Praise Famous Men.* Boston: Houghton Mifflin, 1960. Originally published 1941.

Alabama Coal Operators Association. *Mining Laws of the State of Alabama.* N.p., n.d.

Alabama Library Association Bibliographic Committee. *Twentieth Century Alabama Authors; a Checklist.* N.p., 1966.

Alabama Writers' Project. *Alabama: A Guide to the Deep South, Compiled by Workers of the Writers' Program of the Works Projects Administration in the State of Alabama.* American Guide Series. New York: Hastings House, 1941.

Arnold, Byron. *Folksongs of Alabama.* University, Ala.: University of Alabama Press, 1950.

Bernstein, Irving. *The Lean Years: A History of the American Worker 1920–1933.* Boston: Houghton Mifflin, 1960.

————. *The Turbulent Years: A History of the American Worker 1933–1941.* Boston: Houghton Mifflin, 1970.

Blount County Historical Society. *The Heritage of Blount County.* N.p., 1972.

Boni, Margaret Bradford, ed. *The Fireside Book of Favorite American Songs.* New York: Simon & Schuster, 1952.

"Book Review." *Time* 33 (May 1, 1939):87–88.

Botkin, Benjamin A. "WPA and Folklore Research: 'Bread and Song.' " *Southern Folklore Quarterly* 3 (March, 1939):7–14.

Browne, Ray B. *Popular Beliefs and Practices from Alabama.* University of California Publications. Folklore Studies 9. Berkeley and Los Angeles: University of California Press, 1958.

Caldwell, Erskine. *Tobacco Road.* New York: Charles Scribner's Sons, 1932.

Caldwell, Erskine and Margaret Bourke-White. *You Have Seen Their Faces.* New York: Viking Press, 1937.

Camp, James McIntyre. *The Making, Shaping and Treating of Steel.* 7th ed. Pittsburgh: U.S. Steel Corp., 1957.

Carmer, Carl. *Stars Fell On Alabama.* Illustrated by Cyrus LeRoy Baldridge. New York: Farrar & Rinehart, 1934.

Chapman, H. H., with W. M. Adamson, H. D. Bonham, H. D. Pallister, and E. C. Wright. *The Iron and Steel Industries of the South.* University, Ala.: University of Alabama Press, 1953.

"Child Labor." In *Dictionary of American History,* rev. ed., vol. 3, pp. 23–24. New York: Charles Scribner's Sons, 1976.

Code of Alabama, July 27, 1907. Vol. 3, *Criminal.* Prepared by James J. Mayfield. Nashville, Tenn.: Marshall & Bruce Co., 1907.

Code of Alabama, adopted by Act of the Legislature of Alabama approved July 2, 1940, recompiled. Charlottesville, Va.: Michie Co., 1958.

Code of Alabama, 1975. Vol. 7, *Conservation.* Charlottesville, Va.: Michie Co., 1977.

Conlin, Joseph R. *Big Bill Haywood and the Radical Union Movement.* Syracuse: Syracuse University Press, 1969.

Couch, W. T., ed. *Culture in the South.* Chapel Hill: University of North Carolina Press, 1934.

————. "Landlord and Tenant." *Virginia Quarterly Review* 14 (Spring, 1938):309–12.

Diard, François Ludgere. *The Tree: Being the Strange Case of Charles R. S. Boyington.* Mobile: Gill Printing & Stationery Co., 1949.

Dictionary of American Biography, Supplement Three 1941–1945. New York: Charles Scribner's Sons, 1973.

Dwyer-Shick, Susan. "The Development of Folklore and Folklife Research in the Federal Writers' Project, 1935–1943." *Keystone Folklore Quarterly* 20 (Fall, 1965):5–31.

Edwards, Lawrence. "The Primitive Baptists." Master's thesis, University of Tennessee, 1940.

Fay, Albert H. *A Glossary of the Mining and Mineral Industry*, Bulletin 95. Washington: Department of Interior, Bureau of Mines, 1920.

Federal Writers' Project. *American Stuff: An Anthology of Prose and Verse by members of the Federal Writers' Project, with sixteen prints by the Federal Art Project*. New York: Viking Press, 1937.

————. *Lay My Burden Down: A Folk History of Slavery*. Edited by Ben A. Botkin. Chicago: University of Chicago Press, 1945.

————. *These Are Our Lives, as told by the people and written by members of the Federal Writers' Project of the Works Progress Administration in North Carolina, Tennessee, and Georgia*. Preface by W. T. Couch. Chapel Hill: University of North Carolina Press, 1939.

————. *Slave Narratives: A Folk History of Slavery in the United States from Interviews with Former Slaves*. Vol. 5, *Alabama and Indiana Narratives*, edited by George P. Rawick. Westport, Conn.: Greenwood Publishing Co., 1973. Reprinted from 1941.

Fox, Daniel M. "The Achievement of the Federal Writers' Project." *American Quarterly* 13 (Spring, 1961):3–19.

Green, Archie. *Only a Miner: Studies in Recorded Coal-Mining Songs*. Urbana: University of Illinois Press, 1972.

"Green, Paul (Eliot)." In *Contemporary Authors: A Bio-bibliographical Guide to Current Authors and Their Works*, vols. 5–8 (four volumes in one), first revision, pp. 474–75. Detroit: Gayle Research Co., 1969.

Grubbs, Donald H. *Cry From the Cotton: The Southern Tenant Farmers' Union and the New Deal*. Chapel Hill: University of North Carolina Press, 1971.

Halliwell, Leslie. *The Filmgoer's Companion*. 4th ed. New York: Hill & Wang, 1970.

Hirsch, Jerrold M. "The Federal Writers' Project Southern Life Histories Program: Culture, Bureaucracy and Relief." Paper presented at 1975 American Historical Association annual meeting.

Humphrey, H. B. *Historical Summary of Coal-Mine Explosions in the United States, 1810–1958*, Bulletin 586. Washington: Department of Interior, Bureau of Mines, 1960.

Jennings, Buford, "Contemporary Alabama Writers." Master's thesis, Auburn University, 1931.

Kennedy, David M. *Birth Control in America: The Career of Margaret Sanger*. New Haven: Yale University Press, 1970.

Korson, George. *Coal Dust on the Fiddle: Songs and Stories of the*

Bituminous Industry. Foreword by John Greenway. Hatboro, Pa.:
Folklore Associates, 1965. Reprinted from 1943 edition.

McDonald, William F. *Federal Relief Administration and the Arts:
The Origins and Administrative History of the Arts Projects of the
WPA*. Columbus: Ohio State University Press, 1969.

McWhiney, Grady. "Louisiana Socialists in the Early Twentieth Century: A Study of Rustic Radicalism." *Journal of Southern History* 20
(August, 1954):315–36.

Mangione, Jerry. *The Dream and the Deal: The Federal Writers'
Project, 1935–1943*. Boston: Little, Brown & Co., 1972.

Marks, Henry S. *Who Was Who in Alabama*. Huntsville: Strode
Publishers, 1972.

Marshall, F. Ray. *Labor in the South*. Cambridge: Harvard University
Press, 1967.

Minehan, Thomas. *Boy and Girl Tramps of America*. Illustrated with
photographs by author. New York: Farrar & Rinehart, 1934.

"Minimum Wage Legislation." In *Dictionary of American History*,
rev. ed., vol. 4, pp. 352–53. New York: Charles Scribner's Sons,
1976.

Mitchell, H. L. *Mean Things Happening in This Land: The Life and
Times of H. L. Mitchell, Co-Founder of the Southern Tenant Farmers Union*. Montclair, N.J.: Allanheld, Osmun & Co., 1979.

Nixon, Herman Clarence. *Forty Acres and Steel Mules*. Chapel Hill:
University of North Carolina Press, 1938.

Penkower, Monty. *The Federal Writers' Project: A Study in Government Patronage of the Arts*. Urbana: University of Illinois Press,
1977.

Powell, Evanell K. *WPA Writers' Publications: A Complete Bibliographic Checklist and Price Guide of Items, Major and Minor, of the
Federal Writers' Project and Program*. Palm Beach: n.d.

Richardson, Jesse M., and Herbert R. Padgett, eds. *Alabama Almanac
and Book of Facts 1955–1956*. Birmingham, Ala.: Vulcan Press,
1955.

Rivers of Alabama. Illustrated by Jack B. Hood; Art Editor, E. L. Klein.
Huntsville: Strode Publishers, 1968.

Solomon, Jack and Olivia. *Cracklin Bread and Asfidity: Folk Recipes
and Remedies*. Illustrated by Mark Brewton. University, Ala.: University of Alabama Press, 1979.

Stott, William. *Documentary Expression and Thirties America*. New
York: Oxford University Press, 1973.

Sutherland, Kitty. "The Coosa." In *Rivers of Alabama*, pp. 81–102.
Huntsville: Strode Publishers, 1968.

Sydnor, Charles Sackett. *Slavery in Mississippi.* Gloucester, Mass.: Peter Smith, 1965. Reprinted from 1933.

Terkel, Studs. *Hard Times: An Oral History of the Great Depression.* New York: Pantheon Books, 1970.

Terrill, Tom E., and Jerrold Hirsch, eds. *Such As Us: Southern Voices of the Thirties.* Chapel Hill: University of North Carolina Press, 1978.

Thrasher, Max Bennett. *Tuskegee: Its Story and Its Work.* New York: Negro Universities Press, 1969 reprint.

Ulrich, Mabel S. "Salvaging Culture for the WPA." *Harper's Monthly Magazine* 178 (May, 1939):653–64.

Vance, Rupert B. *Human Factors in Cotton Culture: A Study in the Social Geography of the American South.* Chapel Hill: University of North Carolina Press, 1929.

————. *Human Geography of the South: A Study in Regional Resources and Human Adequacy.* Chapel Hill: University of North Carolina Press, 1932.

White, Newman Ivey. *American Negro Songs.* Cambridge: Harvard University Press, 1928.

————, ed. *The Frank C. Brown Collection of North Carolina Folklore.* 7 vols. Durham, N.C.: Duke University Press, 1952–61.

Wilson, Eugene M. *Alabama Folk Houses.* Montgomery: Alabama Historical Commission, 1975.

Zinn, Howard, ed. *New Deal Thought.* Indianapolis: Bobbs-Merrill Co., 1966.

Index